The Quest for Universal Soci... South

ϵ 13 ᴅ/
ᴢ Ο

Universal social policies have the power to reduce inequ... more cohesive societies. How can countries in the South ... ism? This book answers this question through a compa... Costa Rica, Mauritius, South Korea, and Uruguay, and ... ical account of Costa Rica's successful trajectory. Again: democracy and progressive parties, the authors place ... policy architectures defined as the combination of instruments that dictate the benefits available to people. The volume also explores the role of state actors in building pro-universal architectures. This book will interest advanced students and scholars of human development and public and social policies as well as policymakers eager to promote universal policies across the South.

Gift Aid item

20 70695393 3732

JULIANA MARTÍNEZ FRANZONI is Professor in the Institute for Social Research at the University of Costa Rica.

DIEGO SÁNCHEZ-ANCOCHEA is Associate Professor in the Political Economy of Latin America and Director of the Latin American Centre at the University of Oxford.

The Quest for Universal Social Policy in the South

Actors, Ideas, and Architectures

JULIANA MARTÍNEZ FRANZONI AND
DIEGO SÁNCHEZ-ANCOCHEA

CAMBRIDGE
UNIVERSITY PRESS

CAMBRIDGE
UNIVERSITY PRESS

University Printing House, Cambridge CB2 8BS, United Kingdom

One Liberty Plaza, 20th Floor, New York, NY 10006, USA

477 Williamstown Road, Port Melbourne, VIC 3207, Australia

314-321, 3rd Floor, Plot 3, Splendor Forum, Jasola District Centre, New Delhi - 110025, India

79 Anson Road, #06-04/06, Singapore 079906

Cambridge University Press is part of the University of Cambridge.

It furthers the University's mission by disseminating knowledge in the pursuit of education, learning and research at the highest international levels of excellence.

www.cambridge.org
Information on this title: www.cambridge.org/9781107564893

© Juliana Martínez Franzoni and Diego Sánchez-Ancochea 2016

This publication is in copyright. Subject to statutory exception and to the provisions of relevant collective licensing agreements, no reproduction of any part may take place without the written permission of Cambridge University Press.

First published 2016
First paperback edition 2018

A catalogue record for this publication is available from the British Library

Library of Congress Cataloging in Publication data
Names: Martínez Franzoni, Juliana, author. | Sánchez-Ancochea, Diego, author.
Title: The quest for universal social policy in the south : actors, ideas and architectures /
Juliana Martinez Franzoni, Diego Sanchez-Ancochea.
Description: New York : Cambridge University Press, 2016.
Identifiers: LCCN 2016015460| ISBN 9781107125414 (Hardback) |
ISBN 9781107564893 (Paperback)
Subjects: LCSH: Developing countries–Social policy–Case studies.
Classification: LCC HN980 .M3145 2016 | DDC 306.09172/4–dc23 LC record
available at https://lccn.loc.gov/2016015460

ISBN 978-1-107-12541-4 Hardback
ISBN 978-1-107-56489-3 Paperback

Cambridge University Press has no responsibility for the persistence or accuracy of URLs for external or third-party internet websites referred to in this publication, and does not guarantee that any content on such websites is, or will remain, accurate or appropriate.

Contents

Figures

Tables

Acknowledgements

The research that led to this book started five years ago. Fieldwork, data analysis, a partial rethinking of the entire project, and finally write-up subsequently followed. In the process of completing all these tasks, we met new people and discovered new places, spent time with friends, and enjoyed conversations we treasure about politics, social policy, inequality, and life affairs. Not surprisingly we have much to thank to a significant number of institutions and people without whom this book and the process that led to it would have been impossible. We hope not to forget any of them.

Our intellectual collaboration began in 2006 when together with Maxine Molyneux we received a British Academy grant to organize conferences on economic models, social policy, and inequality in London and Costa Rica. Since then, Maxine has been a tireless supporter, personal friend, and a role model for both of us. We thank her for her valuable advice, including early discussion of the ideas that gave birth to this book as well as more recent feedback on several drafts.

The project received a major push thanks to a British Academy Small Grant and Juliana's Visiting Fellowship at the Kellogg Institute in Notre Dame. Her year-long visit was also made possible by a Fulbright's fellowship for Central American scholars. The British Academy proposal benefited from insightful inputs from Leigh Payne and Tim Power as well as administrative support from personnel at the School of Interdisciplinary Area Studies in Oxford. Scott Mainwaring, Carmelo Mesa-Lago, Mitchell Seligson, and Jorge Vargas Cullell supported Juliana's application to the Kellogg where she could focus on our research in a nourishing environment. At the Kellogg, Robert Fishman and Samuel Valenzuela suggested ways to improve our comparative methodology. Lovely evenings spent with their families helped Juliana and her family cope with the harsh winter. Fulbright happened to have a warm chaperone in their San José headquarters: Ana Lucía Pérez turned complex paperwork into a simple task.

In these initial stages of the project – as well as at other moments more recently – Evelyne Huber was always available and amazingly supportive. She helped us refine the methodology of our British Academy proposal and met often with Juliana during their joint stay at the Kellogg. She has been a great source of encouragement and inspiration for us.

Three institutions were fundamental for the completion of this research from beginning to end. The Instituto de Investigaciones Sociales (IIS) at the Universidad de Costa Rica (UCR) directed by Carmen Coameño provided sustained institutional support throughout the research process. A very special thanks goes to Ciska Raventós, former director of the IIS, who opened the door for Juliana to begin her academic career in Costa Rica. Juliana's junior colleagues, Francisco Robles and Koen Voored, have for several years now shared their warmth and enthusiasm about our work, and Kathia Castro, the Institute's administrative director, has been crucial in dealing with the many administrative "firsts."

The Latin American Centre and the Oxford Department of International Development funded Diego's fieldwork trips to Costa Rica. They have also been amazing homes for him, and many of his colleagues (including Leigh and Tim already mentioned as well as David Doyle, Valpy FitzGerald, Nandini Gooptu, Eduardo Posada-Carbó, Frances Stewart, and Rosemary Thorp) supported this project in diverse ways. We also thank CAF-Development Bank of Latin America, which funded Juliana's trip to Oxford and some of Diego's time in Costa Rica within the agreement CAF-Latin American Centre.

Visiting fellowships for both of us from the program Desigualdades at the Free University of Berlin were instrumental for the completion of the book. Desigualdades-funded stays in Berlin spread throughout 2011, 2012, and 2013. Altogether we had over two months of writing accompanied by long walks in the city and useful conversations with colleagues from the program. All the Desigualdades team was helpful and kind. Special thanks to our friend Barbara Fritz: she encouraged us to apply to the fellowship, supported the application, invited us to her house (where we could talk with Bert as well), and gave us useful feedback.

The project involved intense fieldwork in Costa Rica as well as archival research in New York, Geneva, and London. In Costa Rica, the personnel of the National Assembly archive, Miguel Madrigal Ureña and Luis Felipe Calderón Uriarte, went out of their way to provide all the information on key laws and legislative debates. We also thank Carlos Adrián Ramírez Martín of the Library Enrique Guier Sáenz at the D. Rafael Angel Calderón Guardia Museum. At the Caja Costarricense del Seguro Social we thank Emma Zúñiga for access to historical records. We would also like to acknowledge the support of Geraldine Hawkins at the Franklyn Delano Roosevelt Archives in New York; Remo Becci, Ariel Golan, and Keiko Niimi at the International Labour Organization in Geneva; and the personnel of the Abel-Smith Archives at the London School of Economics.

In Costa Rica, we interviewed dozens of politicians and state and social actors. These conversations helped us refine our arguments and gather valuable information on Costa Rica's policymaking in the last four decades. Those interviews – more than any other piece of data – confirmed to us the quality of the state actor we mention so many times in this book. We are particularly thankful to Jorge Vargas Cullell who gave us sharp pointers on different parts of this project, suggested several people to interview, and has shaped many of our views on Costa Rican politics. He is not only an impressive academic but also a generous friend.

During 2014, Juliana benefited from a fellowship from the Mobility Program of the University of Costa Rica – the first of its kind – to conduct fieldwork in Argentina and Uruguay. Special thanks go to Juany Guzmán and Alberto Cortés, dear friends and during that time directors of the Centro de Investigaciones y Estudios Políticos (UCR), and to Carmen Caamaño, Director of IIS, for their support in opening a door that will benefit many other researchers in the future. The Centro Interdisciplinario para el Estudio de las Politicas Publicas (CIEPP, Argentina) and the Department of Political Science at Universidad de la República (Uruguay) were Juliana's home in the Southern Cone. Ruben Lo Vuolo and Camila Arza at CIEPP and Carmen Midaglia and Maria Ester Mancebo in Montevideo were fantastic hosts. Our research benefited enormously from their intellectual energy, generosity, and personal warmth. We look forward to future collaborations with all of them.

Many colleagues provided feedback in at least some parts of the manuscript or gave us useful ideas and critical bits of data on particular topics. Their work has also been a source of inspiration and informs this book in multiple ways. Colleagues who gave us feedback include (in alphabetical order): Armando Barrientos, Daniel Béland (who read the whole manuscript), Janine Berg Anne-Emanuelle Birn, Mary Clark, David Díaz, David Doyle, Christina Ewig, Fernando Filgueira, Gerardo Hernández, Huck-Ju Kwon, Rubén Lo Vuolo, Lena Lavinas, Carmelo Mesa-Lago, James McGuire, Sheila Page, Jennifer Pribble, Jeremy Seekings, John Stephens, and Enrique Valencia. We also thank the two anonymous reviewers at Cambridge University Press as well as the reviewers of a paper published in *Latin American Politics and Society*, which constituted the basis for Chapter 4.

When venturing to compare three countries other than Costa Rica, we benefited from the help of several colleagues. For Mauritius, Jeremy Seekings sent us his excellent articles on pensions and gave us ideas to think about health care. He also provided constructive comments on the overall project. Erik Erikson's graduate thesis was also very useful. For South Korea, we received feedback from Huck-Ju Kwon, who pointed out inaccuracies in our interpretation of South Korea's current architecture and other parts of the manuscript and who invited us to Seoul. In Uruguay, Fernando Filgueira, Guillermo Fuentes, Carmen Midaglia, and Marcelo Setaro came several times to our rescue and readily shared their time and ideas.

In the course of these past five years, we have received useful feedback in the many seminars we did individually and jointly. These include presentations in the Programa de Acumulación, Distribución y Desigualdad at the IIS (UCR) in Costa Rica, Nuffield College, the Oxford Department of International Development, the University of East Anglia, and the University of Bath in the UK, the Kellogg Institute for International Studies (Notre Dame) and the Watson Institute for International and Public Affairs (Brown) in the United States, the Economic Commission for Latin America and the Caribbean in Mexico, the Banco de la República in Colombia, the Universidad de Pacífico in Peru, the universities of Buenos Aires and San Andrés in Argentina; the Universidad de la República in Uruguay; the Seoul National University in South Korea; and FLACSO, FES and the Universidad de La Habana in Cuba. We also had useful discussions at international conferences where we participated including "The Political Economy of Social Policy in North America: Convergence towards Universalism?" (St Antony's College); "National Development, Social Inclusion and Smart Governance" (Seoul National University); and

"The Transformation of Latin American Social Policy: Dynamics, Models and Outcomes" (University of Bath).

The Latin American Studies Association (LASA) conferences have always been a key professional venue for both us. In Toronto, San Francisco, Washington, Chicago, and Puerto Rico, at least one of us organized panels on social policy where we exchanged ideas on the meaning of universalism and the politics of social policy. They were unique opportunities to receive critical feedback and to feel part of an engaging community of likeminded colleagues. We also received useful comments at conferences of the Society for the Advancement of Socio-economics and, more recently, ISA's Research Committee on Poverty, Welfare and Social Policy (RC19) and the Red de Economía Política de América Latina (REPAL).

The team of research assistants who contributed to the project at different moments was exceptional. Thanks to Rossana Castiglioni's diligent recommendation, we were fortunate to meet Sara Acuña Ávalos who undertook archival work in Santiago de Chile. Luis Ángel Oviedo continues providing us with fantastic statistical support and Donna Harrington edited several versions of many chapters. At the beginning of the project, Ana Luz Sáenz Ramírez helped us with archival research in San José, and Héctor Solano undertook archival research and helped us in the organization of historical data and preliminary analysis of the data presented in Chapter 6. Diana León Espinoza demands special mention and a huge thanks. She helped us with archival research, the management of data sets, general editing, the preparation of the bibliography ... and was a lifesaver at all times!

At Cambridge University Press, we have benefited from John Haslan's guidance, Christofere Fila and Carrie Parkinson's support in the production process, and Jennifer Miles Davis' efficient copyediting. We acknowledge the permission to use parts of old papers in the book granted by *Latin American Politics and Society* and *Latin American Research Review*. We also thank Humberto Jerez at FLACSO México for design of the book cover (and Alicia Puyana for making this collaboration possible) and Fernando Filgueira, Rebeca Gryspan, and Evelyne Huber for their endorsements.

We are particularly indebted to Camila Arza, Jennifer Pribble and Ken Shadlen for reading our manuscript at different stages and for their extreme patience and generosity in helping us improve our argument. This book is definitely better due to their inputs, which, in the case of Ken, a dear friend of Diego, was not only intellectual but emotional as well. We look forward to new projects with them in the future.

We are thankful for our intellectual partnership and friendship. So much so that we are ready to embark on new joint projects to continue learning about research and policy from each other.

Our biggest gratitude goes to our families. Our life partners Rosa and Mauricio have been amazingly supportive during the whole project. They shouldered all domestic duties and caretaking when we were away working on the book and welcomed us back home tired but with a supportive smile. Silvia, Maite and Maya came to accept our absences as well as our busy presence when working together in either of our homes in Oxford and San Isidro. They are all an amazing source of energy and happiness. We did our best to make them part of this project. We know that they enjoyed visiting Berlin, Buenos Aires, and Costa Rica and that they cherish the extended family we built along the way. This book is dedicated to the five of them.

Abbreviations

AFAP	Administradoras de Fondos de Ahorro Provisional (Pension Savings Funds Administrators)
ASSE	Administración de los Servicios de Salud del Estado (State Administrator of Health Services)
AUGE	Plan de Acceso Universal de Garantías Explícitas (Universal Access Plan with Explicit Guarantees)
BPS	Banco de Provision Social (Social Welfare Bank)
BRP	Basic Retirement Pension
CCSS	Caja Costarricense del Seguro Social (Costa Rican Social Insurance Agency)
CCTs	Conditional Cash Transfers
CISS	Conferencia Interamericana de Seguridad Social (Inter-American Conference on Social Security)
CN	Concertación Nacional (National Pact)
COOPESAIN	Cooperativa Autogestionaria de Servidores para la Salud Integral (Self-Management Cooperative for Integral Health)
COOPESALUD	Cooperativa Autogestionaria de Servicios Integrales de Salud (Self-Management Cooperative of Integral Health Services)
COOPESANA	Cooperativa Cogestionaria de Salud de Santa Ana R.L (Health Self-Management Cooperative of Santa Ana)

DFID	Department for International Development
DGSS	Dirección General de Seguridad Social (General Board for Social Security)
DISSE	Dirección de Seguros Sociales por Enfermedad (National Board of Social Insurance)
DRG	Diagnosis Related Groups
EBAIS	Equipos Básicos de Atención Integral en Salud (Basic Comprehensive Health Care Teams)
ECLAC	Economic Commission for Latin America and the Caribbean
FODESAF	Fondo de Desarrollo Social y Asignaciones Familiares (Social Assistance Fund)
FONASA	Fondo Nacional de Salud (National Health Care Fund)
GDP	Gross Domestic Product
GP	General Practitioner
IDS	Institute of Development Studies
IFIs	International Financial Institutions
ILO	International Labour Organization
IMAS	Instituto Mixto de Ayuda Social (Mixed Institute of Social Assistance)
IMF	International Monetary Fund
INA	Instituto Nacional de Aprendizaje (National Learning Institute)
ITCO	Instituto de Tierras y Colonización (Institute of Land and Colonization)
LPT	Ley de Protección al Trabajador (Workers' Protection Law)
MDGs	Millennium Development Goals
MOH	Minister of Health
NBLS	National Basic Living Standard
NHI	National Health Insurance
NHS	National Health System
NPF	National Pension Fund
NPS	National Pension System

NRF	National Resource Fund
NSF	National Savings Fund
OECD	Organization for Economic Co-operation and Development
PAHO	Pan American Health Organization
PANI	Patronato Nacional para la Infancia (Childrens National Agency)
PLN	Partido Liberación Nacional (National Liberation Party)
SIPROCIMECA	Sindicato de Profesionales en Ciencias Médicas de la C.C.S.S. e Instituciones Afines (Union of Medical Professionals of the Costa Rican Social Insurance Agency)
SNAIS	Sistema Nacional Integral de Salud (National Integrated Health System)
SUPEN	Superintendencia de Pensiones (Pensions Supervision Agency)
UCIMED	Universidad de Ciencias Médicas (University of Medical Science)
UM	Unión Médica (Medical Union)
UNICEF	United Nations Children's Fund
UNRISD	United Nations Research Institute for Social Development
USAID	United States Agency for International Development
WHO	World Health Organization
WOP	War on Poverty

PART I

Universalism in the South

1 | *Introduction*

1.1 The Renewed Attention to Universalism

"Health care is a right for everyone in every country, rich and poor. Our commitment is universal," the World Bank's President Jim Yong Kim claimed in early 2014.[1] He is not alone in his call. Policy proposals aimed at achieving universalism have flourished (Filgueira *et al.*, 2006; ILO, 2011; UNRISD, 2010), as has far-reaching policy experimentation (Cotlear *et al.*, 2014; Huber and Stephens, 2012; Martínez Franzoni and Sánchez-Ancochea, 2014; Pribble, 2013). The term has gained traction among policymakers in national and international institutions: the World Health Organization (WHO) is pushing for universal health coverage; the United Nations (UN) is promoting a global social protection floor; and a number of countries across the South, particularly in Latin America, have introduced reforms labeled as universal. The growing attention to full coverage and equity in the post-2015 international agenda has expanded the interest on these goals even further (Fischer, 2012).

This policy attention coincides with the emergence of a new middle class that across the South demands better and more affordable social services (Pezzini, 2012). Economic growth, improved wages, and more access to credit has rapidly expanded the number of the non-poor: in Latin America, for example, the number of people within the middle class is now equal to the amount of those in poverty (Ferreira *et al.*, 2012). And the expansion is far from over: estimates indicate that, across the world, the middle class will increase from 1.8 billion in 2009 to 3.2 billion in 2020 and 4.9 billion in 2030 (Kharas, 2010). Although upward mobility has granted these groups new consumption and investment opportunities, they still share many characteristics with the

---

[1] See www.worldbank.org/en/news/speech/2014/01/14/speech-world-bank-group-president-jim-yong-kim-health-emerging-economies (last accessed December 8, 2014).

poor. They are what the *Financial Times* depicts as "the fragile middle" (Burn-Murdoch and Bernard, 2014): people who are just "one illness away" from falling back into poverty (Krishna, 2010) and in need of high quality services and transfers.

Despite its growing social, academic, and policy relevance, few studies have focused on how universalism should be understood across the South; what its core features are; and how it can be built and sustained. Most comparative literature explains the level, composition, and/or redistributive power of social spending (Haggard and Kaufman, 2008; Segura-Ubiergo, 2007). Others have accounted for social policy reforms in recent decades (Castiglioni, 2005; Madrid, 2003; Mesa-Lago, 2008; Rudra, 2008). None of these lines of inquiry have explicitly addressed the creation and expansion of universalism. Moreover, most studies on the historical determinants of social policy address the presence of democracy, social movements, and left-wing parties (coupled, in some cases, with economic variables) to explain variation (e.g. Sandbrook *et al.*, 2007). These factors may be significant preconditions, contributing to place social policy at the top of the policy agenda. However, the observation of left-wing parties under democratic regimes expanding social spending yet not universalism suggest there are missing links between democratic institutions on the one hand and universalism on the other.

This book is about these missing links. We begin by defining universalism in terms of desirable policy outputs: similar, generous entitlements for all. These, we argue, must be distinguished from the specific instruments that secure them – which may include social insurance and social assistance alike. We then explore the determinants behind universal social policies based on the comparative study of four countries across three continents – Costa Rica, Mauritius, South Korea, and Uruguay – and a detailed analysis of policymaking in Costa Rica. We identify two variables that link democracy and progressive political leadership with universalism. The first is the policy architecture – i.e. the combination of instruments that define who has access to what benefits, and how. In the short run, the more unified these instruments are, the more we expect universal results to be. In the long run, policy architectures create a set of opportunities and constraints for further (positive and negative) change. The second variable is the presence of state actors capable of promoting unified architectures through the adaptation of international ideas. What makes this actor successful in some countries, sectors, and periods yet not others is the combination of the right political, ideational, and bureaucratic resources.

Based on the evidence we present throughout this book, we draw implications for contemporary efforts to promote redistribution. This goal is pressing as the concentration of assets among the very wealthy intensifies across the world (Piketty, 2013; Stiglitz, 2013). Aside from being objectionable on ethical and moral grounds, inequality bears significant costs in terms of economic growth and various social ills (Wilkinson and Pickett, 2009; World Bank, 2006).

To present our argument in this introductory chapter, we first discuss the meaning and importance of universalism (Section 1.2) to then identify gaps in the literature on the determinants of universalism in the South (Section 1.3). In Section 1.4 we justify our selection of policies and briefly address missing links between democracy and universal outputs. In Sections 1.5 and 1.6 we present our methodology and the main arguments, focusing first on the concept of policy architectures and then on state actors and ideas (with democracy and progressive leadership as preconditions). We conclude with a brief overview of the rest of the book.

1.2 The Meaning and Relevance of Universalism

The meaning of universalism in social policy is contentious (Anttonen, Häikiö and Stefánsson, 2012). Following Titmus' (1958) and Esping-Andersen's (1990) typology of welfare states, a dominant approach understands universal social policies as those programs funded with general taxes that everyone receives as a matter of right based on the principle of citizenship (Beland *et al.*, 2014; Esping Andersen and Korpi, 1987). Unfortunately implementing these kinds of policies in the South confronts deep-seated obstacles. High income inequality, concentration of political power among a small elite, weak fiscal capacity, political instability, and macroeconomic volatility have all hindered the creation and expansion of citizen-based, tax-funded programs for all (Sandbrook *et al.*, 2007).

Partly as a response to these problems, recent policy proposals use the term "universal" and "universalism" to refer to programs that seek to reach everyone, even if they entail unequal benefits.[2] For example, in the January 2014 speech we mentioned early in this chapter, the World Bank's president stressed the need for "a special focus on expanding access to vital services for poor women and children." In Mexico, the much heralded creation of Seguro Popular is viewed by authors like Cotlear *et al.* (2014) as a way to reduce segmentation in the present and down the road. Yet the reform may create instead two-tier social systems with notorious differences in generosity between beneficiaries.

In our view, if everyone has access to some health care benefits, but only a few have their cancer treatment covered, there is no universalism to speak of. Neither can we call an education system universal when it combines poor quality public schools, privately managed schools that require co-payments, and private schools with more resources, a better curriculum, and more daily school hours for a small minority. When it comes to pensions, if transfers to the poor are below subsistence levels while the rest of the population receives generous pensions based on previous income levels, we may witness massive coverage yet not universalism.[3]

Moreover, focusing primarily on the poor is unlikely to create the type of cross-class coalitions that are required to support a steady growth of social spending (Korpi and Palmer, 1998). When both the poor and the middle class are incorporated into the same policies, the voice and mobilization capacity of the latter benefit the former as well. This cross-class alliance is not only helpful to broaden access but also to guarantee generosity. The resulting expansion of transfers and services has substantial redistributive effects and creates a virtuous circle for social incorporation (Huber, 2002).

We need an approach to universalism that builds on the maximalist goal but acknowledges that there may be different ways to secure the same benefits for all (e.g. not only general revenues but also social insurance combined with social assistance). Universal social policies are those that reach the entire population with generous transfers and services (see Figure 1.1), without necessarily resorting to markets.

---

[2] "Everyone" may mean the population at large or everybody who is part of a given collective (e.g. young children in the case of pre-primary education or the elderly in the case of pensions).

[3] Even though pensions may be granted for a number of reasons, in this book we use the term to refer to old-age transfers alone.

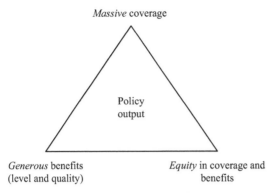

Figure 1.1 Universal Outputs as a Triangle of Coverage, Generosity, and Equity

There are thus three key dimensions in our approach: coverage, generosity, and equity. Massive coverage is relatively straightforward: it takes place when benefits reach most people involved in a given category (e.g. school-age children; pregnant women; the elderly). Ideally, transfers and services should incorporate non-nationals located in the country (regardless of their legal status), even if that ideal has been particularly difficult to sustain in the South and increasingly in the North as well. Generosity refers to the level and quality of benefits involved. The more comprehensive and the better quality benefits are, the more universal the policy output will be. Equity refers to the distribution of coverage and generosity across beneficiaries: countries could secure massive access with an uneven generosity among groups of the population. The more evenly distributed – between rural and urban areas; women and men; and the poor and the non-poor – benefits are, the more universal the results will be.

By introducing a new definition of a concept that has a long tradition, we risk being criticized for muddying the waters. Why should we challenge a rich body of scholarly work that defines universal social policies as those based on the principle of citizenship? Why don't we use terms like "egalitarian social policy" or "redistributive social policy" instead? We believe that giving up the term would not be the best approach for at least two reasons. On the one hand, the term "universal" has a powerful normative value; it is also contested as too many policymakers and some academics nowadays use the term to promote unequal benefits for different groups. On the other hand, as previously discussed, creating citizenship-based programs is difficult. Weak state capacity and electoral pressures conspire against implementing large programs funded through general taxes from scratch. Our approach highlights the potential to secure the desired goals through more pragmatic and diverse means.

Adopting this definition allows us to explore many policy relevant questions: what policy instruments help countries get closer to desired policy *outputs*? Have social insurance and social assistance played a role in building universalism? Have countries secured universalism by relying on non-public providers, and if so, how?

1.3 Explanations of Universalism: Going Beyond Enabling Political Conditions

Until very recently, the comparative political literature on social policy in the South did little to address the building of universalism. In the last decade, however, a growing number of studies have started to pay (often implicit) attention to this issue – largely mirroring the intensive processes of state-building taking place in many of these countries.

In exploring the formation of social policy, studies define their dependent variable in diverse ways. Many scholars still base their claims on the amount of people reached and social spending involved, with few explicitly addressing universalism. For example, in his study of welfare states in Latin America, Segura-Ubiergo (2007: 31) groups countries based on "welfare effort" – measured by coverage and various indicators of social spending. Quantitative indicators of this kind are even more prevalent in econometric analysis, where data availability inhibits more nuanced forms of measurement. Brown and Hunter (1999) focus exclusively on spending in their study of democracy and social policy – an analysis reproduced and updated by Lehoucq (2012).

Following an established tradition started by Titmus' work and boosted by Esping-Andersen's influential analysis of the worlds of welfare capitalism, other studies explore how public money is spent. Authors such as Huber, Mustillo, and Stephens (2008), Rudra (2008), and Rudra and Haggard (2005) distinguish between social security, health care, and education, and explore its different determinants. Most of these authors assume that health care and (primary) education have larger redistributive capacity than pensions, but do not discuss universalism per se.

There are some recent exceptions. In their ambitious study of welfare states in Latin America, East Asia, and Eastern Europe, Haggard and Kaufman (2008) use the term "universal" to refer primarily to coverage, although at times extend the concept to equity. When talking about the welfare state in Eastern Europe under Communism, for example, they argue: "core benefits such as the employment guarantee, healthcare, pensions, and family allowances, all evolved into universal programs. Where benefits were tied to wages (as with pensions), the highly compressed nature of the wage structure meant that they were distributed relatively equally" (p. 143). Overall, however, Haggard and Kaufman do not devote much attention to the meaning or determinants of universalism per se – in fact, neither universal nor universalism appear in their index.

Sandbrook *et al.* (2007) also refer to universal policies in their exploration of social democracy in the periphery. When defining the different types of social-democratic regimes, they refer to "universal entitlements to meet basic needs" in radical social democracies like Kerala, and to "universal and comprehensive welfare state" in classical social democracies like Costa Rica and Mauritius. Yet they make little effort to define these terms rigorously or to distinguish analytically between universal policies and the other components of the social democratic regimes they explore (e.g. state intervention in economic affairs; the structure of the state; and the role of social movements).

Two recent studies on Latin America's welfare policies are more explicit in their definition of universalism. Huber and Stephens (2012) explore the determinants of redistributive social policies in Latin America through a combination of panel data and case studies. Their study focuses on redistributive policies, which they define in terms of basic universalism: flat rate transfers for the bottom three deciles together with "tax financed, flat rate universalism, that is, quality health and education as a right of citizenship" (Huber and Stephens, 2012: 68). Like us, they recognize the role that different policy instruments (including social security and means-testing) can have. Unlike us, however, they put an accent on massive and equal access to basic rather than generous benefits.

Jennifer Pribble's object of study in her book on the role of party politics in welfare reforms in Latin America is the closest to ours. Her definition of universalism includes coverage, transparency, quality, and level of segmentation and financing. She moves away from binary distinctions (universal vs non-universal) and argues that universalism can be reached with different policy instruments (Pribble, 2013). At the same time, her definition involves features we see as part and parcel of policy instruments – rather than outputs – such as transparency and financing.

Moving from the conceptualization of our dependent variable to its determinants, much of the literature underlines the role of democratic institutions in making broad-based policies possible (e.g. Filgueira, 2007a; Huber and Stephens 2012; Lehouqc, 2012; McGuire, 2010; Rudra and Haggard, 2005; Sandbrook *et al.*, 2007; Segura-Ubiergo, 2007). Although often not explicitly defined, democracy for these authors is commonly understood as encompassing a system of government with free and fair elections and freedom of the press. The accent on democracy owes much to Meltzer and Richard (1981): their median voter theorem holds that policy will reflect the preferences of the voter located at the median point in the income distribution. Therefore, "majority rule with a universal franchise would lead to economic redistribution" (Shapiro, Swenson, and Donno, 2008: 1). Electoral competition forces political parties to draw on social spending to increase their constituency. Democratic governments are particularly effective in protecting social spending in times of economic crisis (Avelino, Brown, and Hunter, 2005; Brown and Hunter, 1999). For McGuire (2010), elections and a free press influence positively the amount of spending in primary health – his central dependent variable. Filgueira (2007a) concentrates on the long-term effects of democracy, showing how democratic regimes gradually develop social coalitions and institutional mechanisms that support large social programs. In his view, "early social state formation is highly correlated with early democratic experiments" (p. 141). Social insurance expanded in Argentina and Uruguay under democratic rule during the 1910s and 1920s. Chile's founding push happened under authoritarian rule in the 1920s, but the subsequent expansion took place under democracy.

Democracy also opens spaces for left-wing parties, which will generally favor higher social spending. Huber and Stephens (2012) found that the Latin American countries where left-wing parties prevailed over the past two decades were more likely to stress spending in health and education – which tend to have broad coverage and more redistributive results – rather than in social insurance and social assistance. In Pribble's (2013) account of universalistic social reforms, having left-wing parties is a necessary condition, even if by no means sufficient.

The literature on the period of neoliberal retrenchment of the 1980s and 1990s brought to the center stage other variables – some of which are prominent in our own analysis in the second part of the book. In particular, international pressures, economic and fiscal demands, and domestic technocrats – mostly economists – received significant attention as drivers of social policy change (e.g. Brooks, 2009; Centeno, 1994; Madrid, 2003). New research was built on the notion that retrenchment shrunk ideological differences between right- and left-wing parties and that a global ideational turn accompanied reforms. Presidents often placed policy formation in the hands of technocratic cadres that at times acted outside democratic institutions (Markoff and Montecinos, 1993; Silva, 2010). Processes of diffusion, learning, and emulation of ideas coming from abroad were singled out as drivers of policy reform (Ewig, 2010; Meseguer, 2009; Weyland, 2005).

Nevertheless, the retrenchment literature also recognized the role of democracy and political parties. Domestic coalitions in the context of democratic institutions adapted the set of reforms promoted by the international financial institutions (Weyland, 2007). Scholars also pointed to the role that right-of-center governments played in embracing state downsizing by privatizing, decentralizing, and contracting out social services and transfers (Castiglioni, 2005; Huber, 1996; Kauffman and Segura-Ubiergo, 2001).

There is no doubt that electoral competition and party ideology influence the level of social policy and are fundamental for the promotion of universalism – a claim we confirm in this book. Yet democracy is by no means enough. In Latin America, for example, electoral competition in Chile and Uruguay resulted in unequal social benefits across occupational groups during most of the twentieth century. Uruguay had nine pension funds in 1967, including those for civil servants, and nine autonomous health insurance funds for workers in different manufacturing activities. In exchange for a monthly premium, large parts of the middle class received services from mutual health associations, which spent 3.1 times more resources per person than the public system (Mesa-Lago, 1978). In Chile, social insurance involved ten different funds, with entitlements and obligations contained in more than two thousand legal texts (Mesa-Lago, 1978; Segura-Ubiergo, 2007). Fragmentation inhibited universal outputs and, as a result, deepened market-driven inequalities (Haggard and Kaufman, 2008).

Since the 1980s and under the last wave of democratization, some left-wing administrations have been more willing and capable of delivering redistributive programs than others. As argued by Pribble (2013: 19), some "populist parties of the left/center-left have recently engaged in regressive social policy reforms." In fact, there is a large variance in social policy among democratic countries, both historically (Filgueira, 2007a) and today (Martínez Franzoni, 2008; Pribble, 2011).

Electoral competition and party ideology are thus important contributing factors to universalism but cannot alone explain the direction of social policy change. More broadly, it is problematic to assume that preferences of leading social and political actors translate more or less automatically into policy content.[4] In fact, political leaders and parties can respond to their electorate in many ways – some of which will lead to universal outputs while many others will not. Voters, particularly middle class constituencies, do not necessarily frame their claim for more and better social services as demands for universalism.

In explaining the link between democracy and universalism, we thus need to look at other variables and answer key questions: What features do programs have? What actors are behind program design? What incentives do they have to promote policy instruments that deliver universalism? Addressing these questions – that is, identifying missing links between political preconditions and universal social policy outputs – constitute the main concern of our book.

1.4 How to Explore Missing Links: Our Research Design

Much of the literature on social policy studies social policy regimes (Gough, 2013), understood as the intertwined set of state interventions to secure people's wellbeing. The assumption is that sectors such as education, health care and pensions are organized under a similar rationale. Interventions in specific areas are pieces of a larger puzzle to ensure safe and resourceful life courses for all. Yet considering the whole policy regime when studying universalism is problematic for at

---

[4] The literature on state capacity has a similar problem: it fails to explain how the bureaucracy builds its own policy preferences. A strong bureaucracy may always be a better enforcer of laws already approved (something Itzigsohn, 2000 shows in his comparison of labor laws in Costa Rica and the Dominican Republic), but by itself cannot explain why certain laws are approved in the first place.

least two reasons. First, it is hard to effectively explore missing links between macro-political factors and universal outputs without focusing on specific policies. Second, in most countries we cannot identify a single rationale behind the allocation of public resources that cuts across policy sectors. This common rationale may be present in a few cases like Sweden, Finland, or Norway, but not elsewhere. Take the case of Canada and the United States (Béland and Waddan, 2013). While both are commonly portrayed as liberal welfare state regimes based, primarily, on the analysis of monetary transfers, the differences in their health care systems are striking. Policy regime "inconsistencies" across sectors are probably even more significant across the South.

In this book we thus avoid making claims regarding the overall social policy regime but still seek to identify policy determinants that cut across sectors. To this purpose health care is the primary sector we address, while pensions is our shadow case – a term used by Pribble (2013). The latter validates the relevance of our findings beyond a single sector. Health care and pensions are the two largest programs in most countries. Additionally, considering differences between a transfer program and a service provides a better understanding of the dynamics fostering and inhibiting universalism.

To explore the determinants for the successful promotion of universal outputs in health care and pensions, we chose cases across different regions (Africa, Asia, and Latin America). More specifically, we compare trajectories in four countries that stand out for having created active social policies at one point or another: Costa Rica, Mauritius, South Korea, and Uruguay. As we show in Chapter 3, Uruguay is regarded as a pioneer in social policy in Latin America, if not in the South at large (Filgueira, 2007a; Mesa-Lago, 1978, 2008). Costa Rica and Mauritius have been outliers in their respective regions for several decades because of high investment in health care, education, and pensions (Sandbrook *et al.*, 2007). Our selection of South Korea may be more controversial given that the country's increase in its welfare effort has taken place only recently (Deyo, 1989; ILO, 2007) and under a higher level of gross domestic product (GDP) than the others. However, we are interested in long-term trajectories: at the beginning of the 1960s South Korea had a lower GDP than the other three countries (see Figures 1.2 and 1.3 below). In addition, South Korea's policy change in recent decades has followed – at least rhetorically – a

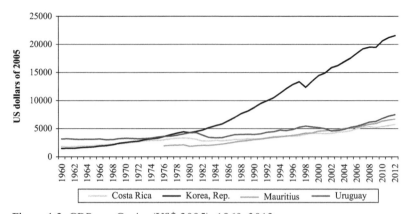

Figure 1.2 GDP per Capita (US$ 2005), 1960–2012
Source: Based on the World Bank's World Development Indicators.

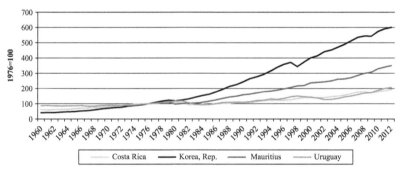

Figure 1.3 GDP per Capita (US$ 2005), 1960–2012 (1976 = 100)
Source: Based on the World Bank's World Development Indicators.

universalistic direction. It is thus a useful case to explore how the initial architecture may constrain subsequent efforts.

In selecting our four cases, we adopt a similar strategy to that of Huber and Stephens in their 2001 study of welfare states in the North. Rather than sampling different welfare state types, they were "guided by [their] theoretical and normative interest in the most generous welfare states … [They focused] on those cases in which labor movements and social democratic parties have had a significant influence on the development of overall regime" (Huber and Stephens, 2001: 113). Huber and Stephens were interested in identifying appropriate political and economic conditions for the promotion of generous social policies in the North, an objective that matches ours for the South. Costa Rica, Mauritius, South Korea, and Uruguay can be considered "best cases" and potential candidates to deliver universal outputs in health care and pensions. However, not all have accomplished this latter task: as we will see in the next section and with more detail in Chapters 3 and 4, Costa Rica advanced more toward equal, generous benefits for a majority of the population than Mauritius and, especially, than South Korea and Uruguay.

The four cases also show diversity across time in terms of political regimes and macro-economic conditions. This variation strengthens our research design because rather than taking the role of democracy as a given, it lets us explore its actual contribution to the building of universalism.

Table 1.1 indicates the variance in terms of political systems. We follow a large body of literature in separating between democracy, semi-democracy, and authoritarian regimes. Focusing primarily on free and fair elections with full suffrage, authoritarian periods take place when these are absent. In semi-democratic periods, there is full electoral competition but some parties are not allowed to participate and/or there is not full suffrage. For example, in Uruguay, Costa Rica, and

Table 1.1 *Periods of Democracy and Authoritarianism in Each of the Four Selected Countries since the Creation of the Foundational Policy Architecture*

Countries	Semi-Democracy	Democracy	Authoritarianism
Costa Rica	1940–1975	1975–present	–
Mauritius	1948–1968*	1968–present	–
South Korea	–	1988–present	1977–1988
Uruguay	1910–1931	1938–1972	1931–1938
		1984–present	1972–1984

Note: By foundational architectures, we mean those shaped by the states in an initial effort to organize social benefits (Chapter 4).
*Between 1948 and 1968 Mauritius was still a colony but with growing political autonomy and democratic deliberation.

Mauritius, women did not have the right to vote until 1931, 1948, and 1953 respectively. In democratic periods, there are free and fair elections with no restrictions on either voters or political parties.

While democratic or semi-democratic rule prevails in our sample, in South Korea and Uruguay there were also periods of authoritarianism. In Chapters 4 and 8, we demonstrate that reforms that advanced the universal objectives of high coverage, generosity, and equity almost always took place during periods of electoral competition – legal changes to integrate different insurance funds in Uruguay during the 1970s being the exception. Progressive parties and politicians interested in social policy were also important for expansionary efforts as the National Liberation Party in Costa Rica; the Labour Party and the Mauritian Social Democratic Party in Mauritius; and the Frente Amplio in Uruguay clearly show.

We thus confirm that electoral competition and progressive parties – led often by charismatic progressive leaders – are important preconditions for universalism. At the same time, their presence is not enough: during most of the twentieth century, Uruguayan health care and pensions were too fragmented to deliver universal outputs. Meanwhile, democratic institutions have done little to prevent increasing inequality in service provision in Mauritius and, more recently, in Costa Rica.

If democracy and progressive parties are insufficient to account for universalism in social policy, what about economic conditions? According to authors such as Eisenstadt (1966), economic modernization promotes growth in social spending, mainly through urbanization, industrialization, aging, and stronger state institutions. A large GDP is often considered a precondition to promote generous, expensive social policies. Finally, some argue that globalization limits the opportunities for pro-universal reforms (Rudra, 2007).

Although GDP growth was indeed important for the expansion of welfare efforts in these countries, it hardly explains diverse trajectories across the four cases. In 1960, the GDP per capita of South Korea, Uruguay, and Costa Rica were not significantly different (see Figure 1.2). And yet, by then policy architectures were already dissimilar, with Costa Rica and, to a lesser extent, Mauritius benefiting from more unified policy instruments than the other two. South Korea's high growth begun in the 1960s, but its attempts at promoting universal reforms came much later. Meanwhile, in Costa Rica and Uruguay a similar economic performance has gone hand in hand with significant differences in social policy outcomes (see Figure 1.3 and Chapter 4). More significantly, Costa Rica has not been an outlier in terms of economic growth in the last fifty years, yet has developed the architecture most favorable to universalism of the four.

1.5 The Influence of Policy Architectures on Universalism

If democracy is only a precondition and economic differences do not explain variations, how can we explain the diversity in universal options? In this book, we identify the policy architectures as the first driver (Figure 1.4). Policy architectures include five different components: eligibility, funding, entitlements, delivery, and regulation of the outside option for specific social policies (e.g. health care, education, pensions).

The notion of policy architecture comes from the Latin American literature on social policy. There, it is used as a relatively loose term that refers to all state institutions and policies involved in social protection (Filgueira *et al.*, 2006). For Filgueira (2007), for example, architectures of social protection comprise principles (e.g. dependence on formal employment), instruments (e.g. payroll taxes), and their interlinks. The term as used by Filgueira and others helps emphasize interrelations between different components of a system, something we also want to highlight. Yet its loose definition tends to overlap with the notions of welfare regime and social policy regime. In contrast, we apply the concept only to specific policy sectors and do our best to justify its components.

In addition to defining the characteristics of specific policies at a given moment in time (see Chapter 3), policy architectures play a more dynamic role (Figure 1.5). Different architectures create distinct

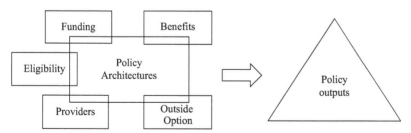

Figure 1.4 Policy Architectures as an Independent Variable in the Short Run

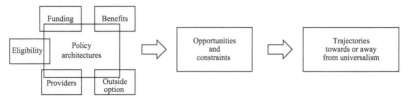

Figure 1.5 Policy Architectures as an Independent Variable in the Long Run

opportunities and constraints for subsequent universalization. This second argument draws on the historical institutional literature on path dependence (Mahoney, 2010), particularly on the concepts of policy legacies and feedbacks. For authors in this tradition, policy change at a certain moment "depends crucially on processes set in motion by the nature of policy in question" (Amenta, 2003: 106). New social programs create actors and coalitions, public institutions, and social expectations that make future changes more or less difficult (Huber and Stephens, 2001; Skocpol, 1992). In the Latin American context, Ewig (2010) expanded the concept of policy legacies beyond its typical focus on class to highlight the way they reinforce gender and race-based privileges as well. More recently and closer to us, Pribble (2013) highlights the role of policy legacies in influencing progressive reforms in Latin America by strengthening specific actors and creating different demands.

By linking the literature on the characteristics of social policy with the historical institutionalist discussion of path dependence, we make a substantial contribution to the study of social policy. The concept of policy architecture allows us to consider short- and long-term implications simultaneously: when designing new programs, policymakers should evaluate the level of unification in the short run but also consider likely trajectories over the long run.

In Chapters 3 and 4, we compare the policy architectures in Mauritius, Costa Rica, South Korea, and Uruguay. The first country funded health care and pensions for all through general taxes. In the other three, social insurance was the most important policy instrument, yet with significantly distinct characteristics. The comparison of the four countries questions the idea that any given policy instrument will always be necessarily more appropriate to reach universalism than others. For example, despite being the closest to the much-praised

"Scandinavian model," the Mauritian architecture has not delivered more universal outputs than the other three social insurance-based cases. In particular, Costa Rica's outputs have been more universal while relying on payroll taxes.

How is it possible to deliver universal outputs through a diverse set of instruments including social insurance and social assistance? We highlight unification as a key feature that must accompany any given policy instrument. Unification takes place when all beneficiaries receive the service or cash transfer in a similar fashion and the state plays a major role in defining benefits, acting as direct provider and effectively regulating the market. By the same token, fragmentation is a major threat to universalism. By fragmentation we mean the existence of diverse mechanisms of access, funding, entitlements, and providers, as well as the presence of a large outside market option. Fragmentation can be policy driven (i.e. led by corporatist arrangements) or market driven (i.e. led by the growing use of private actors in public provision). Rather than a binary category we deal with unification and fragmentation as two ends of a continuum where each of the five dimensions of a country's policy architecture can be placed.

We also show that the existing policy architecture at a given time influences subsequent changes through two main channels. On the one hand, they strengthen some social and state actors over others and create different kinds of economic, political, and social incentives in favor of or against unification. For example, powerful private providers are likely to consolidate fragmentation over time – something Ewig and Kay (2011) show for the Chilean case. On the other hand, policy architectures shape the set of available options that policymakers contemplate when considering reforms. In general, when arrangements are from the onset unified, it is easier to expand them in a pro-universal direction in subsequent stages.

The discussion of policy architectures in Chapters 3 and 4 highlights Costa Rica's exceptionality in comparative perspective. Costa Rica's foundational architecture in the early 1940s did not deliver universal outcomes immediately (e.g. initially informal workers were marginalized, children and stay-at-home women entered only as dependents of insured workers), but had unique features that facilitated the subsequent pro-universal expansion. Social insurance was based on a single fund for all workers and was built "from the bottom up."

At first, mandatory social insurance only covered blue-collar workers under a wage ceiling. Insiders had incentives to support further expansion to higher income groups that could bring larger payroll tax contributions to the system. This became particularly evident in the 1970s, when the wage ceiling was eliminated and the wealthy were legally mandated to join social insurance. The provision of the same high-quality health care benefits for everybody who was insured (whether workers or their dependent family) created incentives for outsiders to join.[5]

During the 1970s, Costa Rica introduced an additional measure that encouraged further unification. To ensure that the poor were incorporated to the services already in place for the non-poor, the government created a Social Assistance Fund (Fondo de Desarrollo y Asignaciones Familiares, FODESAF). FODESAF provided financial resources for programs aimed at improving nutrition, health, non-contributory pensions, and other benefits for the population who, until then, had been marginalized. The new programs were placed under line ministries, therefore avoiding the creation of different institutions devoted to the poor alone.

Finally, we demonstrate that the outside option is a growing threat to universalism across the world. Private supply of social services creates new actors and opportunities for the middle class, thus eroding unification in the other four policy components of the architecture. Empirical evidence presented in Chapters 3, 4, and 7 sustains our call for the effective regulation of the outside option in Chapter 9.

Our findings are based on a small N comparative study, which is the most appropriate research design to explore the role of architectures in shaping universal policy outputs. The small sample allows us to characterize the policy architecture rigorously, considering all five components and their interaction in detail. We are also able to explore the evolution of the policy architecture in each country and sector over the long run, identifying how path dependent mechanisms operate in each

---

[5] Ideally, everyone should have access to transfers and services independently of their labor market status. In particular, all family members should have the same rights as citizens rather than as workers. Yet, as previously discussed, in many countries, providing benefits through social insurance may be easier – a desirable second best. What is important in these cases is that dependent family members receive the *same* benefits than the head of household – exactly what happened in Costa Rica.

case. This would not have been possible with a larger number of cases. Econometric-based studies of social policy are severely constrained by data availability on indicators of outputs that go beyond coverage, and by difficulties to measure the degree of unification of policy architectures.

We are, nonetheless, aware of the challenges of small N analysis and try to minimize them. The first has to do with establishing causality between key variables. We need to demonstrate that policy changes introduced in the four countries were indeed conditioned by the architecture. To this purpose, we use secondary sources to reconstruct changes in architectures over time and show how they influenced subsequent decisions. As we discuss at the end of this book, our argument would benefit from additional research that considers the role of the architecture in other contexts (e.g. countries with low state capacity) and also explores the conditions under which dramatic disruptions are possible under democratic regimes.

The second concern has to do with the extent to which we can generalize our arguments beyond the four countries we compare in this book. The validity of some of the claims we make is based on pair comparisons: the contrast between Costa Rica and Mauritius demonstrates that social security can be more successful than tax-based policies in delivering universal outputs. When compared with South Korea and Uruguay, Costa Rica shows the importance of relying on unified policy instruments. We also discard competing factors – particularly macro-economic ones. Given the variety of comparisons on which we base our claims, we feel confident about its broader applicability.

Our findings are particularly relevant for middle-income countries – from Bolivia to India, China, or Brazil – where most of the world's poor currently live (IDS, 2012).[6] This is the case because promoting universal outputs requires a minimum of state capacity, which may be absent in the poorest countries in the world. Nevertheless, our claim that programs are long-term affairs, our call for more detailed studies of political trajectories, and our accent on state actors may still resonate across the South.

---

[6] This is also where the rise of the new middle class is expected to continue and where the challenges to overcome its fragility will be more intense.

1.6 Policy Architectures as a Dependent Variable: Political Determinants

How are policy architectures initially designed? How are they (re)shaped at key moments? Given its success in promoting universal outputs when compared to the other countries, we decided to explore this question through the Costa Rican case. We resort to a combination of historical institutional methodology and policy process tracing to establish the political determinants for the creation (Chapter 5), expansion (Chapter 6), and contradictory changes (Chapter 7) of its policy architecture. For the first two periods (lasting from the early 1940s to the end of the 1970s) we consider health care and pensions simultaneously, as part and parcel of a single process of policy formation. For the most recent period, we separate the two programs to account for distinct dynamics of transformation.

We concentrate on key moments when health care and pensions underwent significant changes, reconstructing policy decisions around these moments. For each policy and period we establish how the policy architecture was (re)shaped, which actors pushed for change, and where their ideas came from. We pay close attention to counterfactuals: policy options that would have taken the policy architecture in a different direction. We also consider how the previous stage influenced subsequent outcomes to account for the dynamic role of the policy architecture.

The analysis follows a specific type of process tracing that "provides information about context, process, or mechanism, and that contributes distinctive leverage in causal inference" (Collier, Brady, and Seawright, in Mahoney, 2010: 124). We collected a set of causal-process observations (Brady and Collier, 2014) to build a theory of the links between democracy and the unified policy architecture under scrutiny. We include thick descriptions of events in the run-up to the creation of social insurance and show how timing mattered in decision making (Mahoney, 2010). For example, we show how the first draft of the Costa Rican social insurance bill was written in Chile, where a close confidant of the President had travelled, precisely at a time when this country was exploring ways to promote unification of its social insurance funds.

Data sources are statistics, archival records, newspapers, and interviews. Descriptive statistics are used to measure universal outputs over time and link them to economic and social changes. Archival records include primary official sources collected in the Costa Rica's Legislative Assembly and the country's national archives between 2011 and 2012; the International Labour Organization (ILO) archives in Geneva (during short stays in 2012 and 2013); the Archive of the Twentieth Century and the newspaper section at the National Library in Santiago de Chile in 2010; and the Abel-Smith archive at the London School of Economics in 2015. Newspapers include the most prominent and ideologically diverse ones available at each point in time. We focus on the period that immediately preceded and followed the adoption of key policy changes. We also conducted around forty in-depth interviews with the most central actors alive (i.e. politicians, policy experts, bureaucrats, and leaders of various pressure groups) involved in policy debates since the 1970s.

Our analysis reinforces the role of electoral competition as a pre-condition.[7] Elections placed the "social question" in the policy agenda in the 1940s and expanded the influence of progressive political parties during most of the period. The appointment as Presidents of political leaders like Rafael Ángel Calderón Guardia in 1940 and José Figueres in 1970 – a Christian and a Social Democrat, using terminology from the comparative literature – created the political space to undertake important policy reforms.[8]

However, the specific characteristics of social security and of FODESAF can only be fully understood by considering the interaction between key state actors and international ideas (see Figure 1.6). In the 1940s, a small group of experts who were part of the President's inner circle placed social insurance in the policy agenda, designed the initial law, and led the process of implementation. These experts participated in international policy networks and much of their influence came from their access to foreign experiences, ideas, and models. They borrowed the basic features of the new social insurance discussed above

---

[7] Electoral competition in the 1940s took place in the context of a semi-democracy. Although much of the literature fails to mention it, half of the electorate could not vote until 1949, yet competition between left and right was intense and increased attention to social policy.

[8] The role of state capacity is less clear. The Costa Rican state was quite small during the early 1940s and institutions were weak. State capacity in the social realm increased rapidly during the 1950s, 1960s, and 1970s, simultaneously to rather than preceding the expansion of social policy.

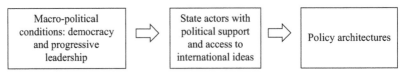

Figure 1.6 Political Determinants of Policy Architectures

Note: As discussed in the previous section, policy architectures in a specific moment in time also shape subsequent policy architectures in an iterative, path-dependent process.

(including its bottom-up and unified character) from abroad. In the 1970s, a team with ideational links to the Economic Commission of Latin America (later renamed Economic Commission of Latin America and the Caribbean; ECLAC) and other international organizations promoted FODESAF. Leading state actors were equally instrumental in managing vetoes, primarily by drawing on incremental adoption and/or implementation.

Our claims about the central role of state actors hold for policy formation since the 1980s. Despite economic obstacles and less supportive global ideas, Costa Rica adopted pro-universal reforms in primary care. At the same time, it failed to reform other components of the health care system to improve service delivery and curb the growth of the outside option. Both failures and successes have been at least in part driven by the existence or absence of politically influential state actors with a coherent agenda (see Chapter 7).

How unique is the Costa Rican social policy process we depict? How relevant are the arguments we make for other countries? Given the dearth of countries in the South where social policy delivers universal outputs, exploring exceptional cases thoroughly is meaningful in its own right. Still, in Chapter 8 we bring in the other three cases to examine the comparative validity of our findings. This robustness test focuses primarily on the historical record in health care but considers the case of pensions when it provides further analytical insights.

Chapter 8 shows that our model travels well and pays-off analytically. Electoral competition matters: under authoritarian conditions, South Korea's foundational architecture in health care provided access to only a small segment of workers. Yet democracy is not enough. In the absence of state actors and/or adequate ideas, democratic Mauritius and Uruguay developed a fragmented foundational architecture. More recently, South Korea and Uruguay have taken steps towards unification thanks to the presence of state actors embedded in international ideas and supported by decision makers.

At the same time, our comparative analysis also helps to refine some of the variables in light of specific national trajectories. First, sometimes – South Korea during the 1990s – policy ideas come from experts active in civil society rather than from within the state. Second, where the policy architecture involves multiple social stakeholders – like in Uruguay – a successful reform may need to have them on board.

1.7 Conclusion

In meeting the challenges of a world with entrenched poverty, a growing middle class, and excessive concentration of income and power at the top, ethical demands and political calculations push in the same direction: towards more attention to universalism in social policy. From an academic perspective, we hope this book helps improve our shared understanding of social policy outputs in democratic contexts across the South. From a policy perspective, we trust that the following chapters make a strong case for pursuing universal outputs through a variety of policy instruments. Calling for a "social protection floor" (ILO, 2012) is a positive yet insufficient step; we need to consider the politics behind the construction of new policies and the best ways to avoid fragmented programs that reproduce inequality.

We show that democratic institutions create opportunities to expand the role of social policy and redistribution, particularly when left-wing parties are elected. Yet the extent to which democracy and left-wing parties deliver universalism will depend on the characteristics of the policy architecture and the existence of progressive state actors with political support and technical expertise. In the presence of the "wrong" policy architectures (with significant fragmentation in access, funding, entitlements, or delivery), it will be rather difficult for countries to ensure similar, high quality services and generous transfers for all.

We are not suggesting that universal social policy outputs can be reached through institutional engineering. The appropriate architectures may only emerge in certain political contexts: politics matters to place social policy concerns in the agenda, open up the space for favorable policy processes, and strengthen key state actors. Moreover, unexpected changes in political conditions can interrupt positive paths at any time. Our point is that architectures are a key ingredient to determine whether social policy delivers generous social programs for all. The more policymakers (and other social actors with technical knowledge) acknowledge their role, the greater the chances to create favorable conditions in the long run.

The next chapter explores how to best define universalism and justifies its policy relevance. Part II is devoted to the comparative study of policy architectures in the short (Chapter 3) and long terms (Chapter 4) through the comparative discussion of Costa Rica, Mauritius, South Korea, and Uruguay. Part III revolves around the building of universalism in Costa Rica during the foundation stage (1940s) in Chapter 5, the expansionary phase (1970s) in Chapter 6, and the contradictory period under market pressures (1990s and 2000s) in Chapter 7. Part IV wraps up and elaborates policy implications. Chapter 8 examines whether our model helps account for the enactment and recent transformations of the social policy architectures in Mauritius, South Korea, and Uruguay. The concluding chapter summarizes the main findings presented in the book and draws some policy implications for progressive policymakers across the South. These lessons, we argue, are relevant for pre-existing policies such health care, pensions, and education, as well as for emerging areas such as early child education and care.

2 | *Universalism in the South: Definition and Relevance*

2.1 Introduction

In November 2013 at a dinner organized by the University of California-San Diego, the former Mexican President, Felipe Calderón, proudly claimed that "now there are doctors, treatments and medicines for every Mexican that needs them." Qualified observers supported his claim (e.g. Frenk, 2006; WHO, 2010). Calderón was boasting about Seguro Popular, a non-contributory health insurance program that since 2003 reached – as a matter of right – families previously excluded from basic medical access. *Seguro Popular*, which by 2015 covered over 50 million Mexicans, embodies a U-turn from the means-tested programs that prevailed across Latin America during the 1980s and 1990s.

Improvements in access to health care are undoubtedly good news. However, given that benefits granted by contributory and non-contributory insurance are unequal, is it accurate to argue that Mexico has established universal health care services? How can countries truly provide everyone with similar, high quality, generous services and transfers?

In this chapter we first discuss how the literature has defined universalism, the problems these definitions pose in the context of the South, and how to move research on the matter forward (Section 2.2). We then explain why universalism is a desirable policy output, discussing its positive impact on poverty reduction and income redistribution, and also in avoiding stigma, nurturing social cohesion, and promoting state-building.[1] Contravening neoclassical economics, generous redistributive

---

[1] We are aware that the full impact of public policy on redistribution depends on both taxes and social spending. In the Nordic countries, for example, social policy has a particularly large positive impact on income distribution because a significant share of the transfers to the wealthy comes back to the state through direct taxes. Unfortunately, in Latin America, redistribution has been limited

social programs in areas like health and education have encouraged rather than harmed economic upgrading in the North (e.g. Sweden, Finland) and the South (e.g. Costa Rica, Mauritius). All throughout, our arguments in favor of universalism draw from the historical experience of a sub-set of countries in Europe and North America but also consider implications for the South. In the last section, we focus on one of the most significant challenges for the promotion of universalism: the fragmentation of social policy driven by a combination of policy design and market expansion.

2.2 What is Universalism? Minimalist and Maximalist Approaches

As a contested concept, universalism takes on a broad range of meanings. On the minimalist end, much of the recent literature – and many policymakers like President Calderón – define universal social policies in terms of coverage, regardless of how generous or equitable such coverage is. Referring to health care, Stuckler *et al.* argue that in developing countries universal health care is equivalent to universal health care *coverage*, defined as "the existence of a legal mandate for universal access to health services and evidence that suggests the vast majority of the population has meaningful access to these services" (Stuckler *et al.*, 2010: 2). A similar approach prevails in the post-Millennium Development Goals (MDGs) agenda, which calls attention to a set of services the poor must receive as a matter of right. For example, the 2012 High Level Panel on Global Sustainability included "universal *access* to affordable sustainable energy" (Hoeven, 2012: 21, own emphasis) while others focused on the creation of an education fund to secure broad access to primary (and eventually secondary) school.

Yet this minimalist definition is neither the only one nor the most commonly used. A broader and more ambitious take – a maximalist one – comes from the academic literature on welfare regimes (Esping-Andersen and Korpi, 1987; Huber and Stephens, 2001). Under this body of research, scholars usually relate universalism to the

---

because taxes are too low and their impact often regressive (Ocampo and Malagón, 2011). Yet given the goals of this book, here we focus exclusively on the social policy discussion.

Scandinavian welfare regime and define it as a policy arrangement characterized by a robust set of services available to everyone on the basis of citizenship principles and funded through general taxes. This definition incorporates both specific instruments (citizenship-based services and transfers) and a set of desired outputs (generous services for all).

Use of this maximalist definition abounds (Korpi and Palme, 1998; Rothstein, 2008). Rothstein (2008) contrasts this approach with liberal welfare regimes and with those where most benefits are concentrated in some privileged groups according to status. The maximalist definition of universalism incorporates a strong normative thrust. Building on the Nordic experience, for example, Danson *et al.* are particularly clear that access to the same benefits in a permanent fashion is a social "right" (Danson *et al.*, 2012: 3). This is, therefore, a literature in which scholars often move from explanatory objectives to policy prescriptions.

Minimalist and maximalist definitions often become entangled in policy and academic debates. Drawing from the minimalist approach, politicians often end up presenting *massive coverage* as a synonym to universalism. Yet if everyone has access to vaccination and primary care while costly transplants are just provided for a few, is this universalism? Can high coverage with fragmentation in service delivery contribute to a sustained reduction of socio-economic inequalities? Or will it erode the most elementary bonds across socio-economic groups? Moreover, policy interventions that prioritize coverage as a stepping stone to promote generosity and equity may never succeed. Instead, they are likely to fuel socio-economic stratification since the better off will exit poor quality services and rely on private options. In this environment, cross-class coalitions endorsing the expansion of social policy are unlikely to emerge.

The maximalist definition of universalism is more useful but, unfortunately, conflates policy outputs with instruments capable of reaching such outputs. This shortcoming may at least partially reflect the enormous influence of Esping-Andersen's work on the three worlds of welfare capitalism (Esping-Andersen, 1990). There, he clustered countries in light of welfare arrangements made of both policy principles and policy instruments. He pointed to Sweden (and more generally the Nordic countries) and Germany (and more broadly continental Europe) as respectively emblematic of social democratic and corporative welfare regimes. The former gives prominence to citizenship, while in the latter entitlements revolve around occupation-based contributions. The former nurtures equality of rights, the latter fuels segmentation and is thus considered less desirable from the point of view of income distribution. In this vein, contributory arrangements become easily conflated to one specific sub-type: occupation-based or Bismarckian. For all the remarkable contributions Esping-Andersen made to our understanding of welfare policies, his typology may have contributed to an oversimplification between levels of analysis in the scholarly work that followed.

Conflating policy instruments and outputs is neither conceptually useful nor normatively appropriate, especially if universalism is to be promoted in poor and unequal societies (Fischer, 2012). If the only road to offering a truly generous set of benefits for all is to rely on services funded through general taxes of up to 50 percent of gross domestic product (GDP) – as in the case of the Nordic countries – universalism in the South becomes beyond reach. As Jennifer Pribble argues, "in the context of contemporary Latin America, the consolidation of such a welfare state is highly unlikely in the short- to medium run" (Pribble, 2013: 8).

In Chapter 3, we show that it is entirely possible that countries reach similar normative goals of equal access to generous social programs for all with alternative policy instruments, particularly contributory measures. By the same token, countries can formally implement policy instruments similar to those in Scandinavia – such as funding based on general revenues – without securing universal outputs. For example, many countries in the South have public health care systems that on paper make every service available to all, but in practice provide low quality services to only a small share of the poor.

2.3 Addressing Universalism as a Policy Output

While the minimalist approach to universalism is too narrow, the maximalist approach mixes policy outputs with the policy instruments required to reach them. Instead, following Hall in his study of economic policy in Britain, it may be analytically clearer to distinguish between policy principles (i.e. the policy outputs pursued) and policy instruments (i.e. how this goal is met), as well as the political conditions surrounding both (Hall, 1993).

In terms of outputs, we rely on a Weberian ideal type based on three dimensions: coverage, generosity (in level and quality), and equity. Social policies deliver universal outputs when they reach the entire population with similarly generous transfers and high quality services.[2] Universalism is therefore not a dichotomous but a continuous variable: few countries perform equally well in all three dimensions simultaneously. By the same token, our threefold definition of universalism is also useful to assess cross-national trajectories.

In distinguishing between policy outputs and the specific ways in which those transfers and services are delivered, we join a previous body of knowledge. Our approach follows Jennifer Pribble's superb research on universal reforms in South America. Like us, she focuses on coverage, quality of services, and the reduction of segmentation these entail (Pribble, 2013).[3] She avoids simplistic dichotomies (universalism vs. non-universalism) and focuses on the (gradual) process behind building expansionary welfare policies.

Fischer also moves away from oversimplifying dichotomies to distinguish degrees "towards stronger or weaker universalistic principles, along with their equalising or disequalising potentials, as well as the institutional obstacles potentially blocking such shifts" (Fischer, 2012: 12). The three categories he considers, however, conflate policy principles (i.e. high coverage), and instruments (i.e. cost/price or who pays for the service and financing or how the services are paid for). Yet in the end his goals are similar to ours: to separate the definition of universalism from a specific historical experience, to establish the possibility of promoting universalism through different channels, and to consider different degrees of universalism.

The output-based definition we propose helps nourish debates regarding how to expand social policy in the South. Two proposals

---

[2] Ours is the type of multi-dimensional definition that Bergh criticizes; in his view, defining universalism in terms of coverage and benefit level "causes problems, because the choice of benefit level is separate from the choice of what groups should be covered by the benefits. Such a definition also makes it difficult to make comparisons between countries and over time" (Bergh, 2004: 750). Yet the interaction between the components is precisely what truly delivers universalism and the lack of comparative data is a shortcoming that future research must seek to overcome.

[3] Pribble also includes transparency and financial sustainability as two other key dimensions of universalism – which we will only discuss indirectly and as part of policy instruments rather than of policy outputs.

have been particularly influential in recent years: "basic universalism" and the "social protection floor." Both address universalism as a policy principle to drive the piecemeal launching of transfers and services for all. They share a similar rationale involving the vertical and horizontal expansion from more to less essential transfers and services. Their main differences are mostly related to their geographical scope and institutional origins.

Basic universalism is a notion set forth by Latin American scholars under the sponsorship of the Inter-American Development Bank in 2006. It refers to a set of essential benefits that governments should guarantee to everyone. By gradually expanding key transfers and services, basic universalism seeks to incrementally deal with the tension between social demands, on the one hand, and fiscal constraints, on the other. Benefit expansion will depend on the improvement in the state's fiscal capacity and the emergence of new stakeholders and electoral support for policy expansion (Molina, 2006). Essential transfers and services are those most capable of reducing inequality by redistributing present and future income: primary education, preventive medicine, and old-age monetary transfers. Targeting has a role to play in narrowing gaps and ensuring access and quality for all (Filgueira *et al.*, 2006).

The social protection floor became an ILO policy recommendation in 2012. Initially, the floor referred to a range of social services including health care, water and sanitation, education, food security, housing, and others (Bachelet, 2011). When passed as ILO Policy Recommendation 202, its scope was narrowed to essential health care and basic income security across the life cycle – i.e. children, adults, and the elderly. Unlike basic universalism, which was basic-ally an inspiring set of ideas following the 2008 global financial crisis, the social protection floor became a policy proposal. By 2012 it had gained the support of the United Nations, the World Bank, the G20 and many international non-governmental organizations (Deacon *et al.*, 2013).

Both of these approaches stress the need for national adaptations to country-specific circumstances; like our analysis, they recognize the importance of combining different policy instruments to achieve universal goals. Both could contribute to consolidate universalism in the South: in particular, the social protection floor has the potential to "give way to the global politics of welfare state rebuilding focused on the alliances that need to be constructed between the poor and the non-poor (especially the middle class) to rebuild bonds of solidarity nationally and internationally" (Deacon, 2010: 1).

Yet their accent on the "basic" and their limited attention to concrete political dynamics and path dependence is worrisome. The social protection floor, for example, recognizes the importance of combining social assistance with social insurance, but does not offer clear political (as opposed to technical) insights into how to do so (Bachelet, 2011). Because social insurance and social assistance have distinct constituencies and institutional settings, policy processes that promote cooperation – for instance by focusing on populations that can be reached through a combination of subsidies and contributions – are crucial. Devoid of this political "backstage" to state building, the social protection floor can easily become an umbrella concept to what in practice are two-tier separate systems for the poor and the non-poor, respectively. Excessive attention to basic services for all can ultimately result in low quality services only used by those who cannot rely on private options. Moreover, if the social protection floor is not accompanied by strong regulations of private services, it could easily perpetuate fragmentation – a point to which we will return in Section 2.5.

2.4 Why is Universalism Important?

Much of the literature that endorses universalism draws heavily on the historical record of Scandinavian countries. Often the arguments are more about favoring the policies specifically adopted by Sweden and neighboring countries than about a more general assessment of outputs. Below, we disentangle arguments based on the Scandinavian countries from those based on accomplishments elsewhere. We go beyond socio-economic claims to consider the political sustainability of social policy and the impact on national identity and state-building. In the process, we explore whether arguments to endorse universalism require the three-dimensional approach we embrace, or whether they hold even when conceiving universalism as broad coverage alone.

2.4.1 Universalism and Redistribution

In recent decades, many policymakers and neoclassical economists have encouraged governments to exclusively implement means-tested programs. These interventions are considered particularly effective in reducing poverty and inequality because they do not waste resources in people who – being capable to rely on the market – can do without state support. According to this view, countries should implement "selective welfare programs that are intended to assist only those who cannot manage economically on their own hand" (Rothstein, 2008: 3).[4]

This argument fails to consider that the middle classes are more likely to support state expansion whenever they directly benefit from it. For example, the European welfare states were primarily established to prevent social unrest among well-organized salaried workers rather than to reach the poor. And yet, the poor greatly benefited from "universal and adequately funded education, health and social insurance programs the middle class want[ed] and finance[d] through the tax system" (Birdsall, 2010: 3). By broadening the number of beneficiaries, social policies for the whole population and with sufficient quality increase political support for social spending, thus creating a redistributive virtuous circle (Huber, 2002; Mkandawire, 2006a).[5]

Much of the literature on this "paradox of redistribution" – programs that incorporate all social groups lead to higher overall spending, thus benefiting the poor more than targeted measures – assumes that the argument is only valid for flat-rate, non-contributory benefits (Danson *et al.*, 2012). Yet Korpi and Palme show that the paradox of redistribution extends to income-related transfers based on social insurance contributions (Korpi and Palme, 1998). In the case of pensions, for example, if public provision relies on non-contributory transfers alone, the middle class and the wealthy will search for complementary market-based solutions. In other words, if transfers are not sufficiently generous, market stratification will challenge public programs – as currently evident in successful developing countries like

---

[4] Even though he did not use the notion per se, Titmuss was the first scholar to make a strong case for universalism back in the late 1950s when distinguishing between institutional and residual regimes. Titmuss also criticized the naivety of the proponents of means-tests, who did not recognize the complexity of targeting. For a collection of some of his best articles, see Abel-Smith and Titmuss (1987).

[5] In fact, there is a risk that targeted programs are sooner or later discontinued. As Moene and Wallerstein (2001) show in a formal model based on self-interested voting, the majority of the population who does not receive benefits will vote for their elimination.

Costa Rica (see Chapter 7 and also Sandbrook *et al.*, 2007). One way around this undesirable stratification is to complement basic pensions for all with income-related social insurance containing redistributive measures such as minimum and maximum replacement rates.

The creation of a cross-class alliance between the poor and different segments of the middle class is not only helpful to broaden access to state policy, but also to guarantee generosity of benefits (Huber, 2002; Mkandawire, 2006a). The middle class has more economic and political resources to voice its concerns than do the poor. In this way, universalism prevents the poor from entering poor programs, namely, those that are under-budgeted, institutionally weak, often discretionary, and prone to political manipulation (Arza, 2012). State personnel in charge of service provision (who belong mostly to the middle class) also develop vested interests in having quality services if they and their families depend on them.

Although all these arguments rely primarily on the experience of wealthy countries, they may be even more valid for the South. First, in these countries there are higher levels of discrimination against the poor (World Bank, 2003) and narrowly targeted pro-poor policies are more unpopular. If social programs are going to be sustained over time and their quality steadily improved, the incorporation of the middle class to any pro-poor coalition is as challenging as it is indispensable. Securing middle class support requires broad coverage and also quality and generosity: these groups will not settle for little and private options are a constant challenge to their loyalty to the public sector. Second, the fact that state revenue capacity is normally low in turn requires broad coalitions that support tax reforms, something that will not happen unless people see clear-cut benefits from such taxes.

Proponents of means-tested policies also fail to consider that people's capacity to stay away from public transfers and services is contingent upon a number of collective and individual factors, from macro-economic and life cycles to accidents and an array of unforeseen circumstances (Krishna, 2010). The assumption that the non-poor will commodify their labor force successfully all throughout their lives and in such a way as to adequately purchase social services is rather problematic given growing volatility, particularly (even if not exclusively) in the South. Because the most relevant social and political distinction is no longer between the poor and the non-poor but between the wealthy and the rest (Birdsall, 2010), means-tested policies draw unrealistic demarcations between deserving and undeserving populations.

The evidence on the contribution of policies that deliver universal outputs to income redistribution is convincing. Along similar lines than the paradox of redistribution argument, Sheila Shaver shows that targeted programs direct a higher share of each dollar to the poor, but that their overall impact on income distribution is lower than in more ambitious programs – largely because they involve fewer resources (Shaver, 1998). This redistributive power is not a function of coverage alone but also of the generosity of benefits involved. In his 2005 book on Europe and the United States, Jonas Pontusson compares the Gini coefficient before and after taxes and transfers in the central economies during the late 1990s. His analysis shows that:

the redistributive effects of the more encompassing welfare states operate through the provision of benefits – services as well as cash payments. *To the extent that they displace private mechanisms, even income differentiated social insurance schemes have important redistributive effects.* On the other hand, programs that specifically target the poor do not seem to enhance the redistributive impact of social spending. (Pontusson, 2005: 179–180, italics added)

Unfortunately the evidence on the redistributive impact of non-targeted social policies in the South is both limited and problematic. Household surveys are not always reliable or comparable and it is difficult to calculate the benefits received by the top 1 and 5 percent of the population which are more often than not either excluded from household surveys or provide unreliable responses. Most studies also fail to incorporate the value of the services and their distribution among social classes (Martínez Franzoni and Sánchez-Ancochea, 2015) or to consider the negative impact of outside private options. Still, the limited available evidence points to the large redistributive capacity of programs that cover a majority of the population with similar benefits. For example, a recent study prepared by CAF-Development Bank of Latin America shows that education – particularly at the primary level – and some health services have a much larger impact on the Gini coefficient than targeted but smaller programs (CAF, 2012; see also Huber and Stephens, 2012). Recent work by ECLAC and the World Bank also shows that those services with the highest coverage and relatively equitable provision – primary education and some health care services – have the highest impact on the reduction of the Gini coefficient (CEPAL, 2007; Goñi *et al.*, 2011).

2.4.2 Universalism and Stigma

Poverty does not only refer to the lack of income and other material resources, but also involves lack of power, physical and social autonomy, and respect (Fraser, 1994; Sennett, 2003; Townsend, 2011). While means-tested programs may reduce short-term income deprivation among the poor in the short-run, they have a negative effect in power structures and people's autonomy.

By signaling who the poor are; by forcing them to provide detailed information about their living conditions to a myriad of state personnel; and by allocating them "second rate" benefits, means-tested programs stigmatize and diminish the social standing of low-income groups even more. As explained by Walker (2011) in a comprehensive review of the perils of means-testing, these kinds of measures can create social divisions between rich and poor and exacerbate the weakness of the latter. When developing her own criticisms of these programs, she relies extensively on Townsend, who was a ferocious critic of targeting. For him,

(selectivity) misconceives the nature of poverty and reinforces the condition it is supposed to alleviate ... It fosters hierarchical relations of superiority and inferiority in society, diminishes rather than enhances the status of the poor, and has the effect of widening social inequalities ... it lumps the unemployed, sick, widowed, aged and others into one undifferentiated and inevitably stigmatized category. (Townsend, 1973: 126, quoted in Walker, 2011: 142)

The cost of stigmatization is particularly high in the case of conditional cash transfers (CCTs) – which by 2009 reached between 750 million and one billion people across the South (DFID, 2011). These programs assume that insufficient use of education and health services results from lack of service demand rather than supply – i.e. the poor are not fully aware of how important these services are. Yet, in practice, enforcing that the poor take their children to school or to medical check-ups in exchange for money constitutes a method of social control. It also questions households' capacity to make decisions in light of context-specific circumstances such as the availability and quality of services. This is why Hanlon *et al.* (2010) argue in favor of "just giving money to the poor": focusing on transfers without conditions.

Policies that cover the whole population and provide similar, equitable benefits enhance the social status of the poor by making them subject of rights. Universalism weakens hierarchies by relying on "one standard of value" for the whole population (Townsend, 1973: 15, cited in Walker 2011). Yet this standard of value must refer to access, quality, and generosity; in fact, having access to only vaccinations when the rich can take care of every other need by relying on markets strengthens rather than weakens social hierarchies.

The argument about the non-stigmatizing effects of universalism is particularly pertinent for non-contributory transfers and services, which do not depend on the position of people in the labor market. In the case of contributory programs, which exclude many low-income groups, avoiding stigma requires decoupling benefits from contributions and creating non-contributory means of access to the programs. One can envision a system where everyone is equal in the eyes of service providers, regardless of their financial contribution and specific type of eligibility criteria.

2.4.3 *Universalism and Management Costs*

Many critics argue that even if universal policies can potentially be more redistributive, states in the South lack the right institutions to implement them effectively. For example, a well-functioning public health system requires nurses, doctors, hospitals, and planning institutions capable of operating in every corner of a given country. Social services depend on a minimally efficient state apparatus, including a Weberian bureaucracy that is capable of organizing effective delivery and avoids discretionary use of state resources (Henderson *et al.*, 2003).

In practice, however, it is unclear whether policies with broad coverage and similar high quality for all require more institutional capabilities than means-tested ones. Social spending with universal aims can have lower management costs than targeted programs and can reduce clientelism (Mkandawire, 2006a; Rowthorn and Kozul-Wright, 1998). Targeting requires sophisticated institutional and technical mechanisms to identify the "deserving" population, making sure that they do not game the system and that the benefits are properly allocated. Policies where there are asymmetric benefits for different groups of beneficiaries also require high technical capacity. This is the case, for example, of many health care programs in the South where different rights to procedures often coexist. It is ironic that programs that advocate a rational use of public resources are at the same time channeling scarce resources to study, control, and monitor the poor and measure errors of inclusion and exclusion.

Administrative simplicity is a powerful reason to have non-contributory and flat pensions for everyone in the South (Willmore, 2007). Even the World Bank – undoing its previous position on the matter – accepted in 2005 that non-contributory pensions for a majority of the population are "probably the best way to provide poverty relief to the elderly. Considering the difficulty of identifying who among the elderly is poor, the principal merit of the program is that its universality avoids the targeting issue" (Holzmann and Hinz, 2005: 95). In countries where broad-based pensions have not been adopted, the integration of different insurance mechanisms within a single institution – a second-best in terms of universalism – can also reduce costs and facilitate management as the Costa Rican experience shows (Chapters 3, 5, and 6).

2.4.4 Universalism and Macro-Social Impacts

Programs that do not simply offer broad coverage, but also generosity (in level and quality) for all, can enhance a sense of belonging to a specific (national) community and become a defining feature of national identity (Béland and Lecours, 2008). Béland and Waddan, for example, emphasize the importance of universal health care for Canada where:

universal health care has long become a core component of social citizenship, as well as a symbol of national identity ... Canada lacks the strong, shared, political myths and symbols ever present in the United States but the country's very different, universal, health care system helps to build a distinct national identity. (Béland and Waddan, 2013: 9)

This is not unlike Costa Rica, where since the 1940s the Costa Rican Social Insurance Agency (Caja Costarricense del Seguro Social, CCSS) has become a national symbol, intertwined with peace, the rule of law, and social democracy. The symbolic status of these institutions can help strengthen a commitment to solidarity and social equality. It also makes the adoption of regressive reforms more difficult. In Canada, political attacks on the universal health system are out of bounds, both at the federal level and in the provinces (Béland and Waddan, 2013). Something similar has happened in Costa Rica where, despite powerful stakeholders seeking regressive reforms, threats to public arrangements have been implicit rather than explicit (see Chapter 7).

Unified programs for the whole population can contribute to social cohesion and to the creation of an inclusive social contract (ECLAC, 2007). Social cohesion appeals to the stability that societies gain from a sense of belonging, membership and shared conditions; these, in turn, rely on social bonds (Hopenhayn, 2007). By providing one of the few spaces for interaction between the wealthy, the middle class, and the poor, state services can nurture these bonds. Generous services that are truly for all shorten social distance and help different socio-economic groups become part of a community and realize their shared problems.

Universalism can strengthen a sense of unity. According to de Neubourg, "the stability of nation states depends … on at least a minimum level of solidarity, shared beliefs, values and preferences on the part of its citizens" (de Neubourg, 2009: 68). He shows how in Europe the creation of generous social programs constituted an important step in the process of state-building; they were particularly important after the Second World War when creating a new sense of community became urgent. In the same way, in many countries across the South, universal policies could contribute to close divisions and heal past conflicts. In Costa Rica not just health insurance but also the education system played this role. Even today, 87 percent of all Costa Ricans attending basic education (primary school plus the first three years of secondary) are enrolled in public institutions (Programa Estado de la Nación, 2013). Social cohesion can contribute to strengthen democracy and trigger other virtuous circles. For Andrenacci and Repetto, social policy is a key component of a strategy that aims at "the construction of societies that are economically integrated, socially cohesive and politically participatory, where differences do not create segmentation" (Andrenacci and Repetto, 2006: 100). Of course, massive coverage alone cannot achieve these goals.

Even if universalism is desirable for social cohesion and state-building, neoclassical economics often highlight its negative impact on economic growth (Pontusson, 2005). The argument is that high marginal tax rates can reduce the incentives to join the labor force and high payroll taxes can make workers prohibitively expensive. Excessive transfers can also reduce effort and productivity. The public provision of social services like health and education can be ineffective, as public providers "have little incentive to improve productivity and to respond to changes in consumer demand" (Pontusson, 2005: 163).

According to critics, policies that pursue universal outputs may also be too expensive for countries with low income per capita, weak tax systems, and insufficient levels of social investment. A Uruguayan Minister appointed under a left-of-center administration criticized the Costa Rican model because "it authorized all the expensive medicines, all the expensive technology and ended up ruining the system and weakening its financial sustainability" (Uy.press, 2013). In fact, if resources are limited and the primary income distribution unequal, the argument goes, it is best to prioritize the poor, leaving everyone else to rely on markets to look after their needs and solve their problems. As Rubén Lo Vuolo puts it in a critical review of pro-market approaches, "the security of the 'non-poor' should no longer be 'social' and should be resolved by private insurance mechanisms" (Lo Vuolo, 2005: 2).

Allegedly, developing "expensive" social programs that cover the whole population with generous benefits is particularly hard under the current global economic order.[6] Globalization has created downward pressure on tax revenues and has made tax expansion difficult for several reasons (Grunberg, 1998; Tanzi, 2004). First, countries across the South compete to attract foreign investment, promising large tax subsidies. Second, the increasing weight of transnational corporations in the world economy has made most domestic-based tax systems obsolete. Adapting taxes to the new global conditions has proven hard because companies manage to avoid taxes through transfer pricing and other tax planning techniques. Third, the reduction of import tariffs induced by trade liberalization has given rise to a fall in public revenues.

---

[6] Globalization can be broadly understood as the "economic interdependence between countries where cross-border linkages among markets and production and financial activities have reached such an extent that economic developments in any one country are influenced to a significant degree by policies and developments outside its boundaries" (Milberg, 1998: 71). For a detailed discussion of globalization and its main effects in Latin America, see CEPAL (2006).

Few of these anti-universalist arguments stand up to close scrutiny. Policies that ensure universal outputs are unlikely to be a net cost on countries; quite the contrary, they usually have a positive impact on sustainable economic growth and competitiveness. As Mkandawire (2006b) argues, social policy and economic development are inter-linked. Social programs not only compensate for the negative effects of external shocks and economic adjustment, but also contribute to the generation of competitive assets. High quality social policies can assist in the accumulation of human capital, expand aggregate demand, and improve social capital. The result is higher economic growth and the creation of new competitive advantages: an argument empirically supported by high growth rates in countries like Costa Rica and Mauritius (Martínez Franzoni and Sánchez-Ancochea, 2013a; Sandbrook *et al.*, 2007).[7]

A more credible criticism of universalism has to do with the obstacles most governments face when seeking to raise taxes. Even in the Costa Rican case, as we show in the second part of this book, introducing tax reforms that make up for the shortage of payroll contributions to social security has been difficult. Yet taxation is primarily a political rather than an economic challenge, which takes us back to the role of broad political coalitions discussed earlier in this section. When those coalitions emerge – something most likely when large segments of society benefit from social services – expanding direct and indirect taxes becomes more feasible.

Moreover, in the last few years expanding taxes in many countries, particularly in Latin America, has been easier due to the commodity boom (Cornia, 2010). As a result, newly elected progressive governments have often managed to fund social policy without challenging the interests of the economic elite. Two emblematic examples in Latin

---

[7] The importance of the historical link between universalism and economic development is clear when the Nordic countries are compared to Latin America. Samuel Valenzuela, for example, tracks the evolution of social programs and economic performance in Chile and Sweden. He demonstrates that the introduction of generous pensions and other social programs in Sweden triggered key socio-economic transformations at the beginning of the twentieth century. In particular, new social programs facilitated the incorporation of women to the formal labor market, the slowing down of demographic growth, and the increase in productivity. Chile's failure to introduce a similar policy package resulted in a more rapid expansion of its population and a less dynamic economic path (Valenzuela, 2006a and 2006b).

America are Chile's health care program to guarantee services for a growing number of sicknesses (AUGE for its Spanish acronym) founded in 2004, and Bolivia's Renta Dignidad – a pension for everybody 60 years of age or more – created in 2008 (see Arza, 2012). The former was funded with copper revenues and the latter primarily with a share of revenues from the direct tax on natural resources.

2.5 Fragmentation of Policy Architectures as a Major Obstacle to Universalism

The creation of universalism has systematically confronted fragmentation of the policy architecture – a concept we discuss with more detail in Chapter 3 – as a threat. By fragmentation we mean a situation where the provision of public social services varies in access and entitlements across groups of people and/or where there is a prominent outside market option. If this is the case, broad coverage can go hand in hand with unequal provision of services. Fragmentation can be driven by the design of state policies (e.g. social insurance programs tailored for specific occupations) or by marketization.

Historically fragmentation reflected policy design, specifically the promotion of social insurance organized along occupational lines. Such insurance was created for income maintenance, not for redistribution. Thus, a diverse set of workers, from teachers to the military and various types of public servants, had every incentive to demand more services exclusively for them, resulting in the vertical rather than horizontal expansion of benefits.

This problem was particularly significant in Latin America where "the urban middle class and some blue-collar workers enjoyed access to relatively generous systems of public protection, but peasants and informal-sector workers were generally excluded" (Haggard and Kaufman, 2008: 1). Entitlements were diverse even among the middle class in the most successful cases (Filgueira, 1998). In Uruguay, in the 1960s large parts of the middle class were members of the mutual insurance health care plans for which they paid a premium (Mesa-Lago, 1978). Mutual organizations spent 4,884 pesos per beneficiary compared to 1,562 pesos in the public system. Argentina created separate funds for civil servants (founded in 1906), railway workers (1919), utility workers (1921), bank employees (1923), and several other groups (Lewis and Lloyd-Sherlock, 2009). Each fund had different benefits and efforts to unify them during the late 1960s and 1970s failed (Huber and Stephens, 2012). In Chile, differences in entitlements were also significant (Mesa-Lago, 1978; Segura-Ubiergo, 2007). This fragmentation made the system segmented rather than universal in terms of outputs and deepened the socio-economic segmentation created in the labor market (Haggard and Kaufman, 2008).

This type of segmentation in outputs was one of the explicit arguments behind pro-market and pro-targeted state reforms promoted during the 1980s and 1990s. While neoliberal reforms indeed weakened what were arguably regressive benefits of previous policies (Rudra, 2007), new types of fragmentation in the policy architecture emerged. CCTs, for example, have enforced the use of basic services, most typically primary school attendance and primary care check-ups, without paying sufficient attention to the characteristics and availability of those services in particular areas. In practice, simply placing new demands on users of most of these programs has not improved the quality of services to the level needed to break the intergenerational reproduction of poverty.[8]

Overcoming segmentation in policy outputs often requires targeting the poor so that they benefit from entitlements others already have. The poor confront a complex set of obstacles that reinforce one another – including asymmetric information, lack of time and human capital, scarce confidence in public servants, and more experience with state repression than with redistribution – which inhibits their adequate appropriation of many services. As Titmuss explained decades ago when referring to Great Britain, "universalism in social welfare, though a needed prerequisite towards reducing and removing formal barriers of social and economic discrimination, does not by itself solve the problem of how to reach the more-difficult-to-reach with better medical care, especially preventive medical care" (Abel-Smith and Titmuss, 1987: 217).

In most cases, countries do better at redistributing when governments implement some kind of "affirmative action" in favor of the poor or what Skocpol called "targeting within universalism". What

---

[8] The World Bank, for example, reports significant differences in school outputs between different income groups and links it to "new forms of inequality, in particular those associated with high variances in quality" (World Bank, 2003: 7). See also CAF (2012).

this means is that governments create programs that provide "extra benefits and services that disproportionally help less privileged people without stigmatizing them" (Skocpol, 1991: 414). Social assistance programs become interlinked to services used by the general population such as health care and education – something that Costa Rica did particularly well (Chapter 6). In contrast, programs targeted to the poor that are delinked from programs accessed by the non-poor or that give access to fewer or lower quality services (e.g. *Seguro Popular* in Mexico, scholarships for private universities in Brazil, old-age cash transfers in El Salvador) nourish fragmentation and deter universalism.

Fragmentation can also result from marketization, which can be defined as the

introduction or strengthening of market incentives and structures ... This process may include diverse elements such as creating markets, encouraging competition among providers, giving greater choice and voice to patients [or consumers more broadly], establishing financial incentives for efficient resource utilization and higher quality of care and shifting decision-making and financial responsibility to service providers. (Agartan, 2012: 458)

Marketization is not a new phenomenon but it has certainly become stronger in recent decades, affecting a growing number of policy sectors from pensions and health care to education. Led by the increasing power of the financial sector, what used to be de-commodified areas of social life have become arenas for profit making. In countries like Turkey, for example, attempts to reduce policy-driven segmentation have gone hand in hand with the expansion of private markets. Unfortunately, this has resulted in increasing stratification and the rich's exiting public services (Agartan, 2012).

Even when the legal design of social policies remains intact, market forces erode universalism in practice – as we will discuss in Chapter 7. The existence of private pension funds creates new savings opportunities for the middle class and the rich, reducing their commitment to public plans. These groups are also likely to exit the public health care system and stop fighting for quality improvements when new private hospitals appear. The expansion of markets also creates new interest groups (such as financial service providers, private hospital owners, and doctors in private practices), which have further incentives to erode the public sector. Even though marketization is particularly harmful when the state has a weak regulatory capacity, current policy debates in England (regarding the National Health Service) and in Germany (regarding the merger between private and public insurance) demonstrates that states can hardly mitigate the pressure of marketization anywhere.

2.6 Conclusion

Providing all citizens with similar, high quality services and generous transfers makes sense for many reasons. It is not only the best way to guarantee social rights for the poor, but also essential to create more integrated societies. It is also likely to help the new middle class consolidate their recent gains. It is urgent at a time when income inequality at the top has become a major policy concern for governments and social movements alike (Oxfam, 2015). Generous services and transfers for all are particularly important when the economic cycle contracts and wages do not keep pace with living costs.

Yet when seeking to establish whether countries in the South have managed to promote universal outputs, it is important to avoid assessing *instruments* in normative terms. More specifically, analysts should not consider large citizen-based programs funded through general taxes as the benchmark against which to assess all other policy instruments. Most countries in the South lack the fiscal and bureaucratic capacity and the political conditions to replicate this approach initially devised by the Scandinavian countries. It may be the case that a combination of various instruments – including social insurance and social assistance – delivers similar outputs and is easier to implement. Of course, this approach is also risky and is as likely to lead to segmentation as to universalism. Under what conditions will these programs deliver the latter and avoid the former is the subject of the next two chapters.

PART II

A Comparative Study of Policy Architectures

3 | Policy Architectures and Universal Outputs Today

3.1 Introduction

In the previous chapter we demonstrated the importance of promoting social policies that deliver universal outputs. Yet this is easier said than done: how can countries in the South build these policies? Much of the political economy literature answers this question by focusing on a small number of countries that managed to establish successful social programs.[1] As we discussed in Chapter 1, the literature links these broad outcomes to the role of democracy (the more the better), partisan ideology (strong left-wing political parties are needed), and the influence of collective actors (unions and other social movements make a difference).

These macro-explanations illuminate key variables behind the building of universalism but also miss other important pieces of the story. They downplay the diverse ways in which countries have pursued this endeavor: even if democracy and political ideology are important preconditions, they cannot explain the specific ways in which policies are shaped and evolve over time. Democratic pressures may, for instance, trigger higher health spending aimed at the poor, but are unlikely to determine the funding and delivery mechanisms or whether benefits set the poor apart from the non-poor.

In this chapter and the next we address the role of policy architectures as an analytical device to study universalism in the South. We define policy architectures as the combination of instruments addressing eligibility, funding, benefits, delivery, and outside market options of specific social programs. The policy architecture is

---

[1] While case studies are sometimes accompanied by cross-country regression analysis, econometric studies tend to focus on the level and composition of social policy rather than on universal policies per se. See, for example, Huber and Stephens (2012) or Segura-Ubiergo (2007).

the blueprint of a policy as defined not just by single components but by the interaction among them.

Architectures influence universal outputs both in the short and the long term. In the short term, they define who receives what and how. Over the long term, by empowering a set of actors and creating incentives for the subsequent expansion of policies, architectures mediate the interaction between democracy and universalism.

In this chapter we look at countries with robust social policies to explore the diversity of architectures and how they constrain universal outputs. As explained in Chapter 1, we focus on Costa Rica, Mauritius, South Korea, and Uruguay – all considered in the literature as successful cases of social development (Huber and Stephens, 2012; McGuire, 2010; Sandbrook *et al.*, 2007; Ringen *et al.*, 2011).

Through this comparison, we make three claims. First, we highlight the diversity of policy architectures and question the idea that, *by definition,* a given architecture will outperform others in terms of enabling universal outputs. Much of the social policy literature argues that policymakers should do their best to emulate the type of policies that the Scandinavian countries implemented over the second half of the twentieth century: citizen-based social programs for all based on general taxes (Huber 2002). Yet the "Scandinavian architecture" may not deliver the expected results and some types of social insurance may perform as well if not better.

Second, we show the importance of studying the interrelation between different components of the policy architecture to explain the obstacles to universalism. Although these obstacles show cross-national variations, they are in most cases driven by the lack of unification across policy components. It is easier to produce universal outputs when everyone enters a single social program in a similar fashion, with the state playing a major role in ordering the sector, providing services and taming the market. We highlight this point by considering Costa Rica's positive performance.

Third, outside options play a prominent role in limiting universal outputs. Having powerful private services undermines the likelihood that the other four policy components will deliver similar, generous benefits for the whole population. This is made clear by the cases of Mauritius and South Korea, where under starkly different architectures universalism has been inhibited by the presence of a strong private sector.

Below we justify our four countries as cases of contemporary success in social policy provision in the South. We then introduce the concept of policy architecture as a useful analytical tool to explore country differences. In Section 3.4, we compare policy architectures in health care services across the four countries. We highlight Costa Rica's success at promoting a unified system, speculating about its positive effect in terms of universal outputs. We contrast these conclusions with pensions as our shadow case.

3.2 Four Best Cases

The literature on social policy regards Costa Rica, Mauritius, Uruguay, and, more recently and to a lesser extent, South Korea, as unique examples of robust social states in the South.[2] Sandbrook *et al.* (2007) consider the first two as "social-democratic pioneers" and also praise Uruguay for promoting generous social policy at different times during the last century. Although South Korea was an exclusionary, authoritarian regime for decades, it is now "indisputably" a welfare state, which has come "about gradually from selective to inclusive protection" (Ringen *et al.*, 2011: 5).

Considered "the closest case to an ... embryonic social democratic welfare state" in Latin America (Filgueira, 2005: 21), Costa Rica has long been praised for its success in expanding health, education, and other social services. Between 1940 and 1980, per capita real spending in health care and education multiplied by three and by eight, respectively (Trejos, 1991). The number of physicians per 1,000 people went from 3.1 in 1950 to 7.8 in 1990; the number of nurses and teachers also expanded rapidly. Welfare efforts covered a growing number of the population: by the 1970s, enrolment rates in primary and secondary education were high and the country did better in terms of human development than almost any other country at a similar level of income per capita (Martínez Franzoni and Sánchez-Ancochea, 2013a). Today Costa Rica is still praised for its prominent attention to public education and health care.

---

[2] When the policy architectures we discuss here were being set in place, all four countries had a relatively low GDP per capita. In 1960 GDP per capita (in dollars of 2005) was 3,151 in Uruguay, 1,842 in Costa Rica, and 1,467 in South Korea (World Development Indicators database). Comparative data for Mauritius is not available until 1976.

Regarded as "Paradise Island" (Carroll and Carroll, 2000), Mauritius is clearly an exceptional case in Africa. Successive administrations "invested heavily in health care and education; and subsidised basic foods" (Carroll and Carroll, 2000: 29). The first government after Independence granted free education to all citizens and human capital accumulated rapidly (Frankel, 2010). Although the economic crisis of the early 1980s forced Mauritius to request support from the International Monetary Fund (IMF) and the World Bank, welfare spending was protected. International institutions "demanded the abolition of free education and free health but Mauritius resisted the pressure and continued to provide these services for free" (Bunwaree, 2005: 7). Coverage grew rapidly: between 1980 and 1997, for example, the gross enrolment rate in primary education increased from 93 percent to 107 percent and attendance in secondary school remained higher than in most other African countries. Despite growing tensions and difficulties, in present times a "largely untargeted social protection system plays an important role in securing favorable outcomes for combating poverty and inequality" (David and Petri, 2013: 4). Mauritius has also been recognized for its strong state institutions (Lange, 2003) and the creation of non-contributory social assistance for the whole population (Seekings, 2011; Willmore, 2006).

Uruguay has been depicted as a "comprehensive social-welfare system" (Haggard and Kaufman, 2008; Huber and Stephens, 2012) but also as a case of "stratified-universalism" (Filgueira, 1998) where broad coverage was historically based on a number of different insurance schemes (Antía *et al.*, 2013; Mesa-Lago, 1978). Still, primary education was mandatory and free from the late nineteenth century and secondary and university education expanded steadily in the twentieth century (Filgueira, 1995). Since the 1950s benefits included "a great expansion of pensions, the introduction of family allowances, the establishment of the first unemployment-compensation programs, and mandatory compensation in case of occupational accidents" (Segura-Ubiergo, 2007: 59). Although the expansion of the social state stagnated during the conservative dictatorship of the 1970s, it has witnessed a rebirth in the last decade with the deepening of a rights-based approach in health, education, and social protection (Pribble, 2013).

South Korea was for decades the antithesis of an ambitious welfare state. Until the late 1980s, social spending was low and devoted to primary and secondary education. Between 1973 and 2000, social spending as percentage of GDP was on average less than a third than in Costa Rica or Uruguay (Martínez Franzoni and Sánchez-Ancochea, 2013a). Not surprisingly, the International Labour Organization (ILO, 2007: 17) warned of "under-investment in social protection" in this and other Asian countries. This was particularly clear in the case of pensions, which were provided through firm-based schemes. Old-age transfers benefited a relatively small share of the population and were implemented along an underdeveloped public safety net (Goodman and Peng, 1996).

Since 1990, South Korea has seen dramatic policy change in health, pensions, unemployment benefits, and social assistance. Public social spending as percentage of GDP more than tripled between 1990 and 2012, from just 2.8 percent to 9.3 percent.[3] As discussed in the next chapter, the expansion of benefits in health care has been particularly impressive: "compared to Germany's 127 years, Belgium's 118, Israel's 84, Austria's 79, Luxembourg's 72, and Japan's 36 years, South Korea achieved the feat of providing health insurance for the entire population in just 12 years, which is faster than any other country in the world" (Kim and Lee, 2010: 144). Although Korea is still far from a European welfare state, the speed and ambition of the changes have been impressive (Kim, 2006; Hwang, 2012).

In all four countries robust social policies have contributed to high levels of human development. Table 3.1 reports data on infant mortality and life expectancy and adds GDP as a control variable. Differences in social dimensions are lower than income partly due to a well-known convergence in health indicators – which also have upward limits. Nevertheless, the fact that South Korea with a GDP per capita at least three times higher than Costa Rica, Mauritius, and Uruguay has social indicators that are only slightly better than the three of them, points to the role of cross-national variance in social policy. Infant mortality under 5 years of age is below 15 per thousand in all cases, lower than both the world average (35 per thousand) and the average for upper middle-income countries (16 per thousand). Performance in life expectancy is also impressive in comparative perspective.

---

[3] Data from the OECD electronic database at http://stats.oecd.org/Index.aspx?DataSetCode=SOCX_AGG (last accessed March 21, 2014).

Table 3.1 *Human Development Indicators, 2012*

Indicators, 2012	Costa Rica	Mauritius	South Korea	Uruguay	Upper-Middle Income	World
Infant mortality age 1 per 1000 live births	9	13	3	6	16	35
Infant mortality under 5 years of age	10	15	4	7	20	48
Life expectancy at birth	79	73	81	77	74	71
GNP per capita (2000 US dollars)	5,716	6,496	21,562	7,497	4,315	7,732

Source: World Development Indicators, 2013.

How have these countries achieved these remarkable results, so elusive elsewhere? In responding to this question, the literature shows a striking consensus concerning the role of democracy – something we will discuss further in Chapter 8. As Sandbrook *et al.* (2007: 123) state, "strong democratic institutions based on a vibrant civil society must develop. These institutions play a pivotal role in motivating politicians to seek equitable socioeconomic development." The influence of democracy on the social state took place from early on: according to Filgueira (2007a: 141), "early social state formation is highly correlated with early democratic experiments." In Uruguay, social insurance expanded under democratic rule during the 1910s and 1920s. The appointment of the Colorado party under the leadership of President José Batlle opened the political space for progressive social legislation and the adoption of new welfare programs (Segura-Ubiergo, 2007). Since then, social policy has expanded as a result of electoral competition, both before and after the democratic breakdown of the 1970s.

In Costa Rica, a country we discuss in more detail in the second part of the book, democracy is also identified as the driver of the social state. In the 1940s, electoral pressures led to the newly elected President

Calderón Guardia to address the social question by pushing for social security (Lehoucq, 2010; Molina, 2008). The subsequent expansion of pensions and health during the 1950s, 1960s, and 1970s has been explained by the dominance of a social-democratic party, the National Liberation Party (Partido Liberación Nacional, PLN), which faced intense electoral competition from conservatives.

According to authors like Carroll and Carroll (2000), Meisenhelder (1997), and Seekings (2011), the gradual emergence of democratic institutions before independence also explains generous social programs in Mauritius. Elections not only forced colonial governments, and later nationalist elites, to be more responsive to a majority of the population, but also consolidated the long-term influence of left-wing coalitions. More recently, electoral pressures have forced governments to maintain entitlements and, in some cases, to backtrack on regressive reform attempts (see Chapter 4).

Proponents of the democratic explanation argue that its contribution to expansionary social policy is clearest in the case of South Korea. During the 1960s and 1970s, the absence of democracy and the persecution of trade unions and social movements was a key factor behind the lack of social rights (Deyo, 1989). Democratization in the 1980s gave more room to left-wing parties and progressive social movements, strengthening pressures to expand social spending (Kwon, 2007). In their analysis of South Korea, Taiwan, Thailand, and the Philippines, Haggard and Kaufman (2008: 256) argue that "parties and politicians scrambled to position themselves with respect to pressing social policy issues, from pensions and health insurance to unemployment, social assistance and rural poverty."

We do not challenge the idea that democracy contributed to the expansion of social policy in all four countries – in fact, we consider it one of the preconditions as discussed in Chapter 8. However, while Costa Rica, Mauritius, South Korea, and Uruguay – and some other cases under democratic rule such as Argentina, Chile, or the state of Kerala in India (Sandbrook *et al.*, 2007) – may have high public spending in social programs, they show significant variations in terms of coverage, generosity, and equity. Because neither democracy nor other political explanations of social policy like the presence of progressive political parties predict this variance in *universal outputs*, we consider an additional set of explanatory factors.

3.3 The Role of Policy Architectures

We explore the missing links between democracy, social policy, and universalism by drawing on a useful analytical device: the policy architecture. Policy architectures have a twofold influence on universal outputs in specific contexts. First, at any given point in time different combinations of policy instruments deliver different levels of universalism. Second, dynamically, architectures create distinct opportunities and constraints for subsequent expansion – some of which will be more universal than others. In the rest of this chapter, we focus on the first role, while we leave dynamic trajectories for Chapter 4.

Policy architectures involve five main components related to who can access what, when, and how (Figure 3.1):

(1) Eligibility (*under what criteria do people benefit?*). This dimension refers to who is entitled to receive benefits and under what criteria. The three eligibility criteria studied in the literature are citizenship, contributions, and need (Esping-Andersen, 1990). Citizenship is associated with belonging or residing in a given nation state. Contributions are related to the insurance of workers directly

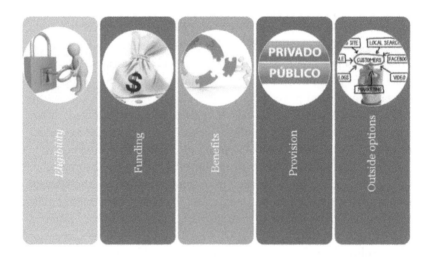

E + F + B + P + OO = Combined degree of unification/fragmentation

Figure 3.1 Dimensions of the Policy Architecture

and of non-workers as economically dependent family members. Assistance responds to economic need. These three criteria can be displayed alone or in different combinations.

(2) Funding (*who pays and how?*). Financial resources may come from general revenues, earmarked taxes, and/or payroll contributions. The latter may involve different degrees of financial commitment by government, employers, and workers. Any of these funding sources may be complemented by co-payments.

(3) Benefits (*who defines them and how?*). States generally stipulate benefits in a statutory fashion. Public agencies can do this in a broad range of ways from assuming that all benefits are included by default to listing everything included or listing only what is excluded. In some countries, businesses and/or workers also participate in the definition of benefits.

(4) Provision (*who does it?*). Delivery can be in the hands of public or private entities and, if private, for- or not-for-profit. Each of these arrangements is driven by particular goals that may favor or inhibit universal policy outputs. These outputs also depend on other factors like efficiency that we will not discuss in detail in this book.

(5) Outside option (*how do governments manage market-based alternatives?*). This component refers to the existence of non-public options available to those who can afford them. The existence of market-based alternatives can trigger exit from state services and transfers (Korpi and Palme, 1998). Within the outside option, we do not only consider out-of-pocket funded private provision, but also the use of public resources for private gains (e.g. doctors' conflicting dual practices).

We argue that building universalism does not depend on a given funding mechanism or a single eligibility criterion. Instead, the likelihood of universal outputs depends on how effectively policy architectures cope with pressures towards fragmentation within and across policy components. For instance, as we address elsewhere in the book (see Chapters 4 and 7), a country may secure unification in four out of five components but fail to reach universal outputs due to the existence of unregulated outside market options that drain public arrangements of resources and "voice". Also, a policy architecture granting a small number of services or limited transfers, even if funded through progressive taxes and delivered by public facilities, is still likely to result in high fragmentation in usage. The implications of a given policy choice for universal outputs should not be assessed in isolation but against the architecture.

In academic and policy debates, there is the well spread notion that Scandinavian countries provide the most desirable road towards universalism (Beland *et al.*, 2014; Huber, 2002). Drawing on the components just discussed, during the second half of the twentieth century, these countries secured universal outputs through a policy architecture that, first, reached all citizens; second, granted generous and high quality benefits funded by general revenues; third, had the state as the actor defining and providing benefits; and finally, kept private provisions in check.

Although these arrangements may be ideal to deliver universal outcomes, implementing them in the South has proven extremely complicated. When poorly funded, services that are allegedly granted for all end up being for the poor alone, run short of funding and provide limited and low quality services. Expanding taxes to deliver better services – the Scandinavian solution to secure equity and quality – has proven particularly difficult across the South. Regulating the private option has also been hard and few governments have understood the negative influence of private providers in the way public transfers and services work.

Can universalism be reached through a different combination of policy instruments than the citizenship-based Scandinavian one? As we illustrate in the following section, the answer is yes. In particular, under the right conditions policy architectures based on a combination of social insurance and social assistance can be successful.

3.4 Policy Architectures in Health Care

We now return to our four cases and establish the extent to which universal outputs are secured through a comparative study of their policy architecture in health care. This comparison also sheds light on the challenges that each country faces – i.e. where the binding constraints are. In undertaking this comparison, we demonstrate the importance of state-driven unification across the key components that make up policy architectures. Table 3.2 describes the policy

Table 3.2 *Current Policy Architectures in Health Care by Country*

Components	Mauritius	Costa Rica	South Korea	Uruguay
(1) What criteria is used for eligibility?	Citizens	Insured (mandatory workers, family, and poor)	Insured (salaried workers, self-employed, family, and poor)	Insured (workers/occupation-based, family, and poor)
(2) Who pays and how?	General revenues	Tripartite contributions and social assistance	Bipartite contribution to single fund + co-payment	Tripartite contribution to single fund + co-payment
(3) Who defines the benefits and how?	State; in theory all services	State; all services	Tripartite committee including trade unions, employers and doctors and hospital managers reviews NHI policies	State; all services
(4) Who/where is care provided?	Public facilities for all	Public facilities for all	Mostly not-for-profit private firms with a minor presence of public providers	Not-for-profit (middle class) and public (poor)
(5) Management of an outside (market) option?	Outside option is large and generally unregulated	Outside option is growing and unregulated	Large number of benefits outside the NHI package	Small number of unregulated private providers.

architecture in each of the four countries. Although there are differences in all components, below we focus on the four that are most significant.

Regarding *eligibility*, only Mauritius pursues the expansion of services through citizen-based principles. The other three cases organize around social insurance. Since the 2000s Costa Rica, South Korea, and Uruguay can claim relatively similar degrees of unification around a single fund.

Funding differences are also significant. Even though in all cases the state subsidizes the poor and the self-employed, there are significant differences among the three countries that rely on social insurance. In Costa Rica and Uruguay state support is more generous and reaches all non-salaried workers. Funding for low-income groups above the poverty line is particularly important if effective access is to be secured and fragmentation avoided.

Another significant difference has to do with the rules establishing *benefits*. In Costa Rica, the state does not limit the services available, which even include expensive treatments for rare diseases. In Uruguay, there is no exclusion list but beneficiaries must share the cost of some services. In South Korea, health insurance comprises only a defined package of services and involves co-payments. Private providers constantly pressure to limit packages because it is more profitable to sell new treatments out-of-pocket. In Mauritius, all benefits are theoretically covered.

The third difference is found in *service provision*. On one end of a continuum, in Costa Rica and Mauritius, services are delivered by public facilities. Fragmentation is low and reflects a standardization of benefits across facilities and protocols. At the other end, South Korean public facilities play a minor role; social insurance relies upon not-for-profit private providers. In 2011, there were only 191 South Korean public hospitals compared to 2,873 private facilities (OECD, 2014). Formal fragmentation is high: providers deliver services in different ways and with different protocols. In between the two extreme situations, Uruguay combines not-for-profit private providers with public facilities. Under the reformed National Health System (NHS), packages are increasingly standardized across providers and fragmentation is tackled by shared protocols.

Finally, there are significant cross-national variations regarding the management of the *outside option*. Mauritius combined at the onset Scandinavian-like arrangements with a large role for private providers. The outside option is also prominent in South Korea where it plays two different roles. On the one hand, private insurance companies are available, particularly for high-income groups. In 2009, private insurance was responsible for 10.6 percent of inpatient services and 5.2 percent of total health spending (Jeong and Shin, 2012). On the other hand, a large number of benefits remain outside the National Health Insurance (NHI) package. In Costa Rica and Uruguay, lower out-of-pocket spending reflects the smaller role of the outside option – although it still poses a significant threat to universal outputs.

The analysis summarized in Table 3.2 demonstrates that what matters for the ultimate – more or less unified – character of the architecture is not just how each component is designed, but also their interaction. Although the differences have diminished over time, they are still significant:

- South Korea and Uruguay historically had policy architectures based on insurance funds organized around firms and occupations (see Chapter 4) and still show more fragmentation across all components. For example, in Uruguay, the poor have access to medical facilities that are different from facilities accessed by middle class individuals. In South Korea, there are still procedures that are not included within the NHI. Co-payments limit effective access to theoretically available procedures for many people.
- In Mauritius, unification is high concerning several components, but a prominent outside option leads to high degrees of fragmentation primarily of funding and benefits.
- Costa Rica is the closest example of a unified state-led system, even if the growth of the private sector has recently become a significant threat. The country has a unified system of social insurance managed by only one institution and funded by tripartite contributions. There are no co-payments and the state is at the center of organizational arrangements, including service delivery.

We now explore the implications that these differences in policy architecture have for universal outputs. Since we are particularly interested in the extent to which countries take care of different groups of the population along occupational or socio-economic lines, we evaluate access, generosity, and equity for salaried workers, the self-employed, and the poor.

To provide a formal operationalization of the three components that comprise social policy outputs, we break down *access* in three categories (one-third = 0; two-thirds = 1; everyone = 2). We measure *generosity* in its two sub-dimensions of level of services covered (basic, non-basic, and full coverage) and fiscal commitment as a proxy measure to quality (low, medium, and high). We evaluate the level of services covered by taking into consideration effective provision. For example, long waiting lists for specialists create problems, particularly for the poor, who are likely to have fewer resources to overcome barriers through discretionary mechanisms. The combination between the level of services available and the fiscal commitments gives way to three options: low-low (= 0); high-low or low-high (= 1); high-high (= 2). *Equity* combines the presence of co-payments and state subsidies (co-payment and no state subsidy = 0; subsidy and co-payments = 1; subsidies without co-payments = 2).

Table 3.3 presents the aggregated coding of countries. Costa Rica scores 17, Uruguay 15, Mauritius 14, and South Korea 12. The coding is primarily based on secondary literature on health care in each of the countries, which we extensively discuss in the next chapter.[4] Even though countries tend to perform similarly across groups, Uruguay does not yet reach the poor in the same way as salaried workers and the self-employed. In South Korea, only 3.7 percent of the population in 2009 were considered very poor and were not required to make co-payments whereas everyone else did, independently of income level.

Costa Rica receives the highest mark because everyone has access to the same services. Generosity is also high in terms of public spending, but faces problems due to growing waiting lists, particularly for specialists. Although in theory these affect all income groups, the poor suffer disproportionally because they have fewer social and financial resources to confront them. Despite significant improvements in recent years, South Korea is still the lowest in the ranking because of low public spending and high co-payments damaging equity.

---

[4] Quantitative data on coverage, degrees of redistribution, or some policy outcomes (e.g. child mortality) would not adequately measure universal outcomes. Measures of the redistributive impact of public spending fail to consider the combined effect of the public sector and the outside option and also do not adequately measure generosity and quality. Outcome indicators depend on many factors other than policy interventions.

Table 3.3 *Index of Universal Outputs per Country by Component, Category, and Total Values*

Country	Salaried	Score	Self-employed	Score	Poor	Score	Total
Costa Rica							
Access	All	2	All	2	All	2	6
Generosity	High-high	2	High-high	2	Low-high	1	5
Equity	High	2	High	2	High	2	6
Total		6		6		5	17
Mauritius							
Access	All	2	All	2	All	2	6
Generosity	High-low	1	High-low	1	Low-low	0	2
Equity	High	2	High	2	High	2	6
Total		5		5		4	14
South Korea							
Access	All	2	All	2	All	2	6
Generosity	High-low	1	High-low	1	High-low	1	3
Equity	Low	0	Medium	1	High	2	3
Total		3		4		5	12
Uruguay							
Access	All	2	All	2	All	2	6
Generosity	High-high	2	High-high	2	High-low	1	5
Equity	Medium	1	Medium	1	High	2	4
Total		5		5		5	15

3.5 The Shared Threat of the Outside Option

In a recent review of the implementation of universal health coverage in the South, the World Bank argues that "delivery [in the different cases analyzed] is undertaken through public, private, for-profit, or not-for-profit providers or a mix of them … (probably the majority) rely to some extent on a mix between public and private providers" (Giedion, Alfonso, and Díaz, 2013: 4) and does not identify problems with this pattern. This technocratic approach overlooks how the existence of an outside option reshapes public services: a prominent private sector, even if efficient in service delivery, has a negative impact on universalism via fragmentation of all other components in both the short and long term.

The outside option refers broadly to the existence of alternatives that drive a larger role for markets in allocating resources. Although often used to refer to private hospitals, outside options can involve many other arrangements. For example, countries may have a liberal practice completely funded by out-of-pocket contributions or the so-called "dual practice" whereby medical professionals have a foot in public and private provision. All these arrangements rely on profit as the organizing principle behind the allocation of resources. Subsequently these arrangements are likely to lead to fragmentation in access (i.e. between those who can and cannot afford to pay); funding (i.e. between sources that reflect rights and those that reflect purchasing capacity); benefits (i.e. between more or less profitable treatments); and provision (i.e. between providers that operate under different rules of the game). All outside options undermine universalism.

Finding a single way to measure the outside option is not easy given its variety and its multiple effects on the other four components. One empirical approximation we consider to be effective is the comparison between of out-of-pocket expenditure and public spending as percentage of GDP. Figure 3.2 considers this indicator as a proxy of equity and compares it to one dimension of generosity measured by public health spending (as percentage of GDP) for all countries with high coverage in child delivery, a basic and much needed service.

Challenges posed by the outside option take on different shapes and degrees across the four cases we discuss. The figure places Mauritius as

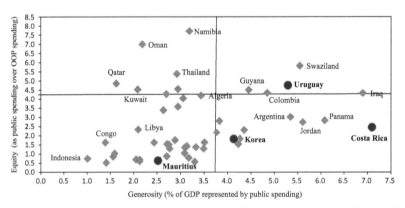

Figure 3.2 Countries with High Newborn Delivery Attended by Professional Personnel: Generosity and Equity in Health Care Provision, 2013
Source: Based on data from WHO (2013)

having the lowest equity and generosity of the four. South Korea follows suit. Costa Rica shows the highest generosity and Uruguay the highest equity, respectively.

The negative implications of the outside option are particularly significant in the case of Mauritius. The historical presence of private hospitals for the upper middle class and the wealthy throughout the country has affected the evolution of public health care over time and – via underfunded and understaffed facilities – influenced the level of coverage, generosity, and equity. Costa Rica has historically managed the outside option better than the other three countries. Yet it is a growing threat as the demand for public services is growing, quality is dropping, and the number of medical professionals entering the labor market each year is rapidly expanding (see Chapter 7).

In South Korea, high out-of-pocket spending results from the delivery of public services by private providers who combine their liberal and NHI practices. Reimbursement takes place per treatment – despite governmental attempts to come up with alternative mechanisms – thus creating incentives to over-consumption of health care services. It also creates pressures to combine treatments included under the NHI with newer and more costly treatments that are not. Altogether incentives are to increase spending on highly sophisticated medical treatments. The result is high private spending with low equity. Indeed, in 2011 South Korea had the third highest private spending among the OECD countries, after Chile and Mexico.

Uruguay is the best performer on out-of-pocket spending measures of the four cases considered. This is partly explained by the small role of private providers operating fully outside state influence and a strong state regulation – introduced with the latest reforms – of the not-for-profit mutual aid sector. Reimbursing mechanisms for these mutual aid societies when operating under the NHS is also beneficial for universalism: providers receive a per capita for each person they manage – unlike South Korea where providers are reimbursed per event. Being in charge of people rather than events reduces fragmentation: guaranteeing that the insured receive all needed treatment as promptly as possible, is in the interest of providers. Uruguay's intelligent regulation of the mutual aid societies contrast with the unregulated approach to the dual practice in Costa Rica and Mauritius, and South Korea's weaker capacity to impose conditions on providers.

3.6 Policy Architectures in Pensions

As we explained in more detail in the introductory chapter, pensions constitute a useful shadow case to explore the analytical leverage of policy architectures as a conceptual tool. Comparing transfers to services (e.g. health care) permits a view of differences and similarities while acknowledging the diversity of obstacles to universal outputs.

Table 3.4 summarizes policy architectures for pensions across the four countries analyzed. Mauritius stands out as the only country with a non-contributory pension for all funded through general taxes. Benefits from non-contributory pensions amount to 20 percent of the average earnings (Vittas, 2003). The complementary contributory pension for salaried workers aims at a replacement rate of 33 percent. Theoretically, this Scandinavian-like policy architecture should be the one most capable of providing universal outputs of the four countries discussed. Yet four features of the Mauritian architecture get in the way of delivering universalism. First, contributory pensions for the self-employed are voluntary and devoid of public subsidies, thus limiting effective access. Second, the government updates the value of pensions based on inflation (rather than average wages) and therefore the replacement rate of social insurance has been much lower than expected, thus reducing generosity. Third, the outside option is significant: by the early 2000s, Mauritius had more than 1,000 private pension schemes, many of which were corporate based, reducing equity. Finally, the existence of a National Savings Fund made of mandatory, capitalization contributions also reduces the redistributive impact of the policy architecture and, again, equity. Confirming our conclusions in previous sections, pensions in Mauritius highlight the importance of considering the policy architecture as a whole: universal non-contributory old-age transfers are extremely important (Barrientos and Lloyd-Sherlock, 2002; Willmore, 2006) but do not by themselves guarantee universal outputs.

Costa Rica, South Korea, and Uruguay base their transfers on a combination of social insurance and means-tested, non-contributory pensions. Yet there are significant differences in the interaction between the two and in their funding sources. In Costa Rica, most pensions are managed by the Costa Rican Social Insurance

Table 3.4 Current Policy Architectures in Pensions: Policy Instruments by Country and Component

Contributions	Mauritius	Costa Rica	South Korea	Uruguay
(1) What criteria make people eligible?	Citizens and insured salaried workers	Salaried workers, the self-employed, and the poor	Salaried workers, the self-employed, and the poor	Salaried workers, the self-employed, and the poor
(2) Who pays and how?	*Non-contributory pensions:* General taxes *Salaried workers:* Bipartite contributions unless there is deficit *Self-employed:* N/A	Payroll and indirect taxes	General taxes	General taxes
		Tripartite contributions	Bipartite contribution to the national pension program	Tripartite contribution to occupation-based funds
(3) Who defines the benefits and how?	State; defined benefit	State-workers contributions State; defined benefit	Workers contributions State; defined benefit	State-workers contributions State: defined benefit
(4) Who provides the transfer?	Public	Public	National Pension program (state managed but without state subsidies)	Public and occupational funds
(5) Management of outside option	Existence of optional private providers as additional tier (funded by workers alone)	Existence of mandatory private providers as additional tier (for salaried workers; funded with public funds and employer contributions)	Existence of private providers as additional tier	Existence of mandatory private providers as additional tier (for salaried workers; funded by their own contributions)

Agency (CCSS).[5] Payroll taxes are the main source of funding for both contributory and non-contributory pensions. The main shortcoming has to do with coverage: non-contributory pensions still do not incorporate all the poor, and contributory pensions for the self-employed, despite their recent expansion, still leave about a third of workers behind.

In South Korea funds for salaried workers and the self-employed have no interaction with non-contributory pensions. Additionally, workers within the contributory system receive limited or no state support, which reduces the opportunities for cross-class subsidies and thus equity. Uruguay has the most fragmented scenario of the four cases as the general fund coexists with several prominent funds for various occupations. Uruguay's advantage is that it has higher coverage overall than do the others. In a sense, the best case scenario would combine the unified architecture found in Costa Rica with Uruguay's high coverage.

To conclude, it is useful to highlight a significant cross-national difference between policy architectures in health care and pensions. Overall fragmentation is higher in pensions than in health care. In the four cases (even if with different degrees), specific occupational groups such as public servants have succeeded in securing more generous old-age transfers than other workers. Additionally, while in the case of health care collectively funded arrangements have made services totally independent from premiums, in pensions, workers' earnings and contributions are always interrelated. Finally, the creation of capitalization pillars in the last two decades – partly driven by a new international environment that was more influential in pensions than in health care – has increased fragmentation much more than in health care.

3.7 Conclusion

In this chapter, we have defined policy architectures as the combination of instruments that address the five key components of specific policy areas: eligibility, funding, benefits, delivery, and outside market options. This concept facilitates comparisons between countries in health care, education, pensions, and other social policy interventions

---

[5] Like the other three countries, Costa Rica has independent funds, but they only cover public teachers and workers in the judiciary.

to determine their place along a continuum between fragmentation on the one hand, and unification on the other. In so doing, we provide evidence that there are different roads to secure universal outputs, which depend more on an adequate combination of policy instruments than on the existence of any specific one. This is clear in the case of Costa Rica where the "wrong" policy instruments (i.e. social insurance) got the country closer to universal outputs than expected.

The comparison between Costa Rica, Mauritius, South Korea, and Uruguay illuminates the specific features policy architectures should have to deliver universal outputs. The more unified all the components of the architecture are, the better for universal outputs, as the Costa Rican case clearly shows. In terms of eligibility, for example, this means that the best instruments are those that incorporate the highest number of people with as few bureaucratic barriers as possible. In terms of funding through payroll taxes, state participation should ideally complement contributions from workers and employees and there should also be cross-subsidies between income groups. Non-contributory mechanisms must be made available to all those who are neither workers nor their relatives as happens in Costa Rica. Benefits should be defined in a transparent and comprehensive manner.

Our analysis also shows the danger of an unregulated private out-side option and thus demonstrates the need to study the public and private sectors simultaneously. This is made particularly clear by the cases of Mauritius and South Korea, where under starkly different architectures, universalism has been inhibited by the presence of a powerful private sector.

In so far as the notion of policy architecture depicts a comprehensive view of all instruments available, it can also help identify the main strengths and weaknesses of social provision in specific contexts. More practically, understanding the sectoral policy architecture can help policymakers devise the best strategies to foster unification. Yet because architectures are in permanent change there are limits as to what we can learn from this kind of static, synchronic analysis. In fact, as a recent comparative analysis of Latin America's health care reminds us, "the journey towards universal health care needs constant learning and adaptation" (Cotlear *et al.*, 2014: 10). Addressing the conditions under which this process of adaptation triggers moves towards unification is precisely the subject of our next chapter.

4 | *The Long-Term Influence of Policy Architectures*

4.1 Introduction

Policy architectures do not only explain the degree of universalism in the short term (as discussed in the previous chapter), but also influence the trajectory of policies over the long run. If social programs exclusively incorporate the better off, pressures to reach out to lower-income groups will be weak. If policies depart from the poor alone, transfers will be low and services will not have sufficient quality to attract wealthier groups. If provision of services is exclusively private, preventing fragmentation and delivering standardized benefits for the whole society is unlikely.

To consider the dynamic role of policy architectures, we introduce the concept of foundational architectures: the blueprint of policy instruments set up by states in an initial effort to organize social benefits.[1] The timing of foundational architectures varies across countries and its identification is more or less straightforward depending on national circumstances. For instance, determining the foundational architecture is relatively easy in Costa Rica: formal state arrangements for health care provision emerged with the creation of the social insurance agency in 1941. Defining the foundational architecture of old-age transfers in Uruguay is much harder due to the blurred boundaries between public and private sectors since inception.

We identify two distinct dynamic roles of policy architectures: first, to empower some actors and create financial and political incentives for subsequent reforms; and second, to constrain the number of possible alternatives that social and state actors can pursue. Our point is not that policy architectures are the sole determinants of universal outputs – democracy and partisan ideology are obviously

---

[1] We ignore initial attempts that may have been exclusively private such as those driven by religious organizations.

important – but that they influence the likelihood and speed of pro-universal reforms.

We develop this argument by describing the foundational architectures and their evolution over time in health care and pensions in Costa Rica, Mauritius, South Korea, and Uruguay. We show that in democratic contexts there were advances as well as set-backs. For example, Costa Rica and Uruguay had electoral competition for most of the first two-thirds of the twentieth century (see Chapter 1), yet social policies in the former resulted in more universal outputs than in the latter. In Mauritius, electoral competition and the presence of left-wing coalitions favored the expansion of health and non-contributory pensions during the second half of the twentieth century. However, the same democratic institutions did little to curb the outside option, which from the onset undermined unified benefits.

By comparing the evolution of policy architectures in all four cases, we also question mono-causal explanations regarding the impact of globalization (see Chapter 1) – thus confirming some of Haggard and Kaufman's (2008) conclusions about the uneven evolution of social policy across the South since the 1980s. During the last three decades, South Korea and Uruguay introduced changes in their policy architectures, which moved them closer to securing universal outputs than ever before. In Uruguay, the 2000–2001 crises triggered reforms that unified the policy architecture. In the late 1990s, South Korea strengthened policy architectures that were favorable to universalism – paradoxically at a time when it was experiencing heavy pressures in favor of austerity from international institutions.

4.2 Health Care

This section discusses the long-term evolution of policy architectures in health care in each of the four countries. We show that Costa Rica's foundational architecture created better conditions to move in a universalist direction. The system was unified across most components of the architecture, even in terms of providers. Social insurance incentivized the incorporation of new groups into a unified, state-led sector. Even if the outside option has become a growing problem in recent years, Costa Rica still maintains the most unified policy architecture of the four cases.

Mauritius constitutes a middle case in terms of the opportunities created by the foundational policy architecture. Like the Scandinavian countries, the Mauritian architecture was based on general revenues and services for all. However, the existence of a large and unregulated outside option constrained unification from early on and has become even more problematic recently.

In contrast, Uruguay and South Korea began with a more fragmented foundational architecture due to the prominence of multiple insurance funds and the active role of private actors. Such fragmentation complicated steps towards universalism. Insiders protected their benefits and, at times, have more incentives to expand their entitlements than to incorporate new groups.

In recent years, the two countries have taken steps towards unification, partly in response to financial bottlenecks in their pre-existing architectures. In that process, Uruguay has benefited from more favorable conditions than South Korea. Private providers were membership-based, not-for-profit organizations with strong incentives to offer affordable services to their members rather than solely to maximize income. Also, throughout the twentieth century the Uruguayan state played an important role in the provision of services, particularly for the poor. In South Korea, health care funds have been unified but insurers and providers have pressured to maintain fragmentation in some areas (e.g. co-payments and a defined basket of benefits).

4.2.1 Costa Rica

Costa Rica's foundational architecture can be located in 1940 when the first Social-Christian president, Rafael Ángel Calderón Guardia, created social insurance under the management of the Costa Rican Social Insurance Agency (CCSS).[2] The new payroll-funded social insurance had three distinctive features that contributed to the subsequent expansion of health care (and pensions). First, it was unified, reaching all workers (and later their families) with the same entitlements, and with a sole, public institution running the system. Second, it started off by insuring urban lower income groups and only later,

---

[2] This section draws on Martínez Franzoni and Sánchez-Ancochea (2014). The term Social-Christian is a translation of the Spanish "Social-cristiano." It refers to politicians that followed the Social Catholic doctrine. At different points in the book, we also refer to Calderón Guardia as Christian-Democrat, which is more consistent with international terminology.

higher income earners (what we call a "bottom-up" expansion).[3] Third, funding was tripartite, with contributions from workers, employers, and the government.

As a way of expanding coverage, in 1955 services were made available to dependent family members of insured workers. Like in the Southern Cone, this vertical expansion was positive for those already entitled to benefits. Unlike the Southern Cone, people reached were not upper-middle class professionals but lower-middle-income families.[4] The change was massive: in the first year, the incorporation of family members resulted in a 54 percentage increase of coverage.

In 1960, the CCSS bureaucrats argued that the combined pressures of growing service demand and state debt jeopardized the financial sustainability of social insurance (Rosenberg, 1983). Given the unified character of arrangements, the creation of new funds that would, for instance, take care of the poor was out of the question. Instead, the CCSS focused on increasing the wage ceiling, which affected relatively high-wage earners. In response to these bureaucratic demands, in 1961 Congress approved a constitutional reform that established the universalization of social insurance in ten years (see Chapter 6).

Coverage expanded gradually during the 1960s, but funding shortages remained. By the early 1970s, the CCSS bureaucrats demanded the full elimination of wage ceilings to increase revenues that funded the required universalization of social insurance. The elimination of the wage ceiling received ample support from the working class: almost all unions favored the decision. The influence of the foundational architecture partly explains their backing: insured workers had incentives to embrace the incorporation of higher income groups who would strengthen services by bringing larger payroll taxes.

In the short term, the increase of the wage ceiling harmed higher wage earners.[5] Yet the fact that social insurance provided a large amount of quality services made their mandatory incorporation if

---

[3] Insurance was initially mandatory for urban workers receiving up to US$54 monthly wages at the 1941 exchange rate.

[4] According to Rosenberg (1979) quoting newspapers from the period, the incorporation of family dependents to social security was also a way to confront the problems of overcrowding and underfunding in hospitals outside the CCSS.

[5] An anonymous full-page advertisement estimated that for workers earning above 1,000 colones per month, the annual payroll contributions would surpass a monthly salary (*La Hora*, 1970).

not attractive, at least bearable. As the Caja Costarricense del Seguro Social (CCSS or Caja) built new hospitals, its facilities became the newest and the best funded and equipped nationwide. According to the Minister of Health between 1970 and 1974, Jose Luis Orlich, "on the one hand, the Caja has good medical treatment thanks to its great facilities and good personnel, which defines a high-quality medicine. On the other hand, the Ministry has extremely poor facilities [and] deteriorated buildings so that we cannot talk about good medicine" (*La Nación*, February 24, 1971: 57). With the removal of wage ceilings and the expansion of mandatory insurance, coverage increased to 85 percent of the total population in 1980 (Mesa-Lago, 1985).

During the 1970s, the Costa Rican government also took action to further incorporate the poor to the health care system. Reforms implemented were consistent with the unified policy architecture already in place. The creation of a primary care program opened the door for the rural poor to access social insurance and receive curative services at the same hospitals than the rest of the population. In 1979, the primary care program was serving 717,500 people (60 percent of the rural population) and 120,000 rural poor had enrolled in social insurance and relied on services at clinics and/or hospitals run by the CCSS (Sáenz *et al.*, 1981). Payroll taxes, which had provided resources to social insurance over the previous three decades, were also drawn to fund transfers and services for the poor through the social assistance fund (Fondo de Desarrollo Social y Asignaciones Familiares, FODESAF).[6]

By the late 1970s, Costa Rica's policy architecture was the most favorable for universalism among our four cases. Different types of insurance – contributory and non-contributory, for workers and for dependent family members – allowed everyone access to the same health care services. Since then, most components of Costa Rica's architecture have remained intact: social insurance is still unified and based on tripartite arrangements and the state plays a central role in running and funding the system and providing services.

Unfortunately, at the same time, a number of emergency measures implemented to confront the economic crisis of the early 1980s and a managerial reform adopted in the 1990s have rapidly broadened the space for private actors. Coverage has remained massive and the level of services high, but cutbacks have badly hurt the quality and equity of

---

[6] FODESAF was also partly funded with newly created sale taxes.

health care. Managerial decisions encouraged a large number of physicians to combine private and public practice, reducing their commitment to the CCSS significantly.

The drop in quality among public facilities, coupled with a larger and more diversified private supply of services, has fuelled a growing reliance on outside options. Between 1991 and 2001, private spending in health care increased by an annual rate of 8 percent compared to 5 percent in public spending (Picado, Acuña, and Santacruz, 2003). In only five years, between 1993 and 1998, the proportion of out-of-pocket spending in total health spending increased five times (Herrero and Durán 2001). Between 2000 and 2009, private spending as a share of the total increased steadily, from 23.2 percent to 32.6 percent. The emergence of a powerful private sector has weakened unified services and could eventually lead to more radical transformations of the policy architecture (e.g. private administration of payroll taxes and facilities).

Costa Rica: The Most Successful Architecture Preceding Recent Setbacks

First decades of the 20th century	The poor rely on religious charity and the non-poor on liberal medical practice (and in charity hospitals when in need of inpatient services).
1941	Creation of the foundational architecture with the introduction of social insurance with three main characteristics: (a) bottom-up incorporation along income lines; (b) unified fund managed by a single institution; and (c) tripartite funding. Also, the outside option is small and shrinking.
1955	The incorporation of family members to health insurance creates financial pressures and political opportunities to expand resources.
1961	Unification is promoted by a constitutional reform mandating the expansion of coverage to all Costa Ricans, including the better off.
1970s	Further unification in access, funding, and providers through the elimination of the wage ceiling, the integration of hospitals, and the enactment of targeted measures to incorporate the poor alongside the non-poor.

(*cont.*)	
1980s– 2000s	Despite formal stability, poorly managed reforms weaken services and expand an array of private providers. As a result, a growing outside option erodes the unified architecture.

4.2.2 Mauritius

We place the foundational architecture of Mauritius in the early 1950s, when newly created democratic institutions still under colonial rule took steps to expand personnel and services.[7] The government opened welfare centers for children and their mothers and increased substantially the number of trained nurses and doctors. In 1959, the Government Medical Service was launched with outpatient services provided by seventy-four doctors in the hospital and in dispensaries all across the island (Titmus and Abel-Smith, 1968). In theory, the service was only free for public servants and low income groups but, in practice, few people paid.

Despite all these improvements, "at the end of the 1950s, health services were in a sorry state. Saturation point in the hospitals had long been surpassed ... In the ambulatory sector, the situation was equally unsatisfactory" with long waiting lists and an insufficient number of doctors (Dommen and Dommen, 1999: 45). Estimations indicated that there was one general practitioner (GP) per 10,000 compared to one per 3,500 in the United Kingdom (Government Medical and Dental Officers Association, undated). The system was limited by low levels of taxation; in particular, less than 8,000 people paid the income tax and most benefited from generous tax exemptions – in fact, the "Income Tax Law provide[d] a system of social security for the rich" (Abel-Smith archive, 1960).

---

[7] In the late 1940s, there were just two public hospitals and six Poor Law Hospitals. Also, thirty-nine public dispensaries across the island delivered some basic services by general practitioners for a few hours per day. Yet the number of medical and nursing staff was still limited, maternity and child welfare were privately managed, and the government focused almost exclusively on the poor (Titmus and Abel-Smith, 1968). Each sugar estate also had its own hospital, which had few doctors and poor infrastructure (Parahoo, 1986).

The government actively supported the private sector, which was responsible for an estimated 40 percent of the total spending in health care (Titmus and Abel-Smith, 1968). In 1960, for example, authorities provided an interest free loan for the construction of the "Clinique Mauricienne" as well as a long lease on the building. This private clinic, which targeted the upper middle class and the wealthy, also received an exception from customs duty in all equipment and inputs (Abel-Smith archive, 1960).

The Mauritian foundational architecture therefore comprised a public network of primary and secondary care facilities, including hospitals, funded through general taxes; and a large outside option including unregulated dual practice – with doctors simultaneously working on the public and private sectors. These two characteristics influenced subsequent developments and consolidated a fragmented architecture.

During the 1970s and 1980s public health made significant progress. Massive campaigns succeeded in eradicating malaria (an effort that had begun in the late 1950s), expanding immunization and diverting additional funding to maternal and child services and health education programs (Republic of Mauritius, 1971; Valaydon, 2002). Additionally, the number of community health centers grew significantly and by the 2000s there were twenty-five area health centers and eighty-one community centers (Sonoo, 2012). In the early 1970s, health centers also became responsible for maternal and child welfare as well as family planning. The building of a new hospital was completed in the early 1970s and new beds were added to the system. The entire population could now receive those services for free.

Yet quality remained a problem at all levels and the upper middle class and the wealthy were in practice never fully incorporated to the national health system. Parahoo (1986) is particularly critical of the state of services at the end of the 1970s. In his account, "health planners decided to build health centers without seriously considering giving them the important role and function that is necessary if the health needs of the people are to be met. Lack of planning is also reflected in the fact that no prior assessment of the health needs of the population was made" (p. 204). There were large waiting lists and insufficient services at the local level and the system was increasingly geared towards curative services provided by hospitals. The number of specialists increased from just four in 1950 to 144 in 1981 with the ratio of non-specialist to specialists decreasing from seven to less than three.

The private sector remained prominent: in 1979 there were six private clinics offering a growing number of services, including laboratory analysis and radiography, without any state regulation. Private practice was geared towards the wealthy and was quantitatively more significant for outpatient than for inpatient services.[8] This lack of commitment to the public system by high income groups became a major driver of fragmentation: "the rich, often the more educated and more powerful, as pressure groups [had] little interest in advocating better health care in hospitals and dispensaries since they hardly use[d] the services of these institutions" (Parahoo, 1986: 238).

Dual medical practice generated significant conflicts of interest: a 1980 report warned that "the same persons who are in a position to determine the level of medical care and efficiency of hospitals and dispensaries also happen to benefit financially if people are forced to rely more and more on private medical services because they are dissatisfied with hospitals and dispensaries" (cited in Parahoo, 1986: 236). Dual practice was poorly controlled in terms of working hours in public facilities and professional fees in private services were unregulated.

During the 1980s and 1990s, the public sector continued to expand and a large proportion of the population relied on its services. Still, problems persisted and the public–private split intensified. By the mid-1990s, child immunization coverage remained at 80 percent (the same as twenty years before); waiting lists in hospitals were significant; and the ratio of nurses to doctors (a good measurement of a country's commitment to basic, preventive health) had dropped (Dommen and Dommen, 1999). A 1995 study showed broad dissatisfaction with health care, with some patients complaining that public doctors – 61 percent of whom also worked in the private sector (UK Monopolies and Merger Commission, in Kaseean and Juwaheer, 2010: 5) – asked them to visit their private practice (Lingayah, 1995: 369).

---

[8] While the number of private doctors was relatively high, the role of inpatient private medical services was not: in 1979 the private hospitals only had 190 beds compared to 2,840 in the public sector and were responsible for only 5.7 percent of all child deliveries (Parahoo 1986: 233).

State authorities were aware of how problematic dual practice was. In the early 1990s, a high-ranking official in the Ministry of Health warned: "There is the problem of private practice. At the time quite a number of doctors who did not have the [legal] privilege of consulting in private were nevertheless resorting to private practice ... Public medical officers – including specialists ... instead of being at their desks, they are in their private offices consulting their patients" (cited in Valaydon, 2002: 198). Valaydon (2002) reports different types of legal and illegal dual practice, including doctors that left early to work in the private sector and health workers paid to handle equipment carelessly by repair companies.

In the 2000s, private providers expanded their role. In 2001 private expenditure already represented 48 percent of the sector's overall spending, increasing to 66 percent in 2008 – significantly higher than in Costa Rica, South Korea, and Uruguay. In the early 2000s there were 14 private clinics, 20 private medical laboratories, and 275 private pharmacies. The private sector had only 14 percent of all beds available in the country (588 out of 4,297) but hired 37 percent of full-time doctors (413 out of 1,107) as well as many others part-time (Ministry of Health, 2002). This expansion of private provision was primarily driven by high-income groups: in the early 2000s, more than half of all out-of-pocket expenditure came from the richest 20 percent of the population (World Health Organization [WHO], 2006).[9]

The expansion of the private sector is likely to deepen in the future for two reasons. First, Mauritius is becoming a medical hub for specialized treatments like in vitro fertilization and hair replacement (Devi, 2008). Health tourism run by private providers is seen as a strategic driver of economic development and its potential impact on the marketization of health care is absent from the public debate (Roychowdhury, 2015). Parallel to this expansion of the outside option, private practice remains unregulated. Second, state support for private options has increased in recent years. A 2012 reform makes it possible for salaried workers (except public employees and very low income workers) to purchase private insurance drawing on their individual accounts in the National Savings Fund. Made up of 2.5 percent payroll contribution, this fund was created in 2006 to provide a lump

---

[9] Private insurance was still relatively unimportant: only 5.8 percent of the whole population had access to private insurance in 2003 (WHO, 2006).

sum at retirement. As a result of the 2012 reform, a large amount of resources will likely be transferred onto private services, further expanding the outside option (*African Business Monitor*, 2012). Additionally, since January 1, 2013, every taxpayer with private health insurance is also entitled to a Rs12,000–36,000 (US$390–1,172) tax relief (Erikson, 2015). Unfortunately, these changes will further consolidate a two-tier system: one for households relying on public services and another for those purchasing medical insurance.

Mauritius: Universal Architecture Undermined by Market-led Fragmentation

First half of 20th century	The poor rely on low quality colonial facilities while the non-poor use private facilities except for inpatient services.
1950s	Foundational architecture is set in place as seventy-four full-time doctors are hired to provide public outpatient and inpatient services. The system is characterized by unification in key components of the architecture (access, funding, benefits, and delivery) together with a powerful outside option. Unregulated dual practice makes things even more problematic.
1970s	Fragmentation driven by the outside option continues: public spending grows and new facilities are built yet insufficient investment and waiting lists limit quality. The upper middle class and the wealthy use private facilities.
1990s and 2000s	There is a significant expansion in out-of-pocket spending and new incentives to rely on private provision. The outside option has therefore gradually eroded other components of the architecture.

4.2.3 *South Korea*

South Korea's foundational architecture can be traced back to 1977, significantly later than in Costa Rica, Mauritius, and Uruguay (Wong, 2004). At that time, the Park Chung-hee regime established mandatory firm-level social insurance in companies with more than 500 workers. Funding was based on mandatory contributions from workers and employers and involved minimum public participation: the state regulated the sector but neither contributed financially nor provided most services.

Parallel to the contributory system for workers in large firms, the government launched a social assistance health care program for the poor (Medicaid). Funded with general taxes, it gave benefits to people who met stringent income and wealth conditions. Medicaid classified the poor into two groups: a minority of people who could not join the labor force because they were too young, too old, or disabled (called "type one") and those capable of working ("type two"). Type one beneficiaries had access to those medical services included in the national health insurance list free of charge; type two beneficiaries had to contribute with co-payments of up to 20 percent of the cost of the service. Both types of beneficiaries paid in full for the substantial number of services excluded from the list (Kwon, 2000).

Gradually, the National Health Insurance (NHI) expanded to all salaried workers through the creation of firm-based insurance societies incorporating increasingly smaller companies. In 1978, government employees and private teachers joined in (with their own insurance societies), followed by companies with over 300 workers in 1979, those with over 100 in 1981, and with over 16 workers in 1983. This expansion was relatively unproblematic: there was no financial burden for the government; contributions from employers and employees were relatively low; and employees from large companies were not affected by the creation of other, insurance societies. Meanwhile, private doctors and providers did benefit from an increasing demand for health care provision (Kwon, 1995: 79).

Some fragmenting features of the NHI had a negative long-term influence on health care arrangements. First, the state aimed to minimize its direct involvement in funding and service provision. As Ringen *et al.* (2011: 73) puts it, "in authoritarian and democratic periods alike . . . the state has enabled itself to both claim ownership of social responsiveness and to pass the buck of practical responsibility on to others." Second, funding was far from unified as insurance contributions were low and were accompanied by co-payments of up to 60 percent of the service cost. Moreover, a significant number of procedures – particularly the latest – were excluded from health insurance. Third, insurance societies were primarily intermediaries: they collected premiums and reimbursed providers but did not attempt to shape service supply and demand. Fourth, service provision was primarily in the hands of private hospitals, which in most cases were owned by one or several physicians (Kwon, 2002). Finally, some insurance societies were in better financial conditions than others.

In 1988, the new democratic government created regional insurance funds for the self-employed.[10] In the following years 134 rural insurance societies and 117 urban insurance societies reached farmers and the urban self-employed (Kim and Lee, 2010). Individual contributions were estimated based on a number of factors, including income, gender, age and the number of dependents (Kwon, 2007). To promote coverage among the self-employed the government was forced to grant them subsidies, equivalent to 46 percent (rural sector) and 34 percent (urban sector) of the premium (Ramesh, 2003).[11]

Low generosity in benefits kept contributions low: most farmers and urban non-salaried workers managed to pay their premiums and the government subsidy was fiscally manageable. During the implementation of the measure, public health expenditure as percentage of gross domestic product (GDP) increased by less than a half percentage point – despite the millions of new subsidized beneficiaries – going from 1 percent in 1987 to 1.4 percent four years later (OECD, 2013). At the same time, co-payments remained high and out-of-pocket expenditure per capita in US dollars (in purchasing power parity) actually increased from 118 in 1987 to 199 in 1991.

Despite claims that by 1989 South Korea had achieved universal health care for all (Peabody, Lee and Bickel, 1995), policy outputs were far from universal: among workers coverage was broad but generosity was low and inequality high. Meanwhile, non-contributory access through Medicaid decreased significantly due to stringent means-testing in the context of high economic growth. Ramesh (2003) shows that in 1999, only 1.6 percent of the Korean population received free services (type 1), well below the total number of poor (10 percent of the population).

---

[10] This decision followed a presidential veto to a 1988 bill that would have incorporated the self-employed and all the existing plans into a single, unified system.

[11] In 1978 the government had made health insurance compulsory for government employees and private teachers, paying for 20 percent of their premiums.

The Asian crisis had a destabilizing effect on these arrangements: in 1997 funds for private industry, school employees, and government reported deficit, while the funds for the self-employed had only a small surplus. By 1998, the combined deficit of all funds was 860 billion won, equivalent to 28 percent of accumulated reserves (Kwon, 2000).

The crisis highlighted the structural problems of having a myriad of relatively small funds.[12] The government then had three options, all involving transformations of the policy architecture: expanding contributions, increasing government subsidies or unifying the system. The first was rather unpopular, particularly because payroll contributions had already increased in previous years and the economy was underperforming. Raising contributions from the self-employed was also hard as most of them were poor and adequate information on their income was hard to obtain. Increasing government subsidies was difficult due to fiscal constraints – some of which came from the post-crisis agreement with the IMF – and the traditional small role of the state in social policy.

In 2000 a Congressional bill unified almost 500 insurance funds into a single insurer, the National Health Insurance (NHI). Pooling contributions had the potential to create progressive redistribution from high-income, mostly healthy salaried workers to the poor, the self-employed and the sick. Additionally, even though the state's financial contribution remained low, it gained a stronger role in coordination and supervision. As a result, "the fiscal deficit and crisis of the NHI has become more of a national agenda than a set of local issues, as in the previous fragmented health insurance system" (Kwon, 2007: 165), making the state the guarantor of last resort in health care.

Yet unification was primarily driven by financial concerns rather than equity (Park, 2011). As critically summarized by Kwon and Holliday (2007: 246), the "NHI reform has had little more than a limited impact on health coverage … Crucially, the merger has not fundamentally changed the benefit package previously offered by multiple insurance societies … The high out-of-pocket payment by patients is very inequitable because it puts a greater burden on the poor and sick."

---

[12] Before the crisis, there was a single insurance society for government and school employees, 142 insurance societies for private salaried workers (60 of which were based on single large companies), 92 for rural self-employed, and 135 for urban self-employed (Kwon, 2002).

High co-payments and private provision of health services – both of which seriously affect generosity and equity – remain the main obstacles to universal outputs. Eliminating the former has not entered the policy agenda and it would require a significant increase in the government's financial commitment. Moreover, despite evidence to the contrary, co-payments have been considered positive tools for containing costs and securing personal responsibility (Ramesh, 2008). Reducing private provision has not been a priority either: in fact, the percentage of beds in private facilities increased from 47 percent of the total in 1980 to 87 percent in the late 1990s when more than 90 percent of the doctors were also in the private sector (Ramesh, 2003).

On a more positive note, the government has sought to tighten regulation as an instrument to contain health care costs. This is clearest in the case of medical prescriptions. Until 2000, prescribing and selling medicines to patients was a significant source of income for doctors. In many clinics, drugs accounted for more than 40 percent of total revenues (Kwon and Reich, 2005): doctors purchased drugs from the NHI and profited from charging patients more than the initial price. The system resulted in a twofold problem: excessive consumption of drugs and cost overruns for the national insurance (Kwon, 2007).[13]

In 2000 authorities succeeded in separating drug prescription from drug sales, but at a high long-term fiscal and political cost. First, after doctors struck in protest, the government was forced to increase their fees by 44 percent (Kwon and Reich, 2005). Second, the reduction in pharmaceutical costs was lower than expected because doctors began prescribing costly branded medicines instead of more convenient generics. Also, at least initially, the number of visits to doctors patients sought to make increased, probably as a way to compensate for the income losses (Kwon, 2007). Third, and most importantly in the long term, the reform created significant animosity between doctors and the government, and reduced the chance of adopting more significant changes.

Indeed, physicians and hospitals succeeded in preventing the government's attempt to modify the NHI's reimbursement mechanism – thus demonstrating the negative effect that private actors have on

---

[13] In the late 1990s, pharmaceutical expenditures represented 31 percent of all health care costs, compared to an average of 20 percent in OECD countries (Kwon and Reich, 2005).

progressive reforms. Reimbursement was historically done per service, creating incentives for providers to go for the most expensive procedures. In the late 1990s, for example, 40 percent of all child deliveries took place through caesarean sections, which had higher profit margins than natural births (Kwon and Reich, 2005). In 1997 a pilot voluntary program began allocating resources for a few procedures, not per services but per diagnosis related groups (DRG) (Kwon, 2007). DRG established payments based on the characteristics of each sickness and the past average costs. Although the pilot program reduced medical expenses and increased cost efficiency, physicians managed to block its expansion by going on strike and pressuring hospitals to oppose the measure. As a result, reimbursement continues to be made based on treatment.

In summary, the foundational architecture has been significantly modified in the past two decades. However, low state funding and prevailing private provision of services are still limiting generosity and equity. Reducing co-payments in the future would require either a significant increase in contributions (which many self-employed could not afford and which it is unclear employers would be willing to pay); an expansion in direct taxes (which would be unpopular and harm the export-led economic model); or more effective profit-containment policies (that private providers are likely to challenge).

South Korea: Reduced Fragmentation Yet Resilient Large Outside Option

1977   Creation of a fragmented foundational architecture: launching of firm-based mandatory insurance (first for workers in companies with more than 500 people, later for smaller companies). Also, a non-contributory, means-tested social assistance program was introduced.

1980s   Expansion of access but without unification of other components: successive expansions of insurance funds to firms with fewer workers.

1988   Expansion of access and funding: incorporation of the self-employed through region-based funds.

2000   Crisis-driven unification of the system, with low generosity and weak regulation of private providers.

4.2.4 Uruguay

Uruguay's foundational architecture can be traced back to 1910 when the government created the National Public Assistance Board (Consejo de la Asistencia Pública Nacional), thus formalizing public sanitation for the poor.[14] This push resulted in the rapid expansion of public hospitals: nine out twelve hospitals in place in Montevideo in 1930, and thirty-three out of thirty-eight operating in the rest of the country were established after 1900 (Barrán, 1992: 71). Meanwhile the middle class relied on a non-regulated, non-for-profit outside option based on mutual aid associations (Morás, 2000; Setaro, 2013) while the for-profit, out-of-pocket outside option was small and affordable only to the wealthy.[15]

In the early 1940s, the state began to worry about health services for the middle class. Rather than getting involved in service provision, starting in 1943 the government began overseeing mutual aid societies (Filgueira, 1995).[16] From then onwards, these societies were required to obtain state permits to operate and were subject to various regulations – for example, their governing bodies had to include medical professionals. At the same time, mutual societies benefited from fiscal exemptions on account of the public service they provided.

By the late 1940s, Uruguay's architecture was thus highly segmented. First, the poor were set apart from the non-poor and services for them were of lower quality. Second, since mutual aid societies were prepaid and relied on fees, both benefits and fees stratified the middle

---

[14] The middle class rarely contemplated accessing public hospitals. For example, in a survey conducted among public servants and published by the newspaper *La Razón* in 1911, one explained that: "while the working man can, under certain circumstances, rely on the Sociedades de Beneficiencia, the [white-collar] employee faces a moral incompatibility to do it" (Barrán, 1992: 73).

[15] These organizations offered health care services since the mid-nineteenth century, first to their members (usually European migrants) and then to everyone who joined in exchange for a monthly fee. The Asociación Española was created in 1853; the Sociedad Francesa de Socorros in 1862; La Fraternidad in 1866; Circulo Napolitano in 1880; Círculo Católico de Obreros in 1885; and the Centro Asistencial del Sindicato Médico del Uruguay in 1935 (Setaro, 2004). In Montevideo, membership of these mutual aid associations increased from just 2.4 percent in 1885 to 61.5 percent in 1930 (Barran, 1992).

[16] Law 10.384, February 13, 1943. Available at www.parlamento.gub.uy/leyes/AccesoTextoLey.asp?Ley=10384&Anchor=. This legal framework remained untouched until the late 1960s when the state started regulating fees.

class. In subsequent decades, this architecture expanded benefits among the middle class, but did not contribute to standardize the generosity and equity of services.

During the 1970s and 1980s increased state involvement made health services more efficient and less dispersed. In the early 1970s, the government mandated that all salaried workers be affiliated to a mutual aid association. In 1975 – under an authoritarian military government – the National Board of Social Insurance (Dirección de Seguros Sociales por Enfermedad, DISSE) centralized fees: each worker contributes a fixed amount and employers and the state paid the rest. The state thus began subsidizing the middle class since "the employee's contribution, deducted from salary, was considerably less than he/she would have had to pay for individual membership" (Filgueira, 1995: 25).[17] In 1979 the National Resource Fund (NRF) was established to fund catastrophic sickness such as kidney transplants and cardiac surgeries for everyone, regardless of whether they were insured or relied on national public services. Funded with a small share of payroll contributions (Castiglioni, 2000; Pribble, 2013), the NRF took care of the high cost diseases that could bankrupt small mutual aid societies.

In 1987, the state administrator of health services (the Administración de los Servicios de Salud del Estado, ASSE) began operations. The ASSE grouped all public hospitals, clinics, and health centers across the country and was funded through general revenues. Access was means-tested and required a free service card. This measure was primarily a managerial reorganization of the public provision, but also represented the first attempt to cover the non-poor who did not have easy access to mutual aid societies. Beneficiaries included workers unable to make co-payments as well as spouses and children of workers unable to pay complementary premiums (Filgueira, 1995). In 2006, just 20 percent of the population was under the poverty line, but 40 percent used the ASSE, with many paying a small co-payment (Arbulo et al., 2012).

These changes made Uruguay's health care system more efficient and increased the state's capacity to shape the policy architecture, particularly concerning financial sources and provision. Yet they did not question the role of mutual aid societies in the architecture; in fact,

---

[17] Funding came from 3 percent of the wages from active and retired workers, 5 percent of the wage paid by employers, and a complementary contribution made by employers if needed to reach the monthly fee. These contributions were complemented by general revenues (Arbulo et al., 2012).

the creation of the NRF and the growing state subsidies secured their financial health. Moreover, the architecture was still unable to provide the same levels of generosity to all beneficiaries and equity was low. About one million people relied on public hospitals, which received 25 percent of the total health care budget, while 1.4 million relied on mutual aid societies which received 75 percent of all funding, including state subsidies.[18] State subsidies benefited the middle class disproportionally and high co-payments forced many people to rely on the public sector.[19]

A more significant reform of Uruguay's policy architecture took place under the left-wing government of the Frente Amplio in 2008.[20] The preceding policy architecture played a double role then: it simultaneously created strong incentives for change and constrained the range of all feasible options.

Financial pressures were an important incentive for reform (Fuentes, 2010). The rise of health care costs and the growing dependence on state subsidies compromised the sustainability of many mutual aid societies. The economic crisis of 2001–2002 exacerbated the tensions over public subsidies, which were neither enough to contain co-payments nor to assure quality of services. The insured complained about both costs and quality while the non-insured (low-income) population suffered from the reduction in public resources.

The delicate fiscal situation made a further expansion of state subsidies difficult. Withdrawing or reducing state financial involvement would have been rather unpopular – not only among beneficiaries

---

[18] In addition, about 250,000 people had access through the military and police force. The total population with access was estimated in 2,650,000 out of 2,900,000 people residing in the country (Filgueira, 1995). The upper class mostly relied on out-of-pocket rather than prepaid private services (Arbulo *et al.*, 2012).

[19] Price regulation went through various stages. In the 1980s the fees for drugs, emergencies, and outpatient services were regulated. Co-payments were then intended to control demand. Only later did they become a crucial funding source for providers: in 1992 prices were liberalized, co-payments raised – e.g. doubled within two years for drugs – and extended to other services. In 1995, the state reintroduced maximum prices and in 2001 prices were lowered for basic medical services (Arbulo *et al.*, 2012).

[20] Promoting health equity was one of the central objectives of the Frente. Its ideas reflected a long-term negotiation with key collective actors close to the party, including medical professionals and mutual aid societies (Pérez, 2009; Pribble, 2013).

but also among personnel at the mutual aid societies. The best option was thus to pursue a more decisive unification of the sector.

Mutual aid societies – a cornerstone of Uruguay's foundational architecture – had a prominent role in making reform possible. First, they were increasingly dependent on state funds and thus had vested interests in measures that improve their funding situation. Second, their diversity, including significant differences between large mutual funds in Montevideo and smaller ones in the rest of country, strengthened the government's negotiating capacity (Pribble, 2013). Third, the main objective of mutual aid societies was not to increase profits but to maintain their membership and personnel.

The creation of the National Health System (Sistema Nacional Integral de Salud, SNAIS) in 2008 made a significant contribution towards unification. This effort included mandatory insurance for previously excluded groups: children and teenagers were to be funded by an increase in premiums and public subsidies (Fuentes, 2013). Over the counter, direct insurance was eliminated and all revenues channeled to a national health care fund (Fondo Nacional de Salud, FONASA) operated by the Social Welfare Bank (Banco de Provision Social, BPS). FONASA transfers resources to providers based on a per capita estimate which considers age and health risks, therefore removing adverse selection and increasing equity. FONASA pays similar amounts to the mutual societies and the public provider – thus narrowing the historical inequality of the system. Resource transfers to providers was made dependent on compliance with an Integral Benefit Plan.

In 2009 the public sector and health care providers agreed on a given number of yearly check-ups for people 65 years of age or over without any co-payments (República Oriental del Uruguay [ROU], 2012, in Papadópulos, 2013). Finally, contributions were made more progressive by differentiating monthly fees according to income levels and the presence of children – fees range between 3 percent and 8 percent of monthly wages.

The reform clearly enhanced universal outputs: between 2007 and 2008, 500,000 new beneficiaries were reached by SNAIS and granted generous services. Nevertheless, the foundational architecture constrained how far governmental efforts could go. The role of mutual aid societies as the main providers of health care services went unchallenged. Leaders behind the reform understood that the societies' central position in health care provision could not be easily questioned (Pribble, 2013). In fact, the changes actually made them financially stronger and responsible for a larger proportion of low-income people – thus reducing the resources for public providers. Additionally, opportunities for cross-subsidies from the middle class to the poor remain low.

The government's attempts to force mutual aid societies to guarantee emergency services failed in the face of pressures from private providers. These services remained out-of-pocket (Pérez, 2009) and therefore unequally available. Funding has also stayed more regressive than initially planned. The original idea was not to rely on payroll contributions but on a personal income tax that was debated by Congress in parallel to the health care reform. Yet the government avoided bundling both reforms out of fear that failure to change taxes could have a negative effect on the health care agenda. A subsequent reform introduced in 2010 set a maximum payroll tax, making funding even less progressive.[21]

Uruguay: From Growing Fragmentation to Gradual Unification

1910   Creation of a fragmented foundational architecture characterized by non-regulated mutual aid societies for the middle class and public health for the poor.

1943   Consolidation of fragmentation as the state begins regulating mutual aid societies. A two-tiered system under which the state funds and provides services only to the poor is consolidated.

1970/   Partial unification of funding under social insurance is driven
1975   by financial considerations. Insurance for salaried workers becomes mandatory. Management of payroll contributions is unified but delivery of services remains fragmented. The state becomes a key financial contributor.

1979   Unification of a small component of the basket of services: the National Resource Fund centralizes the funding of all

---

[21] In principle, each year people should not pay more than the assumed value of the benefit they will receive with an extra margin of 25 percent (Arbulo *et al.*, 2012). Exceeding contributions will be returned to the insured.

> *(cont.)*
>   catastrophic illnesses to reduce costs and risks for mutual aid
>   societies.
> 2008 Unification and expansion of access and funding: the National
>   Health System unifies contributions from the public sector and
>   mutual aid societies. A more effective payment for services
>   based on per capita is introduced as well as mandatory
>   insurance for children and teenagers.

4.3 Pensions as a Shadow Case

Like in health care, the initial foundational architecture and its subsequent trajectory in pensions show significant differences between
Costa Rica and Mauritius, on the one hand, and South Korea and
Uruguay, on the other. The first two were from the onset more
unified, which facilitated advances towards more universal outcomes
over time. The creation of complementary pillars in the last two
decades has eroded equity, but has not radically modified the policy
architecture.

Uruguay began with a large number of funds organized around
occupations, which the state gradually and painfully tried to unify.
Like in health care, financial bottlenecks encouraged this process of
unification, which, nevertheless, took several decades. Pensions have
become more generous and equitable but some historical inequalities
remain. South Korea struggled to extend old-age pensions to the
self-employed from the beginning. Also, low state involvement and
insufficient contributions limited generosity and equity. The recent
creation of a non-contributory pension for the lower income population has not significantly reduced the fragmentation of the policy
architecture.

4.3.1 Costa Rica

The inception and expansion of old-age pensions followed a similar
logic to that of health care as depicted in the previous section. The
1941 Social Insurance Law mandated the creation of two programs
aimed at providing health insurance and pensions. A payroll

contribution would fund both: in the case of health care, resources were largely invested; in the case of pensions, the agency enacted a partial capitalization fund. The newly created pension insurance had positive features for the promotion of universal outputs: it first incorporated low-income workers to a mostly unified system.

We say "mostly unified" to highlight one major difference with the foundational architecture in health care. In the case of pensions, a few groups, including workers in the municipality of San Jose and other public employees, succeeded in protecting the occupational plans they already had. So even if seven out of every ten salaried workers ended up insured under the single collective fund, fragmentation was larger than in health care. Driven by the policy architecture, the proportion of people covered grew, but at a slower pace than health care. For example, the program was launched in 1947, six years later than for health care. By 1963, the latter reached twice as many people as pensions (31 percent and 16 percent of the occupied population, respectively). During the 1950s and 1960s the wage ceiling was lower in pensions than in health care – which meant that a larger proportion of middle and high income workers were not obliged to contribute – and was removed later as well. These differences in timing are not surprising: for a still young population, improving health care was more pressing than protecting the elderly.

During the 1970s and under the same mandate to universalize health insurance, a large proportion of the poor population received pensions. The policy architecture influenced this means-tested, non-contributory pension in at least three ways. The new pension was, first, promoted by the CCSS as a way to reach a population unable to pay their premiums. Second, it was partly funded through payroll taxes in the context of the creation of FODESAF. This established a rather unusual mechanism of cross-subsidy between salaried workers and the poor, which is not found in the other three countries we study. Third, the new regime was administered by the CCSS and seen as part of a single pension system.

By the mid-1980s, a majority of Costa Ricans had access to a pension granted by the CCSS and funded primarily through payroll taxes. Yet there were still two significant shortcomings: the incorporation of the self-employed to the system was voluntary and the coverage and generosity of non-contributory pensions was low. At the same time, international pressures to expand private participation in pensions intensified – just like in the rest of the South. Responses to these challenges were partly conditioned by the policy architecture, which influenced priorities and limited the scope of feasible reforms (Chapter 7).

The 2000 Workers' Protection Law (Ley de Protección del Trabajador, LPT) created new instruments to improve the collection of contributions and made insurance mandatory for the self-employed (Martínez Franzoni and Mesa-Lago, 2003). The LPT also established that non-contributory pensions had to be at least equal to half of the lowest contributory pension. In 2005, replacement rates were made progressive (the higher the income, the lower the rate) and gender equity enhanced through the creation of a reduced pension for people with a shorter labor record. The 2005 reform also expanded social insurance revenues and increased membership among the self-employed: their insurance became mandatory but new benefits for people with shorter labor histories created additional incentives to join.

The architecture also played a role in limiting the type of market-friendly reforms promoted by international organizations. In 2000, the LPT made individual savings mandatory for all salaried workers and turned them into the second pillar to the collective fund run by the CCSS. This reform had negative effects upon universal outputs, but did not go as far as in other Latin American countries. The reform did not question the tripartite contributions from the state, employers, and workers. Moreover, the role of the social insurance agency remained significant: contrary to other countries, most notably Chile, the CCSS was allowed to run individual funds (in competition with the private sector) and the reform was sold as one that reinforced the state's prominent role.

Costa Rica: Unified Social Insurance as a Road Towards Universal Outputs in Old-Age Pensions

1941– 1947	Creation of a unified foundational architecture with the implementation of social insurance, including old-age pensions.
1975	Expansion of unified access with the creation of non-contributory pensions managed by the CCSS, honoring the mandate to universalize social insurance.

> (*cont.*)
> 2000   Expansion in access and benefits and simultaneous growth of
>   the private pillar. Legally binding increase in the value of the
>   non-contributory pension; insurance for the self-employed
>   made mandatory; and individual capitalization savings made
>   compulsory for salaried workers.

4.3.2 Mauritius

Mauritius' foundational architecture in pensions dates back to 1950 with the creation of a non-contributory universal pension (Seekings, 2007, 2011). This initial arrangement partly shaped all subsequent measures and remains a central component of the overall architecture.[22] The new program provided a maximum monthly income of 15 rupees for people 65 years of age and over. The pension was initially means-tested and granted to people whose income was under 15 rupees. At the same time, a small number of private insurance funds in large companies endured (Mootoosamy, 1981).

Responding to social opposition, the government expanded the cut-off point to 30 rupees in December 1950 (Willmore, 2006). As a result, four-fifths of the Mauritian population started benefiting from the new program. For the following twenty-six years, changes to old-age transfers primarily revolved around expanding non-contributory pensions to the whole population. Three steps were particularly significant (Willmore, 2003, 2006):

- In 1953, the qualifying age for women went from 65 to 60 years, the maximum pension increased to Rs 20 per month and the income ceiling for eligibility grew to Rs 35.
- In 1958, pensions became universal partly as a way to reduce administration costs. Tax arrangements ensured that the measure had progressive effects: pensions were at that time considered

---

[22] Prior to 1950 a non-contributory pension system for public servants was already in place. It was founded in 1859 for high-ranking officials and extended in 1905 to all other public employees. Some large companies also had contributory private pension funds, which reached a small percentage of the total working population.

taxable income and through income taxes the high-income groups returned much of the benefit to the state (Willmore, 2003).

- In 1965, the minimum age for men to receive pensions was also lowered to 60 years of age. To compensate for the increasing costs associate with a larger number of eligible people, a mild form of targeting affecting just 5 percent of all beneficiaries was introduced.

In 1976 the government created the National Pension Fund (NPF) as a contributory pension for salaried workers regardless of occupations (contrary to the case of Uruguay) and firm size (contrary to the case of South Korea). Payments were based on a "notional defined contribution": with the 3 percent contribution from workers and 6 percent contribution from employers, beneficiaries acquired points, which were then used to calculate their pension.[23] The Ministry of Social Security and National Solidarity administered the NPF and the Ministry of Finance controlled the level of contributions and benefits and the type of investments made (World Bank, 2004).

Like in Scandinavian countries (Korpi and Palme, 1998), the new pension was clearly considered a complement to the non-contributory transfer – thus expanding more than modifying the previous architecture. The value of the points accumulated by a person over 40 working years was expected to equal a replacement rate of about one-third of his or her average lifetime earnings (World Bank, 2004). The reform did not target the self-employed. Although they could voluntarily join the system, they lacked the state subsidy that in other countries like Costa Rica compensates the absence of employers' contributions.

Simultaneously to the creation of a contributory pension, the government strengthened the non-contributory benefit, now renamed basic retirement pension (BRP). From 1976 onwards, the real value of the benefit expanded rapidly, particularly for people 70 years of age and over. Aiming to reach around 20 percent of average income (World Bank, 2004), by 2004 the average pension was 2.7 times higher than in 1978 and represented a higher percentage of GDP per capita (Willmore, 2006).

By the late 1980s, Mauritius' policy architecture in pensions included non-contributory pensions for all complemented by contributory pensions for salaried workers. Unfortunately, the latter involved

---

[23] There was also a ceiling in the contribution: in 2000 it was equal to a monthly salary of Rs5,535 (US$220) (Willmore, 2003).

low contributions, lacked state subsidies, and failed to deliver reasonable replacement rates.

Coping with the weakness of the contributory regime would have required public subsidies and a significant increase in payroll contributions. Rather than following this avenue, the government – influenced by the international environment – embraced reforms that further increased fragmentation. In 1994 the National Savings Fund (NSF) was enacted: it involved a 2.5 percent contribution from private and public employers as a defined contribution scheme based on individual capitalization accounts. This system has eroded solidarity since it only benefits formal employers and directly links contributions and benefits.

The outside option has also become prominent, partly due to the inadequate replacement rate of public pensions. The number of private plans has expanded rapidly: according to the OECD (2013: 7), "the Mauritian environment has also seen considerable growth of multi-employer or 'umbrella' funds ... Most of the large trade unions have established national defined contribution schemes and have negotiated an option for their members to belong to such funds, as opposed to membership of an employer-sponsored fund. [Personal] pension plans have gained in importance in recent years."

At the same time, the influence of the foundational architecture is evident in the politics of non-contributory pensions, which have remained popular. In 2004, as a response to World Bank recommendations, the government imposed a narrow targeting in the BRP. Months later, the governing coalition lost the general elections partly as a result of this decision, which the new government promptly reversed.

Mauritius: the Long-Term but Incomplete Role of Non-Contributory Pensions for All

1950   Creation of a unified foundational architecture based on non-contributory pensions with very broad targeting.
1958   Growth of access when non-contributory pensions are extended to the whole population.
1976   Implementation of insurance-based pension for salaried workers (with low benefits) to complement non-contributory pensions.
1994   Growing fragmentation with the creation of a capitalization account for salaried workers (NSF).

4.3.3 South Korea

South Korea's foundational architecture in pensions has its origins in 1986 with the creation of the National Pension System (NPS).[24] The NPS set mandatory insurance for employees in firms with ten workers or more. By 1990 the NPS reached 16 percent of the working population, mostly relatively well-off industrial workers. Entitlements were theoretically high: only twenty years of contributions were supposed to deliver a 70 percent replacement rate (Kim and Choi, 2013). However, low contributions and relaxed withdrawal rules lowered replacement rates in practice.

Once the foundational architecture was in place the expansion after democratization ran parallel to that of health insurance: in 1992 contributions became mandatory for firms with more than 5 employees and in 1995 the NPS reached farmers, fishermen, and the self-employed in rural areas. Such expansion did not confront major obstacles since it increased the size of the pension fund (thus expanding growth-enhancing savings) without costing much to companies and workers, since contributions were low, or to the state, which did not provide any subsidies (Kwon, 1995).

Yet by the mid-1990s the limits of the existing policy architecture were evident. The combination of low contributions, no state subsidy, and high replacement rates challenged the financial sustainability of the system. In 1995, the public think tank Korea Development Institute published a report arguing that the national pension funds would be depleted by 2033 (Choi, 2008). Also, the lack of public subsidies and weak state controls resulted in incomplete coverage for the self-employed – despite mandatory contributions.

The 1997 East Asian financial crisis further aggravated the problems, placing pensions at the center of the policy agenda. Changes in all components of the architecture were then discussed. Proposals for incremental parametric changes competed with a radical transformation of the system designed by the World Bank, which included a sharp reduction of benefits. The World Bank proposed splitting current

---

[24] Like the other three countries, South Korea created special pension funds for some groups prior to that date: in 1960 the Government Employees Pension Scheme was introduced covering initially 237,000 people. The military personnel were initially included in this scheme but three years later created its own fund. In 1973, the government introduced the Private School Teachers Pension Scheme (Moon, 2008).

pensions into two components: the basic pension (that would remain a collective fund) and the earnings-related pension, which would become an individual account managed by private companies.

The reform finally adopted expanded mandatory insurance and introduced only parametric changes – a nice illustration of how architectures constrain decision making. Replacement rates were reduced (from 70 percent to 60 percent) and pensions were expanded to the urban self-employed and to workers in small firms. In addition, payroll contributions were increased to 9 percent and the number of years required for full benefits increased from twenty to forty.

State involvement remained low and most of the self-employed were forced to pay premiums equivalent to the combined contribution paid by employers and employees.[25] Thus, the reform was hardly a "direct route to reach greater national integrity and social solidarity" as authors like Hwang (2007:10) argue, and actually consolidated previous shortcomings of low generosity and limited equity.

Low-income groups remained excluded until the creation of two new programs that partly transformed the policy architecture (Moon, 2008). In 1999, the National Basic Living Standard Security Act created a means-tested, narrowly targeted social assistance transfer for people of all ages (hereafter the NBLS). Since more than one-quarter of its recipients have been senior households, the NBLS have in practice become the "zero-pillar" of old-age pensions (Moon, 2008). This new transfer expanded the role of the state but low access limited its impact on universal outputs. The actual number of recipients is less than 10 percent of senior households of 65 years of age and over, and benefits correspond to only a quarter of the official poverty line.

In 2007, a new non-contributory means-tested program, the Basic Old Age Pension Scheme, was introduced. Unlike the narrow targeting of the NBLS, this pension has benefited the poorest 70 percent of people 65 years of age and over. It is defined as compensation for people's dedication to national development and child rearing. The pension entails a monthly fixed amount equal to 5 percent of the value of the national pension (expected to reach 10 percent in future years) (Kim, 2013).

Yet the impact of these two policies on Korea's policy architecture and their contribution to universal outputs should not be exaggerated.

---

[25] Only farmers and fishermen received a subsidy, which was one-third of their contribution before 2007 and increased to half of their contribution since then.

The combination of means-testing and low replacement rates results in small benefits for a large segment of the older population and does little to reduce poverty among the elderly.[26] The new programs have not entailed an expansion of insurance among the self-employed. Coverage is now particularly low in small firms, which tend to have a higher proportion of non-regular workers. Indeed, in companies with fewer than ten workers more than half of employees are not insured, compared to just 4 percent in companies with 100 workers or more (OECD, 2013). Also, some of the workers in large firms benefit from firm-based private pension plans and high-income groups have significant outside private options (OECD, 2009).

South Korea: Expanded Access with Low Benefits in Old-Age Pensions

1986	Creation of a fragmented foundational architecture with the adoption of a bipartite pension system for salaried workers.
1995	Expansion of pensions to the self-employed with minimum state support improves access but with fragmentation of funding and benefits.
1999/ 2000	Growth of (segmented) coverage with the creation of a basic income for the poorest 70 percent of the population including the elderly poor.
1999/ 2000	Further growth of coverage with the creation of a non-contributory pension for the poor. Yet problems of generosity and equity remain.

4.3.4 Uruguay

A gradual and cumbersome process of state involvement in a myriad of old-age funds makes the identification of the foundational architecture of pensions in Uruguay challenging. We locate it in 1919 when both a

---

[26] The poverty rate is three times higher among the elderly between 66 and 75 years of age than among the overall population, for which it is 15 percent. This contrasts with the OECD as a whole, where the proportion of the population and the elderly living in poverty are about the same.

state-driven means-tested, non-contributory pension and the Public Utilities Pension Fund – partly funded through taxes – were created. The tax-funded, non-contributory pension was targeted to the elderly poor 60 years of age and over. The Public Utilities Pension Fund covered workers from the railway, telegraph, streetcar, telephone, and gas companies (Mesa-Lago, 1978). This fund joined other occupation-based private pensions, which had been created in the late nineteenth century with contributions from employers and employees.

Regardless of its exact date of inception, the foundational architecture had three main characteristics: different funds with diverse benefits; tripartite contributions, with the state acting often as guarantor;[27] and a non-contributory pension for the poor.

During the following fifty years, the policy architecture remained relatively stable but pension funds grew rapidly. Expansion was particularly fast during the period 1920–1940, resulting in the coverage of a large number of blue- and white-collar workers in the manufacturing and service sectors (Mesa-Lago, 1978). Such expansion deepened occupational fragmentation in contributions and benefits.

During the 1960s, the limits of a fragmented architecture became evident: funds started to run deficits and required higher state subsidies, partly as a result of excessive benefits and unsound investments (García Repetto, 2011). In response to these problems, insurance became mandatory and a newly created tripartite agency, the BPS (to which we referred when discussing health care) attempted to unify all funds in 1967. Yet the initial fragmentation inhibited unification: the BPS managed to group – yet not to merge – several funds (industry and commerce, domestic service, and most of the public sector) but many others (including those for the military, private banks, university professionals, and lawyers) opted out. Overall, "no progress appears to have been made in centralizing the collection and distribution of social security, [and] in establishing uniform and rational standards for the various benefits" (Mesa-Lago, 1978: 83).

The state's struggle to unify and rationalize the system continued during the 1970s. The authoritarian military government sought to

---

[27] García Repetto (2011: 5) explains heterogeneous state involvement across funds. For example, the Industry and Trade Fund was formally a collective capitalization system but in practice became "intergenerational pay-as-you-go model with high dependence from the state." On the other hand, in the Banking Fund, the state had a managerial role but never acted as guarantor.

deepen centralization to secure the funds' financial stability while avoiding the growth of the public deficit (Filgueira, 1995). The BPS was replaced by the General Board for Social Security (Dirección General de Seguridad Social, DGSS) within the Ministry of Labor and Social Security. The DGSS sought to consolidate not only old-age funds, but also a myriad of other programs like health care, child and maternity care, and family allowances (Mesa-Lago, 1985). The DGSS was responsible for ordering and managing all benefits and coordinating all the para-state retirement funds (Castiglioni, 2000). Again, this attempt at integrating different programs faced significant constraints: right after the return to democracy, for example, the funds for notaries, bank workers, and university professionals recovered their managerial independence.

By the mid-1980s, Uruguay had a more unified system than in the 1920s, but there were still some independent funds with a variety of benefits. Also, non-contributory pensions were low. Demands for higher benefits grew after democratization: a 1989 national referendum guaranteed the real value of old-age pensions by linking it to public workers' wages. A 1990 Law established that no pension could be under the minimum wage (Papadópulos, 1992), thus also helping to improve generosity among those at the bottom. During the 2000s, non-contributory pensions continued to grow and became less discretionary. A full transfer is set at US$360 if the beneficiary lives with family members and more if living alone. Depending on the person's income, benefits can be full or partial – in which case the subsidy entails the amount needed to reach the US$360 cut-off point (Papadópulos, 2013). The measure has helped to decrease the incidence of poverty among people 65 years of age and over.

In 2007–2008, additional reforms expanded the number of options to access pensions (e.g. for people of the required age without enough years of contribution), which had positive consequences for equity. In addition, women were granted a year of contributions for each child raised to acknowledge income gaps and the "double shift" of unpaid work at home.[28]

---

[28] A subsequent reform established that replacement rates should be estimated based on the last ten working years (and not the last three) or the best twenty wages during the worker's historical life (Papadópulos, 2013). This measure prevents workers from over-declaring wages at the end of their careers. It also improves pensions for the unskilled and more vulnerable workers, whose wages tend to stagnate after a certain age.

All these measures have increased coverage and expanded pensions at the bottom. To date, Uruguay has one of the highest coverage in Latin America (about 80 percent of the economically active population), next to Brazil, Argentina, and Bolivia, and the system has become more equitable. Nevertheless, the powerful role of the foundational architecture and the difficulties in overcoming fragmentation are still evident. Uruguay has independent funds, which provide particularly generous benefits to specific groups. Benefits also remain unequal because of the uneven amount of contributions workers are capable of making before they reach 65 years of age (Forteza *et al.*, 2009). In particular, the decision to raise the minimum number of years required to get a pension to thirty-five is likely to reduce the proportion of beneficiaries (Buchelli *et al.*, 2006).[29]

The introduction of an individual savings account in 1995 was also consistent with historical fragmentation. Following internationally dominant paradigms and responding to funding problems, the government created individual accounts run by the Pension Savings Funds Administrators (Administradoras de Fondos de Ahorro Provisional, AFAPs). The reform deepened fragmentation for at least two reasons. First, it eliminated all redistribution between individuals, since each person contributes according to his or her wages and benefits match contributions. This means that inequalities in the labor market – such as income gaps between women and men – are fully reflected in old-age transfers. Second, it has opened the door to the private sector, which will likely become a growing actor in the pension system and will push for further marketization.

Uruguay: the Long and Painstaking Task of Reducing Fragmentation

1919	Creation of the first non-contributory pension and a major fund for public companies.
1919–1967	Expansion of an architecture based on fragmented, mostly tripartite funds and a reduced non-contributory, targeted pension.

---

[29] Data precedes the formalization of labor relations that has taken place since 2005. Still, it is unlikely that such formalization will solve the problem.

(cont.)	
1967– 1980s	Gradual moves towards unification of funds, largely driven by funding shortages.
1980s– 2013	Introduction of pro-universal parametric reforms but also a capitalization pillar, which makes access and generosity more unequal.

4.4 Conclusion

Policy architectures do not simply deliver more or less universal outputs at a given point in time; they also influence a country's trajectory over the long term. By picking and choosing who to incorporate first to state benefits, and by creating different incentives for subsequent expansion, they either facilitate or hamper pro-universal reforms. In so doing, architectures reflect the interests of different stakeholders.

To be clear, we are not arguing that policy architectures determine a specific path – that would be too mechanical an argument – or that they are always the most relevant trigger for change – political actors in democratic contexts and international ideas certainly matter. Our argument is that the features of the initial blueprint of any social program influence the likelihood of reaching universal outputs and the speed of advances. As a result, when governments across the South introduce new programs, they should give serious consideration to the political dynamics the initial designs will create. This is particularly important for emerging policies that are built from scratch like those addressing care.

Among the four countries we have examined, Mauritius seemed the best candidate to deliver universal outputs: it created a tax-funded public health care system and non-contributory pensions for all. However, the existence of a powerful outside option in health, the lack of generosity of non-contributory pensions and the shortcomings of the complementary contributory pension limited the expected positive effects. The case makes it clear that citizen-based architectures are not always better for universalism than those based on social insurance.

In practice, the Costa Rican architecture was the most successful in promoting a universalist path. Costa Rica's state-led unified social insurance dealt better with the tensions between fragmentation and unification than the architecture in the other three countries. The contrast with South Korea is particularly significant. There, the lack of state involvement in service provision and the reluctance to increase public spending were initial features of the architecture that still harm the delivery of universal outputs over half a century later.

Costa Rica is relevant for another important reason: it has experienced a growing market-led fragmentation during the last two decades at a time when, paradoxically, South Korea and Uruguay have made progress towards unification. Before we study this paradox, we must first explain the determinants of Costa Rica's uniquely successful foundational architecture. How did Costa Rica create it? How did it evolve over time? How was it able to secure state-led unification in a context of low GDP per capita? Can electoral competition and ideology by itself explain it? In the following three chapters, we tackle these questions from a comparative perspective. We show that democracy was a contributing factor, but not a driver of the architecture. Instead, we focus on the interaction between state actors and international ideas in shaping the initial architecture in the 1940s and its development in the 1970s. We also explain the state's growing incapacity to avoid fragmentation by considering the interplay between state experts and changing international ideas since the 1980s.

PART III

Building Universalism in Costa Rica

5 | *The Foundations of the Policy Architecture in the 1940s*

5.1 Introduction

In the previous two chapters, we showed Costa Rica's comparative success in enacting a unified policy architecture, capable of delivering universal outputs. This accomplishment did not happen overnight but instead took place in successive stages of incremental change. In this and the next two chapters we address policy drivers behind each stage, to then compare our conclusions with the experience of the other three countries in Chapter 8.

Our analysis begins in 1941 with the creation of social insurance for health care and pensions. As discussed in the preceding chapter, this new program had features that largely shaped its subsequent trajectory. These included the provision of the same benefits to all workers (and later their families) and the incorporation of urban, relatively low-income earners first, and only later higher income earners – what we call a "bottom-up" expansion.

Electoral competition and progressive leadership were preconditions for the foundation of social insurance. The 1941 Presidential elections were dominated by debates on how to confront poverty and improve living standards for a majority of the Costa Rican population. The election of the first Christian-Democrat president was pivotal in reshaping debates about this "social question." Yet these two variables do not adequately explain why the new government focused on social insurance or where the key characteristics of its architecture originated.

In this chapter we show that state actors drove the design, adoption, and implementation of Costa Rica's unique architecture. We highlight the role of a small group of experts who shared two characteristics.

Most of this chapter is based on the authors' article "Filling In the Missing Link Between Universalism and Democracy: The Case of Costa Rica", *Latin American Politics and Society*, 56(4): 98–118 (Winter 2014). We thank LAPS for the permission to reproduce it.

First, they had close access to top decision makers and received their full support. Second, all members of the group were involved in international policy networks and much of their influence came from their access to international experiences, ideas, and models – like similar groups of policy experts in more recent times (Weyland, 2004). Their participation in international organizations, conferences, and publications played an important role in spreading and adapting global norms domestically (see Sugiyama 2011 for an account of similar processes since the 2000s).

State actors – both this group of experts and also political leaders – also succeeded in managing vetoes. Although the absence of a large industrial labor force in Costa Rica may have inhibited strong social actors (Segura-Ubiergo 2007) social pressures still existed. Unions grew in close alliance with the Communist Party, and the economic elite – primarily coffee growers and traders – had significant influence. State actors accommodated different demands by appealing to piecemeal implementation without harming the building blocks of social insurance.

In the rest of this chapter we explore the drivers of Costa Rica's foundational architecture through a qualitative analysis of primary official sources and newspapers.[1] We acknowledge the role of electoral competition as a precondition for the creation of social insurance, but demonstrate that accounting for the features of the policy architecture requires looking beyond democracy. Paying attention to specific laws, we reconstruct the policy process and offer a rich, empirical account of actors and ideas shaping this policy architecture.

5.2 The 1941 Law

To reconstruct drivers behind the foundational architecture, we break down the policy process into agenda setting, policy adoption, and policy

---

[1] We often contrast and complement our analysis with Rosenberg's (1979, 1981) path-breaking description of Costa Rica's social insurance. His study identified the bureaucracy as the driving force behind social insurance. As we break down the analysis of the policy process into stages, we dispute the bureaucracy's central role regarding agenda setting and adoption. Second, we give a more prominent role than Rosenberg to international policy environments, their actors and ideas, and how they played into the domestic policy process. Third, we focus on the characteristics of the policy architecture and, in subsequent chapters, explore its influence over time.

implementation. These are distinguishable stages of policymaking that cover the framing of actual problems, formal enactment of solutions into policy, and their ultimate operation. These stages often overlap, are not always coherent, and usually lead to a non-linear and often messy policy progress. We neither expect a mechanical sequence across stages nor give the policy process explanatory power; we treat it as an analytic tool to evaluate the role of different actors.

5.2.1 Agenda Setting

Why did social insurance end up at the center stage of the Costa Rican policy agenda in the early 1940s? How did the overall concern with social insurance translate into a design that went beyond Catholic ideas of income maintenance for high-income formal workers? Dominant explanations have focused on electoral competition (Molina, 2008), visionary leadership (Segura-Ubiergo, 2007: 208), and the views of domestic, nationally contained policymakers (Rosenberg, 1983). Some of these factors were indeed significant preconditions; each fails to explain the outcome on its own.

Electoral competition provided an enabling environment for reforms. The arrival to power of President Rafael Ángel Calderón Guardia, the first Social Catholic president in Costa Rica during the twentieth century, granted a renewed attention to the "social question." Yet Calderón must not be singled out as a unique leader and social insurance should not be seen as his "almost personal project" (Segura-Ubiergo, 2007: 208). Rather, Calderón was embedded in a historical period where policy changes reflected ongoing struggles between Christian Democrats and Communists. Following key encyclicals written by Leon XII and Pius XI (including the 1931 *Quadragesimo Anno*), Catholic politicians worldwide viewed social insurance as a policy instrument to build class collaboration and achieve social peace.

Calderón was also responding to the increasing influence of the Costa Rican Communist Party, whose electoral support had grown from 5 percent in 1934 to 10 percent in 1940 (Molina, 2007). By 1940 with its daily newspaper, increasing union strength, reformist policy program, and representation in Congress, the party gave new prominence to the social agenda (Molina 2007) – yet not necessarily, in our view, to the enactment of social insurance.

Even if important, Calderón's ascent to power and the concern with the social question cannot satisfactorily explain the growing attention to social insurance. During the first year of the new administration, social concerns translated in the public delivery of goods (e.g. shoes for the poor), not in the promulgation of social insurance. Notably, only once during his candidacy, the night before the elections did Calderón address social insurance publicly (Creedman, 1994). Molina (2007) argues that this lack of electoral attention sought to avoid a needless confrontation with the oligarchy. However, we found no evidence that social insurance responded to demands from below in any of the newspapers we analyzed. Instead, at the time societal pressures revolved around basic labor rights (see also Rosenberg, 1981).

To understand why social insurance entered the policy process and why it did not benefit high-income workers, we must turn to the role of an advisory group close to the President. This inner circle was mostly comprised of physicians and lawyers (Rosenberg, 1981; Molina, 2008).[2] Creedman (1994) lists the Secretary of Health and Sanitation, Mario Luján; Solón Nuñez, formerly Secretary of Health and Sanitation for over fifteen years; Rafael Calderón Muñoz, father of the president; and lawyer Guillermo Padilla. Additionally, Rosenberg (1981) mentions Jorge Volio, Carlos María Jiménez, José Albertazzi Luján, and Francisco Calderón Guardia, the president's brother and Secretary of Interior and Public Security. Most of these individuals had studied in France or Belgium, right before the First World War or during the interwar period. They were familiar with Communist, Fascist, and Catholic debates about the role of the state in managing class conflict and nourishing class collaboration. They were also well informed about changing regional and international debates on social insurance. Regardless of their political trajectory, they all had the president's ear and worked more or less autonomously in different policy areas like public health, labor policy, and social insurance.

---

[2] In Latin America, a whole generation of physicians entered into politics in the 1930s and promoted new social programs (Palmer, 2003). Calderón Guardia was born in 1900 and graduated in 1927. Chile's Salvador Allende was born in 1908 and graduated in 1933. Others were Arnulfo Arias in Panama, Ramón Grau San Martín in Cuba, and Jucelino Kubitschek in Brazil. In Costa Rica, the frontrunner in the 1940 election, Ricardo Moreno Cañas, was also a physician. He was assassinated by a patient and his martyrdom helped Calderón win the election by exciting public sympathy for the profession.

Across these areas, these experts plugged Costa Rican policy formation into an international environment, designing policies that followed international prescriptions (Secretaría de Gobernación, Policía, Trabajo y Previsión Social, 1941).

Any discussion of the role of international ideas in shaping Costa Rica's social insurance must take into account two distinct aspects: the global policy environment on this issue and the specific mechanisms through which Costa Ricans accessed those ideas. Worldwide, the International Labour Organization (ILO) provided legitimacy to the design of social insurance systems. Initially it supported the creation of multiple, occupationally based funds, but by the mid-1930s the ILO accepted a single, mandatory fund for all workers as an alternative path (International Labor Review, 1936: II, 654). By the early 1940s, Oswald Stein, a leading expert at the ILO based in Geneva, was endorsing a unified system as the best way to expand social insurance (Seekings, 2010).

While the ILO shaped the global policy environment and legitimized some national experiences over others, it lacked direct influence on the policy architecture for at least two reasons. First, latecomers like Costa Rica were crafting social insurance schemes at a time when the ILO personnel were fleeing from Nazi Europe to Canada and could not easily provide technical advice. Second, between the mid-1920s and mid-1940s, Costa Rica was the only Latin American country not to be a member of the ILO.[3] Costa Ricans were thus barely exposed to the organization's ideas directly.

Instead, international ideas entered Costa Rican policy formation through Chile. During the 1920s, Calderón's advisers like the Costa Rica Secretary of Health Mario Luján, and Calderón's main technical advisor on social security, Guillermo Padilla, met several Chileans while studying in France. One of them was Miguel Etchebarne, who by 1941 was the head of the Chilean social insurance agency.[4] Padilla – a lawyer who had been involved in public affairs – travelled to

---

[3] Costa Rica was a member from 1920 to 1927. It participated as an observer from 1936 until 1944 when it rejoined the organization (ILO, NATLEX database, www.ilo.org/dyn/natlex/natlex_browse.home, accessed January 2011).

[4] Etchebarne finished medical school in Paris in 1928. Together with Salvador Allende, he was a cabinet member in the Popular Front governments made of the Socialist, Communist, and Radical parties: between 1938 and 1939 Etchebarne was Minister of Health. In December 1939 Allende took over this position and Etehebarne became Head of Social Insurance (Diccionario Biográfico de Chile, 1942).

Chile that year and wrote the first draft of the social security law while in Santiago. His stay in Chile influenced the contents of this draft through several channels.

First, Padilla met with key Chilean experts. In addition to Etchebarne and actuaries involved in the day-to-day operations of the social insurance fund, Padilla discussed matters with Moisés Poblete Troncoso, a prominent Chilean policy expert. A lawyer by training, Poblete Troncoso had led a failed drive to create a fully unified social security system in the mid-1920s (Borsutsky, 2002). He was later recruited by the ILO and at the beginning of 1940 toured Central America, visiting Costa Rica and meeting presidential candidate Calderón Guardia and other leaders (Poblete Troncoso, 1940).

Chilean experts like Poblete were attuned to heated international debates on how to build social insurance. In 1936 Chile hosted the ILO-sponsored Labor Conference of American States, which recommended that social insurance became compulsory, extended to all workers (including the self-employed) and seek to prevent, cure and manage social risks. Governments were also advised to establish wage limits exempting the better off from social insurance (International Labor Review, 1936: II, 654).

Second, Padilla also learned from the Chilean Seguro Obrero and his failures (Poblete Troncoso, 1940: 15–18). In his own words years later: "[from the Chilean experience I learned] the need to apply social insurance in an integral way to prevent the dispersion of similar funds that suddenly become antagonistic and also the need to give a strong economic support to the institution to secure stability" (Padilla, 1966). Although no records of these exchanges remain, it is likely that these lessons came from Poblete.

Third, Chilean experts put Padilla in contact with Oswald Stein, the ILO Chief of Social Security and probably the most important global expert on social security at the time. Stein arrived in Chile in 1941 only a few weeks after Padilla Castro had returned to Costa Rica. Moisés Poblete shared Padilla's draft with Stein, who read it and sent a letter to Padilla. In his letter, Stein congratulated him for a project that "echoing the experiences of other countries, particularly Chile and Peru, provides innovative solutions ... adapted to the prevailing conditions in the country." He also offered to share cross-national experiences that could facilitate Costa Rica's design process (Caja Costarricense de Seguro Social [CCSS], 1943: 2).

The Chilean influence was explicitly recognized when the law was introduced to Congress. The author of the legal document manifested that "we do not aim at making this an innovative project. Guidelines ... we propose are the same all over the place" (Secretaría Gobernación, Policía, Trabajo y Previsión Social, 1941: 1). The influence of external experiences and contacts was stressed again once the system was in place (e.g. CCSS, 1943). According to the social insurance agency, the Chilean government "gave its most generous cooperation so that our country could learn from the useful experience on social insurance that Chile had accumulated" (CCSS, 1942a).

5.2.2 Policy Adoption

Padilla also played a prominent role in the legislative process, this time accompanied by other prominent members of the President's inner group. For example, legislator Ernesto Marten, with close ties to the President, mediated relations between Congress and the Executive (Rosenberg, 1983). Neither political parties nor civil society contributed much during this stage. Legislators left untouched the overall orientation and most policy instruments included in the initial draft. This is evident in Table 5.1, which distinguishes initial contents ("draft") from changes introduced during the legislative process ("bill"). Most changes were aimed at simplifying the legislation. For example, the final bill eliminated many details regarding benefits in line with the Executive's belief that the social insurance agency should introduce changes as it went along (Secretaría de Gobernación, Policía, Trabajo y Previsión Social, 1941: 5).

All issues concerning implementation were left to the brand new CCSS. Postponing controversial matters (including the implementation date of health insurance and when and how rural workers would be insured) and turning them into a sequence of decisions was effective in buffering potential conflicts.

Civil society played a minimal role in the legislative process and seldom questioned the basic architecture of social security. Through *Trabajo*, the Communist Party called "the Costa Rican people" and the "working class" to mobilize in support of social security and the "progressive attitude" of the Costa Rican president (*Trabajo*, October 18, 1941: 1, 4). Yet no newspaper provides evidence of mobilizations actually occurring. Unions were not directly involved and the

Table 5.1 *Social Insurance: Presidential Draft and Bill Approved by Congress*

Dimensions		Draft	Bill
Target groups	Occupations expected to have mandatory insurance	Blue- and white-collar workers, public employees, domestic workers, interns	A lower and single wage ceiling for white-collar and the self-employed Started with salaried workers that were easiest to reach Left anything else up to the new agency
	Special funds	Mandatory insurance for new employees in occupations with special funds	Unchanged
Benefits/ Services	Benefits	Social insurance addressed all risks	Eliminated detailed account for each program Health care insurance must be launched first Timing to pass ordinances (introduced by the Communist Party)
	Provision	Incremental transfer of services from Secretary of Sanitation and coordination of charity institutions	
Funding	Contributions		Board established contributions and Executive approved them Contributions by employees cannot exceed those of employers*
	Enforcement	Created body of inspectors	

Table 5.1 (*cont.*)

Dimensions	Draft	Bill
Use of resources		External board controlled investment (Finance Minister, National Insurance, and Costa Rican banks)
Governance Board		Executive appointed board; composition of board follows banks
Management		In charge of personnel, wages, budget and fees for board members

*The draft mentioned this point in the introduction but lacked a specific article for it. The article added in the bill was submitted by the Communist leader Manuel Mora.

Communist Party made few substantive suggestions. Newspapers also indicate that only official actors, mostly bureaucrats and appointed officials, were called to the commission (Congreso Constitucional, 1941a, 1941b; *La Tribuna*, October 22, 1941).

The only request to be spared from joining the new program came from the judiciary and concerned pensions. The bill established that all special regimes would be maintained but that the newly hired would enter the unified system (Congreso Constitucional, 1941b; *Diario de Costa Rica*, October 2, 1941). The judiciary claimed that this was a threat to the financial sustainability of their special fund and an attack on the independence between state powers.[5]

Meanwhile, the business sector did not act in an organized fashion nor did it advocate against social insurance. We reviewed the three main Costa Rican newspapers in search of the private sector's official position but could not find any public statements for the period 1941 to 1943. There are only a few articles in the pro-government *Tribuna* with comments from entrepreneurs and they generally present supporting statements from specific companies (*La Tribuna*, October 21, 1941; September 25, 1942). The opposition newspaper does not have any reference either

[5] This fact reinforces our claim in Chapter 3 that pressures towards fragmentation in pensions have always been more intense than in health care.

for or against the new program. Even the United Fruit Company indicated its willingness to pay social insurance for the workers in the manufacturing activities the company had in Costa Rica (*Diario de Costa Rica*, March 11, 1942).

The lack of policy influence coming from pressure groups – which contrasts with the political landscape in Uruguay and the rest of the Southern Cone – facilitated the passing of the law without major changes. Yet the political skills displayed by proponents of social insurance to prevent and manage vetoes was also significant. Wage ceilings and the willingness to lower them reassured physicians – traditionally opposed to public health in Latin America because of its effects on their private clientele (Poveda, 1973) – that social insurance would not threaten their liberal practice (Rosenberg, 1981). During the legislative process the wage ceiling was set at 1941 US$50 per month, 17 dollars under the ceiling initially drafted in the bill.[6] The initial exclusion from social security of all employees that worked less than 180 days per year – which was the case of many coffee laborers, particularly in small and medium plantations – eased business opposition.

5.2.3 Policy Implementation

In most countries in the South, the transformation of laws into actual policies is riddled with difficulties. Lack of resources and capable bureaucracies can render new programs totally ineffective. Influential collective actors seek to shape the new programs in their own interest, while a majority of the population remains uninterested. These difficulties were at play in Peru in the 1930s, Mexico in 1943, and Guatemala in 1946 (Dion, 2010; Mesa-Lago, 1978; Rosenberg, 1981).

Costa Rica benefited from the relative weakness of actors who could have torpedoed social insurance. A significant part of the traditional coffee elite, which was either German or had ties to German families, was weakened by the domestic consequences of global geopolitical changes (Shifter, 1979). Service and manufacturing firms in the urban sector had a limited economic weight and unimpressive collective action and mobilization capacity. For instance, the Chamber of Industries was

---

[6] With this ceiling, most low- and middle-income workers were granted coverage (Rosenberg, 1981).

not created until 1943, after the actual approval and implementation of social insurance. Opposition to the government intensified a few years later when the number of business-led strikes in urban areas increased. These strikes, however, generally targeted other policy measures like the Labor Code and the Social Guarantees (Yashar, 1997).

Some civil society actors actually endorsed the government's proposal to enact social security. More specifically, the Catholic Church and the Communist Party, at that time part of the governing coalition, played a role in shaping public opinion favorable to social insurance. For example, upon request from the President of the Republic in April 1942, the Archbishop of San Jose published a pastoral letter – to be read in every Church across the country during Sunday mass – entitled "The Catholic Church Supports Social Insurance." Social insurance led the Communist Party to reassess its views on government, and recognize its capacity to introduce progressive policies. *Trabajo*, the official newspaper of the party, devoted a considerable number of articles to encourage support from the working class to health care insurance. On May 1, Labor Day, unions had a sign supporting the social security program (Díaz-Arias, 2009).

The Communist newspaper also praised employers "who are excellent and pay" and encouraged union delegates to oversee the payment of payroll taxes by, for example, going to the capital city of San Jose to check that employers had indeed transferred all the contributions (*Trabajo*, September 12, 1942: 3–4). This effort coincided with the launch of a campaign by the Costa Rican Social Insurance Agency (Caja Costarricense del Seguro Social, CCSS, or Caja) against noncompliance among employers, stressing sanctions and praising dutiful employers (*Diario de Costa Rica*, September 18, 1942: 5).

There were, nevertheless, some vetoes – more so for pensions than for health care. A few groups of workers, including public employees at the capital's municipal government[7], a public bank,[8] and customs[9] demanded that their special status be maintained. They succeeded in protecting their special pension regimes. Still, an

---

[7] Local governments had different views (*La Tribuna*, July 2, 1942: 2; *Diario de Costa Rica*, August 5, 1942: 1; *Diario de Costa Rica*, July 30, 1942: 1). The social insurance agency opposed segregation (*Diario de Costa Rica*, July 21, 1942: 1) as did the general public (see *Diario de Costa Rica*, July 21, 1942: 4).
[8] *La Tribuna*, September 25, 1942: 5.
[9] Diario de Costa Rica, August 2, 1943: 9.

overwhelming majority of workers were insured under the single collective fund and, in the long run, only two additional regimes remained in place.

Progressive experts next to the President played important roles throughout the implementation stage. Those in leading positions with the new Board of the CCSS – including Padilla who was initially second in command and constantly appealed to his ties to the President (CCSS, 1942a) – confronted opposition by broadening social support through the rapid expansion of services. Just a few months after launching the program, the largest hospital in the country looked after an average of 25 insured people per day (*Trabajo*, February 6, 1943). By December of 1942, the insured rose to 14,000, with more than 10 percent of them receiving health care services directly provided by the new agency (CCSS, 1942b). Eight physicians hired by the social insurance agency worked at facilities overseen by the Ministry of Public Sanitation and prescribed medicines available there or in private pharmacies (Rosenberg, 1983). Services were initially provided to workers residing in the four largest cities of the Central Valley, but by the end of 1943 reached two small towns as well.[10]

Policymakers close to President Calderón also handled initial appointments. Padilla recalled the selection of a few – in his words – progressive students from the School of Law at the University of Costa Rica (Rosenberg, 1983). They ran two critical departments: one was in charge of explaining the benefits of social insurance for all (CCSS, 1943: 141); the other ensured the collection of payroll taxes. Postponing the launching of old-age insurance, the new agency set payroll taxes below the legal limit (*Trabajo*, September 12, 1942: 3–4). Before the first contributions were collected, funding for the social security agency was drawn from increased taxes on alcohol and drinks (*La Tribuna*, August 27, 1942) in the considerable amount of US$177,000 for the first twelve months.

Just two years after the approval of the founding law, the CCSS pushed for the expansion of eligibility and further degrees of institutional autonomy. A law designed by the Caja leadership and backed by high-level ILO experts was approved in 1943. It established coverage

---

[10] This expansion reflected social demands to cover locations other than the capital city (*Trabajo*, April 3, 1943: 1; *Trabajo*, May 9, 1942: 2, 4; *Diario de Costa Rica*, September 2, 1943: 2; *Diario de Costa Rica*, September 9, 1943: 2).

for *all* manual and white-collar salaried workers as a necessary step for the financial sustainability of social insurance. The bill also secured financial and managerial autonomy from the Executive Office (Secretaría de Gobernación, Policía, Trabajo y Previsión Social, 1943). Such autonomy was established in the presidential draft sent to Congress in 1941 but was later eliminated, creating instead an external body to oversee decisions made by the social insurance board. The 1943 reform was mentioned only twice in newspapers and was seldom debated publicly.[11]

5.3 Managing the Outside Option: the Conflicts with the Physicians

Until 1941, most physicians shared time between a charity hospital (either the San Juan de Dios in the country's capital or any of the smaller five hospitals located in Cartago, Alajuela, Heredia, Liberia, and Quepos) and their private practice. The creation of social insurance potentially threatened their interests but it was regarded at first as an exclusive solution for the low-income population and thus too insignificant to worry about. In Clark's words "when the CCSS was founded in 1943, nobody foresaw that virtually all Costa Rican doctors would one day be state employees" (Clark, 2005: 130). Moreover, the CCSS initially sub-contracted services from the most important charity hospital, the San Juan de Dios (Jaramillo, 2003).

Conflicts between the medical profession and the CCSS soon exploded. In the eyes of the social insurance agency, the sub-contracting arrangement with the San Juan de Dios did not work properly: doctors charged excessive fees to insured patients and the costs of medicines were higher than in private pharmacies. As a result, the CCSS decided to expand its own facilities, launching outpatient services in 1943 and inpatient services in 1945 (Jaramillo, 2003: 216). In March of 1945, the Hospital Policlínico of the social insurance had fifty workers, including administrators, nurses, cleaners, and pharmacists. Twenty doctors worked part-time. The number of beds also increased rapidly from 29 in 1945 to 200 in 1952.

In 1944, the Costa Rican doctors created the Medical Union (Unión Médica, UM) to represent their interests. The UM was initially led by

---

[11] Unions supported this measure as one badly needed for social insurance to accomplish its goals (*Diario de Costa Rica*, September 5, 1943: 13).

Antonio Peña Chavarría, the director of the Hospital San Juan de Dios and a Conservative opposition leader. The new union did not oppose the growth of social insurance and allowed all its members to work for the CCSS in the first instance (Rosenberg, 1983).

Yet relations between the UM and the Caja quickly deteriorated. The main source of conflict was the 1945 CCSS decision to reach the wealthy by eliminating the wage ceiling. This decision – promoted by Padilla himself – was seen as a significant threat on the doctors' liberal practice. As the president of the UM warned days after the proposal was announced, "as a collective service, social insurance limits doctors' private initiative. Even if it is good for social groups with limited life chances, it is worrying from the perspective of the doctors [and] for high income groups who can pay for private medical services" (quoted in Rosenberg, 1983: 89). For the UM, it made more sense to first increase services to the working class as a whole and only later expand it to higher income groups – an argument shared by the Communist Party.

The subsequent negotiation between the doctors and the CCSS failed as the UM also opposed the expansion of the wage ceiling from 400 to 600 colones. The UM launched a successful strike that paralyzed all social insurance services for three days. In the end, the CCSS was forced to withdraw its proposal and its general manager resigned.

In the short-term, the strike represented a victory for doctors and their efforts to protect their private practice and by extension the outside option. It also turned them into a strong collective actor for decades to come. Yet, despite their initial success, in the following years, the interaction between the social insurance agency and medical professionals contributed to a sharp reduction in the outside option.

First, the Caja continued to hire physicians until it became the main employer of doctors in Costa Rica. In 1950, the Census reported 265 physicians (for a total population of 800,875). Between 1950 and 1955, the Caja employed two-thirds of the 65 newly registered physicians in the country, the number of its doctors increasing from 101 to 146. Although there is no accessible information on the changes in the numbers of full-time CCSS doctors over time, there are indications that it increased rapidly. The incorporation of dependent family members to social insurance in 1957 increased the demand for doctors significantly: the number of insured family members went from

42,813 in 1955 to 584,826 in 1969 (Miranda Gutiérrez and Asís Beirute, 1989: 22–31 and Rosenberg, 1983: 205). This was a major contribution to the rapid growth of the total number of physicians in Costa Rica, which multiplied by 2.5 between 1951 and 1969.

Second, the socio-economic background of doctors became more diverse and their commitment to the state stronger. Until the Second World War, most physicians were trained in Europe. During and after the War, an increasing number were trained in Mexico, El Salvador, and in South America, primarily Argentina and Chile. In 1961, the University of Costa Rica started its own program, thus increasing access to lower middle class students to the profession.

Third, the social insurance agency expanded facilities, including modern equipment and its own infrastructure, across the country. More importantly, it became more sophisticated in terms of the services it offered and provided many opportunities for the professional development of doctors (see Chapter 6).

5.4 Conclusion

In the early 1940s Costa Rica embraced a foundational architecture that in subsequent years triggered a pro-universal expansion of social policy. Social insurance constituted a step forward in all five components of the policy architecture by providing access to low-income workers along income/class rather than occupational lines; successfully enforcing payroll taxes; having benefits defined by the new CCSS; rapidly expanding public facilities; and progressively reducing the role of private practice.

Rather than delivering universal outputs immediately, the foundational architecture created the incentives for pro-universal expansion. The implementation of a unified fund from the very onset limited opportunities for fragmentation. The early incorporation of low and lower-middle income workers incentivized the subsequent bottom-up expansion to the better off. The brand new public bureaucracy in charge of regulation and service provision became a powerful stakeholder interested in further expanding social insurance. Policymakers eager to promote universalism across the South should keep these features of the policy architecture in mind.

While acknowledging the importance of democracy and weak social veto actors as preconditions for social insurance, we have shown that they cannot, by themselves, account for these specific features. Instead, we need to focus on the state and consider the role of a small group of experts. They comfortably interacted with political actors such as the President as well as with global policy prescriptions. They became intermediaries and adaptors of international ideas, drawing on them to shape domestic policy debates and policy design. State actors also contributed to effectively manage vetoes from interest groups that, although weaker than in the Southern Cone, did exist. Combining macro-factors with a detailed analysis of state actors, we can fill the missing link between democracy and universalism.

The timing of the initial programs and the role of international ideas brought by policy experts to domestic debates is fundamental when explaining differences between Costa Rica and the other three cases discussed in previous chapters. In particular, the fact that Uruguay founded its health care and pensions systems during the first decades of the twentieth century while Costa Rica did it at a time when unified insurance funds had become a dominant policy idea is particularly important (see also Chapter 8). Meanwhile, differences between the Costa Rican and the Mauritian architecture can only be understood if we consider the differences between the roles of the ILO and the British administration in the diffusion of international ideas.

We must also recognize that by the 1940s, Costa Rica had taken only the first step toward universalism. The system still needed to expand, state institutions had to be strengthened, and the outside option kept in check. How did this happen? How did the foundational architecture lead to further developments? How did state actors use the opportunities created by the initial architecture to deepen the features that favored universalism? These are the questions we will address in the next chapter where we discuss the expansion of social policy in the 1970s.

6 | Moving Further Towards Unification in the 1970s

6.1 Introduction

By the early 1970s a growing number of Costa Rican workers and their families received equal, generous social benefits. Yet Costa Rica's social policy architecture still confronted major limitations. On the one hand, health care insurance was underfunded. On the other hand, the poor and the self-employed had "second class" access to curative health care services and lacked protection in old age. Many high-income workers were also uninsured. Had the architecture remained restricted to salaried workers and their families, Costa Rica would not have become an exceptional case of universalism in the South.

During the crucial decade of the 1970s, these problems were largely resolved thanks to three interrelated changes. First, by eliminating wage ceilings in payroll contributions, mandatory social security extended to high income groups and temporarily tackled its funding problems. Second, the transfer of all hospitals to the Caja Costarricense del Seguro Social (Costa Rican Social Insurance Agency, CCSS or Caja) enhanced the unification of service provision and created incentives for the incorporation of the poor to social insurance. Third, this incorporation was also facilitated by new programs such as rural and community health, which were funded through a path-breaking social assistance fund (Fondo de Desarrollo Social y Asignaciones Familares, FODESAF). Created in 1975, FODESAF generated a new income stream that enabled institutions such as the Ministry of Health and the Caja to reach the poor. Funded benefits included non-contributory pensions and preventive and primary health care as well as school luncheons and technical training. Unlike the social assistance funds created across Latin America after 1982, FODESAF funded affirmative action measures without fragmenting benefits into a two-tier system.

How did Costa Rica manage to eliminate wage ceilings, thus increasing the tax burden for some of the most powerful groups in society?

Why was the restructuring of health care – a difficult bureaucratic undertaking – successful? How were the poor incorporated to the same programs as the rest of the population? We acknowledge the contribution made by electoral competition, social pressures, and progressive partisanship in the context of a volatile international environment. Progressive politicians in Costa Rica and abroad were responding to growing social mobilization in the rural sector and to international pressures to deal with the "communist threat." Across Latin America, governments were pushed to extend social protection to the rural poor – a large group who lived in deplorable living conditions but were fundamental for the production of primary exports (Mallet, 1980). Concerns about the spread of Communism after the 1959 Cuban revolution also led the US to enact the "Alliance for Progress."[1]

In Costa Rica, José Figueres made the "war against misery" his main motto in the 1970 Presidential campaign.[2] There was, however, no indication that he was committed to implementing difficult measures such as the unification of service provision. In fact, in his inaugural speech as president, he only referred to social policy when talking about the creation of an anti-poverty national emergency plan (Figueres, 1970). The latter resulted in a private – public partnership (the Mixed Institute of Social Assistance, or Instituto Mixto de Ayuda Social, IMAS) to transfer cash to people under extreme poverty – a rather fragmenting measure in so far as it was decoupled from any effort to incorporate recipients to services and transfers received by everyone else.

Political leadership and ideology can thus not explain the specific reforms adopted. Instead, to account for these policy changes, we must turn our attention to state actors. A close policy community of experts attuned to international ideas and supported by political leaders led key

---

[1] Attention to poverty in the Americas was enhanced by events in the United States. Following President Lyndon Johnson's (1963–1969) call for an "unconditional war on poverty" (WOP) in his 1964 State of the Union address, social policies towards the underprivileged received renewed attention. Many programs continued under the Republican administration of Richard Nixon (1969–1974). The WOP was based on the notion that prosperity and growth alone could not deal with the roots of poverty.

[2] President José Figueres led the winning side in the civil war that took place in Costa Rica in 1948 and was the head of a provisional government in 1949. Founder of the social-democratic Partido Liberación Nacional (National Liberation Party, PLN), he was elected president in 1953 and again in 1970, remaining a major figure in Costa Rican politics until his death in 1990. Between 1974 and 1978, the President was Daniel Oduber, another historical leader of the PLN.

transformations. They all shared a belief in the equity-enhancing role of state intervention, even if often disagreed on the optimum instruments.[3] These state actors were also skillful in managing and defusing potential vetoes through a mixture of gradualism and appeasement.

In designing their responses, state actors were influenced by the pre-existing architecture, which created incentives for change and shaped available policy alternatives. For instance, maintaining the prominence of payroll taxes and removing wage ceilings was easier than relying exclusively on new taxes. The size and power of the CCSS explains why all hospitals were transferred to the social insurance agency instead of remaining under the Ministry of Health. A strong Caja also limited the growth of the outside option. In this chapter we also show that some changes in the architecture brought about others: the elimination of the wage ceilings led to the unification of hospitals, which then placed the needs of the poor at the heart of the policy agenda. These changes in turn influenced the subsequent creation of the rural health program and of FODESAF.

Below we first discuss the policy process behind the removal of wage ceilings and the restructuring of the health care sector. Second, we explain measures aimed at the social incorporation of the poor: the expansion of curative health care, the creation of the rural health program and the enactment of FODESAF. Throughout the chapter, we trace relevant connections between different measures and identify the actors behind policy design.

6.2 Expansion and Unification: the Removal of the Wage Ceiling and the Integration of Hospitals

In November 1970 social insurance became mandatory for all salaried workers with contributions calculated on their full wage. This decision resulted in the incorporation of all workers earning US$145 (1,000 colones) or more – mainly administrative staff and professionals – and

---

[3] Our claim has to do with specific state actors and not with state capacity itself. In fact, we reject a simplistic view of the Costa Rican state as an autonomous entity with strong bureaucratic capacity and a clear short- and long-term project (see also Martínez Franzoni and Sánchez-Ancochea, 2013a). During this period, the process of policy design was slow and controversial even among actors with a shared vision. Far from a given, state autonomy was shaped and reshaped by these state actors through their policy decisions.

their families to the CCSS.[4] The increase in the proportion of the insured population soon triggered a second change: the integration of all hospitals under a single institution.

These reforms were driven by a select group of well-connected state actors embedded in international policy communities. This close network included politically appointed experts in at least three key institutions: the Caja (e.g. Guido Miranda), the Ministry of Labor (particularly, the Minister Danilo Jiménez Veiga), and the Ministry of Health (e.g. Edgar Mohs and Lenín Sáenz). Contrary to the 1940s, it also incorporated a few high-ranking bureaucrats from the Caja such as its chief actuary, Álvaro Vindas.

Debates concerning the elimination of the wage ceilings and the integration of hospitals were intertwined and involved the same actors and institutional settings. We, nevertheless, discuss them separately to carefully disentangle the main driving forces behind each. To facilitate the analysis, Figure 6.1 presents the timeline of the main milestones discussed in this chapter. The circles refer to legislative moments, while the squares incorporate executive decisions.

6.3 Expansion of Eligibility and Unification of Funding: Mandatory Insurance Reaches the Better Off

Since the 1950s social insurance had experienced funding shortages. The growth in the demand for health care services; the incorporation of economically dependent family members; and the government's cumulative failure to honor its contribution, increased pressures to expand revenues (Rosenberg, 1983).[5] Periodic bureaucratic demands to increase the wage ceiling ultimately triggered the introduction of a constitutional mandate to universalize social insurance in 1961. Proposed by the PLN, the constitutional reform has often been portrayed as an attempt to enhance this party's influence on social security (Gutiérrez

---

[4] The wage ceiling equated to 70 percent of the household food basket, which was equivalent in 1977 to US$208 in rural areas and US$223 in urban areas (Mata and Murillo, 1980).

[5] The state made two types of payments: as employer it contributed to fund health care and pensions for civil servants. Additionally, it made a 2 percent contribution (which dropped to 0.25 percent in 1974) for all workers. The government consistently failed to meet this second obligation and, as a result, accumulated a growing debt to the Caja (CCSS, 2014).

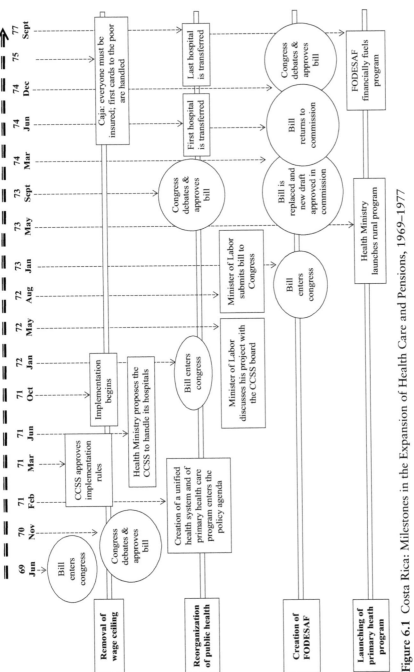

Figure 6.1 Costa Rica: Milestones in the Expansion of Health Care and Pensions, 1969–1977

Góngora in McGuire, 2010).[6] Yet more than a programmatic initiative, the amendment responded to financial requests from Caja officials (Rosenberg, 1983).[7] The commitment to full coverage in the space of ten years was an attempt to meet the Caja's demands gradually.

In the short term, the constitutional amendment did not deliver full access to services. Coverage did expand continuously: between 1963 and 1973 it increased from 29% of the economically active population to 50% and from 22% of the total population to 60% (Rosenberg, 1979). New facilities were built and better services added. However, social insurance for most salaried workers still coexisted with private outpatient services for the better off and public sanitation for the poor.[8]

Resource shortages became acute during the late 1960s as the unpaid debts of the public sector with the Caja increased (Legislative Assembly, 1969). The potential elimination of the wage ceiling moved again to the center stage of the policy agenda (CCSS, 1969a: 6). A report prepared for the Board by Álvaro Vindas, the Caja's chief actuary, shaped the subsequent debate (CCSS, 1969b). The "Vindas report" argued that removing wage ceilings would give the CCSS enough resources to extend social insurance to all salaried workers.[9] It discussed additional measures, including the expansion of services to the whole population. The self-employed would join contributory social insurance on voluntary bases and a new, complementary program would look after the poor.

In June 1969, the PLN legislator and former board member of the Caja, José Luis Molina Quesada, introduced in Congress the bill to remove the wage ceiling. He stressed that his proposal reflected a consensus within the social insurance board of directors (Molina Quesada in Legislative Assembly, 1969) – a claim supported in writing a few days later by the Caja's general manager (CCSS, 1969c). The

[6] Interview #1.

[7] The initial proposal was pushed by Enrique Obregón, a progressive PLN deputy. It demanded that at least 10 percent of annual public spending was devoted to social insurance. Yet the Caja sought to maintain a more flexible system, pressuring to change the wage ceiling without establishing a fixed target. The terms of the reform were ultimately agreed between prominent PLN legislators and the Caja vice-manager, Rodrigo Fournier.

[8] In 1972, the hospitals of the CCSS had 1,265 beds and attended 22% of all patients compared to 5,984 and 78% in the public hospitals (Legislative Assembly, 1972).

[9] For the Caja bureaucracy this measure was regarded as more effective than the tax on cigarettes the government was proposing (CCSS, 1969a).

congressional debate started immediately, but was soon postponed as Costa Rica entered into an electoral period. Deliberations restarted in June 1970 in the Commission of Economic Affairs (CCSS, 1970a).

Along the way and following Vindas' views, the elimination of the wage ceiling was reframed as a step towards reaching the whole population and not just as an instrument to increase funding. About a month before the bill was voted in Congress, state officials from the CCSS argued for the "elimination of the ceilings to social insurance contributions, because without this measure we could not think about new programs," including the expansion of services to all (*La Hora*, March 26, 1971: 8). The draft established mandatory coverage for all salaried workers; proposed voluntary insurance for self-employed workers, and gave the CCSS freedom to choose how to service the poor (Legislative Assembly, 1969).

In March 1971, the law was approved with the support of all legislators but one. The Minister of Labor and Chairman of the CCSS Board, Danilo Jiménez Veiga, played a crucial role in securing this overwhelming legislative majority. He lobbied Congress for a larger budget for the institution and also pushed for a sustained increase in the number of people with access to social insurance. Like most other key state actors in this period, Jiménez Veiga had a progressive agenda and close links to international policy circles. After serving at the International Labour Organization (ILO) for twenty years in Istanbul, Peru, and Mexico, he had returned to Costa Rica in 1970.[10] Jiménez Veiga was also a pragmatist as reflected in his claim that "the biggest changes that Costa Rica and the whole world have undertaken in areas like education, health care and social insurance have never waited for all optimum conditions" (Legislative Assembly, 1969: 74).

6.3.1 Unification of Benefits and Provision: Public Hospitals under a Single Roof

The elimination of wage ceilings gave the CCSS much needed resources, but also created new service demands. To respond to this challenge, the board of directors of the CCSS assessed alternative

---

[10] Jiménez Veiga was a controversial figure in the PLN because he had not been in the social-democratic camp during the 1948 Civil War, supporting Communist trade unions instead. By 1970, however, he had married President Figueres' daughter and had become part of his inner circle.

Table 6.1 *Measures to Reorganize the Delivery of Health Services, 1960s*

Year	Proposal	Proponent/s	Contents
1961	Physicians commissioned legislative report "Analysis of the medical situation in Costa Rica"	Carlos Arrea Baixench, Guido Miranda Gutiérrez, and Fernando Trejos Escalante	Unification under a new agency (National Health Institute) or under the CCSS
1961	Draft bill	Rodrigo Loría Cortes	Creation of a national health service as an autonomous agency in charge of all hospitals, including the Caja ones
1962	Non-legislative report on the "Reorganization of medicine in our country"	Guido Miranda Gutiérrez	Preventive care should remain under the Ministry of Health; all hospitals should be integrated, under either the Ministry of Health or the CCSS
1962	National plan to integrate medical services of the CCSS	CCSS	The Caja would gradually absorb all medical services; the Ministry of Health would remain as coordinating agency
1965	Basic agreement between the Caja and the Ministry		Development of preventive medicine for the insured and the non-insured through tailored-made programs starting in San Jose and then expanding nationwide; in practice very little was done
1965	Report commissioned by the government and the Caja	Pan American Health Organization (PAHO)	Creation of a high level commission and a working group to coordinate efforts in health care
1968	Draft bills to create a national health system	Fernando Guzmán Mata and Fernando Trejos Escalante	The Caja would provide basic services to the whole population and develop a national pension system.

Source: Ministry of Health and PAHO (1977).

options.[11] One suggestion – defended passionately by Caja's board member from the conservative opposition, Miguel Barzuna Sauma – was to give the insured population medical choice, including access to private practitioners (CCSS, 1970b). A second option was to rely on services delivered by public hospitals managed by autonomous boards. Yet these hospitals were short of medicines, infrastructure, and equipment (Rosero-Bixby, 1986) and could hardly deliver the quality of services the CCSS expected. The third option was to transfer all medical facilities to the Caja (CCSS, 1970c) – which would then become responsible for the non-insured population as well.

As shown in Table 6.1, debates about the reorganization and integration of Costa Rica's hospital network were not new. Yet previous proposals had generally lacked support among key state agencies and political actors. The CCSS (by the 1960s the dominant player in the system) repeatedly opposed the creation of new state agencies (CCSS, 1962). In addition, none of these proposals had Presidential support – a precondition for change.

Internationally, in the 1960s the dominant belief was that services for the insured and the rest of the population should remain separate. Social insurance experts, in particular, aimed to keep a clear separation between the poor and the (non-poor) insured population. For example, when visiting Costa Rica in 1959, the General Secretary of the Inter-American Conference on Social Security (Conferencia Interamericana de Seguridad Social, CISS) advised the board of directors of the CCSS to coordinate public sanitation interventions with the Ministry of Health without blurring the boundaries between the two institutions. The CISS drew from Spain, where social insurance turned down the extreme poor to avoid "diluting efforts that diminish the level of protection granted to the insured" (Martí Bufill, 1960: article 3).

Chile's failure to create a National Health System during the 1950s was rather influential.[12] Lessons from the Chilean fiasco came through Guido Miranda, who travelled to Chile in 1960 and two years later organized a Chilean Medical Week.[13] Based on his insights, the Caja's board concluded that emulating the Chilean National System was

---

[11] These options were further developed in the first National Health Plan in 1971 (Interview #2).
[12] Interview #3.
[13] Interview #1. Miranda was an internationally trained doctor who had worked in the San Juan de Dios in the early 1950s and joined the Mexico Hospital upon its

undesirable because "after 10 years of operation of this Service, Chile faces a reality more complex and difficult than prior to the creation of this organism" (CCSS, 1962: 2).

By the early 1970s, however, the international environment had changed significantly. The need to grant preventive and primary health for the poor and the non-poor simultaneously and integrate components of health care became part of the global consensus. In 1972 the World Health Organization (WHO) established the Office for Health Service Strengthening, which aimed to promote integrated health systems. The WHO also increased the number of projects on "basic health services" from 85 in 1965 to 156 in 1971 (Cueto, 2004). The appointment of Halfan Mahler – an enthusiastic supporter of integrating primary health care in national systems – as Director General of the WHO in 1973 moved this agenda along (Litsios, 2002).

Costa Rica's pre-existing policy architecture also influenced state actors' decision to transfer all hospitals to the Caja rather than to an alternative institution. The Caja had more resources and political clout than the Ministry of Health and was in charge of the most modern facilities, including the brand new Mexico hospital.[14] According to Antonio Jara, quoting a doctor from the hospital San Juan de Dios he interviewed:

the medical consultation in [a public hospital managed by the Ministry of Health] was full of financial hardship with permanent suffering, that is ... there was almost nothing available ... the experience was an agony for the patients and ... for me. In the afternoons, I had consultation in the Clorito Picado [part of the CCSS facilities] ... In that consultation as general practitioner, I could prescribe any medicine of the ones we had in the book, which was a thick book of 3 or 4 centimeters, while the one in the San Juan de Dios only had thirty pages. (Jara, 2002: 27)

The notion of giving up its facilities was totally foreign to the CCSS and would have entailed a U-turn in its intense process of institutional building.

While a growing consensus emerged about the transfer of all hospitals to the CCSS, there were still heated debates about timing

foundation in 1969. In the 1980s, he would become head of the CCSS (see Chapter 7).

[14] Interview #2.

and human and financial resources. The Minister of Health, José Luis Orlich, was eager to proceed rapidly and transfer all hospitals immediately (CCSS, 1970d). Danilo Jiménez Veiga endorsed a more gradual, piecemeal process led by the Caja. In his view, each hospital should only be transferred when funding was secured and all parties involved had agreed on the labor conditions for all personnel involved.

Successive negotiations between the CCSS and the Ministry of Health followed. Not surprisingly, when the bill was finally approved in August 1973 it primarily reflected the preferences of the Caja: the transfer of hospitals would be gradual and the Caja would define its actual timing. This institution would also receive all resources until then managed by each hospital (a combination of lottery income and other taxes). The law also established that additional resources would be created, something that did not happen.

The transfer of all hospitals, which concluded in 1977, illustrates the positive influence of the policy architecture in the context of a favorable international environment. Alternative reform options would have led to fragmentation of the policy architecture. Had some hospitals remained outside social insurance, services would have become fragmented based on income and occupational affiliation.[15] The separation between provision and funding would have also created severe financial shortages.

6.3.2 *State Actors and Veto Management*

Business chambers, professional associations, and trade unions were not involved in the design of the two reforms just discussed. Still, various groups tried to derail those measures that could affect them negatively, at times endangering the unification drive. Like in the past, state actors coped with vetoes through two main instruments: gradualism and delegation of crucial decisions regarding implementation to the CCSS and the Ministry of Health.

Business chambers posed a threat to the unification of eligibility and funding. Opposition to the elimination of the wage ceiling was bitter. An editorial of the *Diario de Costa Rica* reproduced in *La Nación* on March 16, 1971 warned,

---

[15] Geographical location remained a fragmenting criteria and one that the health care reform enacted during the 1990s sought to overcome (see Chapter 7).

if the reform to article 3 of the Constitution is approved, the country may sink. Companies will suffer, workers will witness a reduction in their salaries, and basic health services will not improve – because there are no doctors, nurses and hospitals to improve them – and at the end we will suffer economic and social chaos. (*La Nación*, February 24, 1971)

Rafael Angel Arguedas from the National Union of Traders echoed these arguments a day later, claiming that "we as entrepreneurs will have to seriously think about liquidating our companies as a response to a fiscal voracity that is increasingly unbearable and that will become even worse with the elimination of the ceilings" (*La Hora*, March 26, 1971). In response to these protests the Minister of Labor, Jiménez Veiga, conducted negotiations with the business sector. He first committed to a gradual removal of wage ceilings (*La Hora*, March 17, 1971) and, in view of legislative opposition to such measure, announced the gradual expansion of services.

An even more significant threat came from the Medical Association (Colegio de Médicos), which aimed to maintain the fragmentation of providers and protect the outside option.[16] As in the 1940s, their main concern was the impact of the reform upon medical choice (see Chapter 5). Policymakers reassured doctors that under no circumstances would the CCSS force physicians to work for the public sector, while simultaneously closing the door to contracting out. Legislators Jenaro Valverde Marín (PLN) and Guillermo Jiménez Ramírez (from the opposition Partido Unidad Nacional) together with the manager of the Caja, Rodrigo Fournier, also agreed with the Colegio that physicians from other countries would only be involved in cases of emergency (Legislative Assembly, 1969).

In their effort to remove the wage ceiling, state actors benefited from trade union support. Newspapers reported eighteen unions and federations expressing their views to the legislative commission, and only one voicing opposition to the measure (*La Nación*, March 9–16, 1971; *La Prensa Libre*, March 10–16, 1971). Some trade unions stressed the positive effects of the measure on solidarity; others emphasized the positive impact of additional resources on service

---

[16] Physicians were by then organized in this professional association and two unions: the Medical Union, whose influence we have already discussed in the previous chapter, and the union of the medical professionals of the CCSS (SIPROCIMECA).

quality. Only a minority disputed the latter claim. For the trade union of the National Bank of Costa Rica, for example, "it is impossible to secure a total universalization of the system, using a mandatory payroll tax ... before reviewing the way the Caja works to provide beneficiaries a better service" (Legislative Assembly, 1969: 14). Teachers unions worried that the reform would shrink their pensions – confirming that unifying pensions was throughout each stage harder than unifying health care. The Minister of Labor played a key role in assuring unions that their pensions would be untouched (*La Hora*, March 26, 1971: 1, 5; *La Prensa Libre*, March 26, 1971: 2).

The transfer of hospitals to the Caja also faced opposition. The hospitals run by the Ministry of Health had their own management boards (Juntas de Protección Social) with representation from the Catholic Church and various civil society organizations. Several of these boards believed that the transfer would increase bureaucracy and reduce hospital autonomy. State actors responded to these pressures with a mixture of gradualism and pragmatism: the Caja first took over the hospitals where there was less opposition. It also allowed the Juntas to remain involved in hospital operations through fundraising activities (*La Nación*, November 1, 1974: 6).

Opposition to the transfer of hospitals became more intense during the implementation stage. For example, just days before the transfer, the director of the San Juan de Dios, Manrique Soto Pacheco, claimed that the change would never happen.[17] On the day of the transfer, Soto Pacheco bluntly said: "it is disturbing ... that a system that has kept for more than a century a medical trajectory in favor of the class with the fewest resources is now replaced by a mechanism of mandatory economic participation, where the place of the indigent has not been well defined" (Hospitales de Costa Rica, 1977: 3). Physicians' resistance to a Caja takeover reflected their strong antipathy to state intervention and some concern about working conditions. Yet the transfer resulted in higher wages and better working conditions for a majority of the doctors involved. In July of 1974 a bill established that all personnel could be rehired under the (better) terms of the Caja (Legislative Assembly, 1974a).

[17] Interview #5.

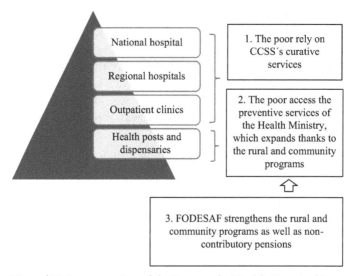

Figure 6.2 Incorporation of the Poor to the Health Care Architecture

6.4 The Non-Insured and the Rural Poor

During the 1970s, Costa Rica also advanced towards incorporating the poor to health care and pensions. In the case of health insurance, three measures contributed to this positive outcome by expanding eligibility and unifying funding, entitlements and service delivery. Figure 6.2 illustrates the interrelations among measures.

First, the poor were incorporated to the CCSS through a non-contributory insurance program. This mechanism ensured access to the same curative services and providers that the rest of the population enjoyed. Second, the Ministry of Health launched a rural health program for the rural poor in 1973. Third, the government enacted FODESAF to facilitate poor Costa Ricans' access to services already available for the rest of the population. FODESAF funded the rural health care program as well as non-contributory pensions for the low-income uninsured population.[18]

What were the drivers behind Costa Rica's success in incorporating the poor in this way? Rural mobilization in the context of electoral competition was a significant precondition. Between 1971 and 1974,

---

[18] Years later FODESAF would fund the non-contributive health insurance as well.

2,240 households illegally occupied more than 91,000 hectares of agricultural land (Cortés and León, 2008). At the same time, progressive movements with ties to the then illegal Communist Party and other small, leftist parties became active in the rural sector (Martínez Franzoni and Sánchez-Ancochea, 2013a). As a result, political leaders from the ruling PLN became concerned about violence and their decreasing influence in some parts of the country.

Yet political leadership and electoral competition hardly drove reforms. The PLN's primary response to rural demands was not expansionary social policy but job creation, land distribution, and food and housing programs (Hernández-Naranjo, 2010). Instead, we turn once again our attention to the role of state actors, including those we mentioned in the previous section. Most of them had a medical background but were also astute political operatives or had close ties with politicians. Much of their ideational inputs came from international policy ideas.

The previous policy architecture also played a role in shaping the new measures. The incorporation of the poor to social insurance was part of the chain of decisions reviewed in the previous section: the transfer of all hospitals to the CCSS forced this institution to take responsibility for the poor. A new publicly funded insurance program – state insurance – was the chosen mechanism. The funding needs of the rural health program and the CCSS's drive to create non-contributory pensions incentivized the creation of FODESAF, which was financed primarily through payroll taxes.

6.4.1 Insuring the Poor through the CCSS

Before the 1970s, the hospitals under the Minister of Health treated two types of uninsured population: those who could afford paying for out-of-pocket services and those who could not. Not surprisingly, the removal of the wage ceiling and the integration of hospitals under the social insurance agency placed access to health care services among the latter at the top of the political agenda.

In 1968 the Vindas report triggered an intense debate within the board of directors of the CCSS about what to do with the lowest income families. Some board members argued for a restrictive definition of universalism, while the President of the Board and Minister of Labor, Jiménez Veiga, supported Vindas' basic principles. He adopted his usual pragmatic and gradualist approach: mandatory insurance would first reach salaried workers to subsequently focus on the rest (CCSS, 1970e).

The law that transferred hospitals to the Caja was negotiated between this institution and the Ministry of Health. Its various components fueled unification regarding eligibility, funding, entitlements, and delivery (Legislative Assembly, 1973a). Concerning eligibility, the law required the CCSS to provide non-contributory curative services to low-income uninsured through state insurance (Legislative Assembly, 1974b; Mohs, 1983: 48).

Concerning funding, the Ministry of Health was required to transfer resources that would take care of services for the poor and identify additional funding sources when needed. The Technical Council for Socio-Medical Assistance (Consejo Técnico de Asistencia Médico-Social), a department of the Ministry of Health, was initially in charge of collecting all resources (Mohs, 1983: 48). The Caja began receiving income from the national lottery, which was previously channeled to charity hospitals, and from indirect taxes on cigarettes and other products. As a result, the share of payroll taxes in the Caja's total revenues decreased (Casas and Vargas, 1980). Yet there was still a significant gap between revenues and needs: by 1980 the total amount of resources the Ministry of Health transferred to the CCSS was about 55 percent of the resources devoted to service provision for the poor (CCSS, 2014). Resources from the national budget were to close this gap, but the state debt with social insurance grew rather than narrowed.

The gap between spending and resources did not have a negative impact on entitlements: after the 1970s reforms, the poor remained insured and received the same services as everyone else.[19] Legal changes required the CCSS to provide the poor with curative services in outpatient clinics and regional and national hospitals. The Ministry of Health remained in change of preventive services – including basic primary care – through its dispensaries, health posts, and rural and community programs. By 1977, 197,538 people (9.5 percent of the total population and 12.5 percent of the insured population) were served through state insurance. This included people in extreme poverty, with serious disabilities, and/or the elderly without contributory insurance (Vargas *et al.*, 1979).

---

[19] The Caja was only able to secure entitlements by raising payroll taxes.

In summary, rather than a well-designed plan from the PLN leadership, the incorporation of the poor to the Caja's curative services was an extension of the unification of hospitals. The unification made the Caja responsible for the uninsured, thus adding pressure for the universalization of the system. Expanded rights for the poor resulted from pragmatic state actors interested in solving demands that followed from other changes in the policy architecture.

6.4.2 Expanding the State to the Rural Poor: the Rural Community Program

By 1970 an estimated 40 percent of the Costa Rican population was still rural, scattered across the country, mostly poor and with limited contact with health care services.[20] Malnutrition, parasites, diarrhea, and other threats led to serious illness that could not be solved through curative facilities. Moreover, many rural Costa Ricans probably did not even know they had legal access to social insurance after the unification of hospitals in 1973.

To face these challenges, the Costa Rican government created a new rural program that complemented efforts in other areas. Initially designed in 1971 and launched in 1973, the program aimed to deliver basic health services to geographical areas with population under 2,000, first by relying on existing health posts and later by setting new ones (Ministry of Health, 1973). An auxiliary nurse and a health assistant with six-month training teamed up to provide services, including sanitation, community organization, and periodic door to door visits for vaccination and check-ups (Casas and Vargas, 1980; Morgan, 1990).

The driving force behind the program was a group of state actors within the Ministry of Health. Although Minister Orlich did not have particular interest in the rural health program, he supported his advisers and collaborators.[21] They included Lenín Sáenz, Antonio Rodríguez Aragonez, Eliecer Valverde, Oscar Alfaro, and Edgar Mohs, all doctors who were also behind the elaboration of the first National Health Plan in 1971.[22] They were all successful professionals who also had political clout: they had been involved in political campaigns and

---

[20] Interview #6.   [21] Interviews #2, #7, and #3.
[22] When the rural program was launched, Mohs was vice-minister; Valverde was director general of the Ministry; and Sáenz and Aragonez coordinated the Councils of Technical-Medical Assistance and of Sanitation. Mohs, Valverde

had close links to the PLN leadership.[23] The group was attuned with international ideas regarding the central role of Ministries of Health in preventive and primary health care services (Villegas, 1977).

Indeed, Costa Rica's efforts were embedded in an international trend sponsored by USAID, the United Nations Children's Fund (UNICEF), and PAHO, which had already reached neighboring countries like Guatemala. PAHO hosted a particularly influential meeting of the Ministers of Health in Santiago de Chile in 1973. Their recommendations included the creation of "minimum integral services ... including services to the sick in emergency situations, health care of mothers and children under 5 years of age, including nutritional, family and community education for a hygienic life; vaccination; basic sanitation; statistical registration, and reference of patients to more complex units" (Ministry of Health, 1973: 6–7).

As we have also seen in previous sections, the success of Costa Rica's state actors can be partly explained by their pragmatic approach. The rural community program initially drew from personnel involved in the ongoing National Service for the Eradication of Malaria (Villegas, 2004).[24] Lesson from the anti-malaria interventions taught state actors that the main health problems stemmed from sanitation issues that curative services were unable to solve. For instance, diarrhea among children was a major cause of dehydration, but drinking non-potable water worsened their condition.[25] As a top official explained to us, before being into politics "I was in the hospital ... [There] children died on us like flies ... They would leave the hospital to return the following week."[26] The rural health program addressed both the symptoms and their environmental and social underlying causes.[27]

Yet ensuring access to hospitals was still important. In fact, Costa Rica's rural program – in contrast to programs in neighboring countries – was fully integrated with other health care services. Increasing access to primary health promoted the incorporation of the poor to the Caja hospitals – becoming a push factor towards full universalization

---

and Sáenz had studied abroad in Mexico and Chile and participated actively in international networks.

[23] The first three were part of the inner circle of the Minister. Mohs, a young and promising pediatrician, was appointed by President Figueres; Sáenz was appointed by Vice-President Manuel Aguilar Bonilla; Rodríguez Aragonez was selected by Orlich after an call (various interviews).

[24] Interview #8.   [25] Interview #6.   [26] Interview #3.   [27] Interview #9.

Table 6.2 *Rural Health Program: Number of Posts and Coverage, 1973–1983*

Year	Number of health posts	Covered population (thousands)	% of rural population covered
1973	50	115	10.3
1975	140	360	30.8
1977	251	650	56.1
1979	287	717	59.7*
1981	294	640	50.9
1983	301	777	57.9

Source: Mata and Rosero (1988)
*Equivalent to 95 percent coverage of the rural dispersed population (those living in communities of 500 people or less).

of social security. According to Casas and Vargas (1980: 269), one of the tasks of the rural centers was to "refer acute and chronically ill patients to the CCSS clinics and hospitals."

The second difference between the Costa Rican program and others was the large pool of resources available. Initially the new program had limited funding and risked becoming the kind of small intervention typical of other Latin American countries. Yet the creation of FODE-SAF in 1974 was a breakthrough that allowed for rapid expansion. Under the leadership of the new Minister of Health, Herman Weinstock, the number of health posts multiplied fivefold from 50 in 1973 to 251 in 1977 and the number of beneficiaries from 115,000 to 650,000 (Table 6.2). In 1976 the program expanded to urban slumps under the name of community health (Minister of Health, 1971; Rosero-Bixby, 1991).

By the late 1970s Costa Rica had become a showcase of "health without wealth" and one of three candidates to host the international conference on health that finally took place in Alma Atta (Litsios, 2002). Between 1972 and 1980, infant mortality decreased by an annual average of 12.9% per year, compared to only 2.3% per year in the previous seventeen years. Costa Rica's success had much to do with how intertwined the program was to the larger health care architecture: 41% of the reduction in infant mortality between 1971 and 1980 resulted from primary care interventions but another 32% can be explained by secondary (curative) services (Rosero-Bixby, 1986).

6.4.3 *Services for the Poor Instead of Transfers to the Insured: the Creation of FODESAF*

The creation of FODESAF was rather convoluted. In January 1973 President Figueres sent to Congress a bill creating family allowances. Following earlier initiatives across the world, the project targeted insured workers who received low wages and had three or more children. By increasing entitlements among the insured but doing nothing for the uninsured, the approval of this initial proposal would have deepened segmented instead of universal outputs.

Yet the law that was enacted almost two years later was radically different. FODESAF became a financially powerful social fund that supported anti-poverty interventions made by a range of state agencies. By funding the poor's incorporation to services everyone else already received, it constituted an affirmative action measure for the economically disadvantaged. In this way, FODESAF became a prominent instrument towards the unification of policy architectures in health care and pensions.

Below we identify the main drivers behind the policy process from the initial design to the enactment of the fund. We give credit to the supporting role of President Daniel Oduber (1974–1978), a formidable politician. However we stress even more the contribution of a group of state experts around Vice-President Carlos Manuel Castillo. We also acknowledge the importance of pressures coming from the architecture, particularly regarding funding needs.

Cash Transfers to Low-Income Insured Workers:
the Initial 1973 Project
The first approach to family allowances was the brainchild of the Minister of Labor, Danilo Jiménez Veiga (CCSS, 1972). As a former ILO official, he conceived social policy as a right directly linked to people's employment status.[28] The bill Jiménez Veiga drafted was attuned with the standard notion of family allowance as a tool to secure a minimum income for working families with dependent children. Cash transfers of this kind had spread in many parts of the world during the first half of the twentieth century: by 1950, more than thirty countries, including Argentina (for public employees), Brazil, Uruguay, and Chile had a family allowance program and "regular

---

[28] Interview #9.

cash payments in respect to family responsibilities ... [had] become a major and probably permanent element in national income security schemes" (Vadakin, 1958: 17).

The bill entered Congress in January 1973 and was passed onto the Commission of Social Affairs. Although the ruling PLN had a Congressional majority, legislative action only took place a year later. Why was not the law put to a vote? For former legislators and policymakers we interviewed, the lack of legislative progress reflected disagreements between President Figueres and Oduber, then president of Congress.[29] Yet this explanation is at best incomplete. Oduber had actually resigned from Congress in March 1973 – two months before the project entered into the Committee – to run for president in the 1974 elections. There is no indication that he was against the broad objectives of the project: Oduber and his inner circle had explicitly recognized the need to complement the labor income of families with children with public transfers.[30]

Instead, the failure of this version of family allowances had more to do with the lack of leadership from state actors. Right after submitting the bill to the Legislative Assembly and in a rather unexpected fashion, the Minister of Labor, Jiménez Veiga, stepped down. His resignation left the bill without the support and political advocacy of any powerful state actor in the Executive or in Congress.

From Traditional Family Allowances to a Revolutionary Social Fund: the 1974 Bill

After Oduber was elected President in February 1974 the project underwent a substantive shift. Benefits were still framed as family allowances, but now added in-kind services to previous cash transfers. Resources – raised by the doubling of payroll taxes – were ring-fenced to anti-poverty programs run by various public institutions (Legislative Assembly, 1973b). Yet this second version of the bill was not put up to a Congressional vote either. Between February and May, the inner circle of the President-elect worked on refining its contents: services were expanded and transfers shrank in response to disturbing malnutrition and rural poverty.[31]

[29] Interview #9 and interview #10.
[30] This shows in the 1968 political manifesto launched by Oduber and other prominent young leaders. "Patio de Agua. Manifiesto Democrático para una Revolución Social," January 6, 1968, available at http://mapasdecostarica.info/edel/Patio_de_Agua.pdf (last accessed March 17, 2015).
[31] Interview #11.

Table 6.3 *Successive Changes in the Law, January 1973–1 December 1974*

Dimension	(1) Initial draft Standard family allowances	(2) Transitional draft Standard family allowances and in-kind transfers	(3) Bill In-kind transfers
Timing	Enters Congress in January 1973	Enters Congress in March 1974	Approved in December 1974
Beneficiaries	Low-income salaried workers insured with children under 18 (mostly urban)	Workers under a minimum wage with children under 18 and people without income	Poor Costa Ricans
Benefits	Monetary transfers	Monetary transfers and services	Services, non-contributory pension (20% of the overall funding) and monetary transfers for workers under minimum wage with children under 18
Funding source	Payroll taxes (7%)	Doubling of payroll taxes (from 7 to 15%)	Increase the payroll tax in 5 percentage points and use of a third of all income from the sale tax
Policy domain	Social insurance (under the CCSS)	Labor (under Labor Ministry)	Social (under Labor Ministry)

The draft presented to the Committee of Social Affairs in May of 1974 was a radical departure from Jiménez Veiga's original idea (see Table 6.3). Recipients were no longer defined as workers but as "poor Costa Ricans" and the fund was conceived as a social instrument rather than as part of labor policy or social insurance. The list of public agencies that would receive funding expanded and the source of funding also changed: many sales taxes were added to complement payroll taxes.[32]

How did the government come up with a program that made such a decisive contribution to the unification of the policy architecture? Presidential preferences are part of the answer: during the campaign, Oduber had seen striking rural poverty. He was a savvy politician aware that dealing with the agrarian poor was crucial to realigning the electoral bases of the PLN. As such, he devoted much of his political capital to tackling malnutrition and improving rural living conditions – including access to land and housing.[33] The family allowance program was a valuable policy instrument to do just that. As Oduber himself put it when he finally signed the law months later, the "social revolution" that had begun in the 1940s included wage-earners exclusively; during his government it was time to give priority to "marginal" groups (*La Nación*, December 6, 1974; *La República*, December 5, 1974).

Yet the final version of the policy, including the definition of whom to include and how, was designed by state actors led by Vice-President-elect and prominent economist Carlos Manuel Castillo. The group included the Ministers of Education, Health, and Labor and the leaders of several autonomous institutions as well as many technical advisers. Doctor Kyra del Castillo was the executive secretary of an internal commission created to discuss the new fund and later one of the leaders behind its implementation.[34] Malnutrition was seen as a priority and interventions to reduce it were considerably expanded.

---

[32] They included the Children's National Agency (Patronato Nacional para la Infancia, PANI) and the National Learning Institute (Instituto Nacional de Aprendizaje, INA). Later the Institute of Land and Colonization (Instituto de Tierras y Colonización, ITCO) and a new nutrition clinic were also included.

[33] Interview #2.

[34] Interview #11. During the signing of the law in December 1974, Oduber also talked about a commission created to explore the issue: there was a "commission formed by Alvaro Jenkins, Danilo Jimenez and doctor Weinstock in the Ministry of Health together with Dr Fernando Guzmán Mata, Dr Kyra del Castillo and other colleagues … They have been studying the problems that we may find in

Other state actors within Oduber's inner circle were also involved in the design of FODESAF. According to a then junior member of the administration, the President's network of advisers and collaborators was "spectacular" and technical knowledge was more valued than in previous administrations. This network was organized in three different groups. The first one included some of the Ministers with high technical expertise, including Vice-President Castillo and the Minister of Health, Weinstock. The second was a "shadow" cabinet with senior advisers like Fernando Naranjo, Federico Vargas, and Rodolfo Quirós – some of whom later became ministers. Finally, there was a younger group of technical advisers such as Luis Libermann, Rodrigo Bolaños, and Luis Fernando Díaz, who collaborated with Kyra del Castillo and Guido Bonilla in the design and implementation of FODESAF.[35]

Many of these key state actors had been trained abroad and had collaborated with international agencies. Vice-President Castillo, for example, worked at the Economic Commission for Latin America and the Caribbean (ECLAC) and in Central American regional institutions. The bill as enacted was more in line with ongoing international debates on social development and basic needs than the initial family allowances proposal, which responded to an older social assistance framework. FODESAF was embedded within the United Nation's call for social development in the 1969 General Assembly and the comprehensive perspective on development approved in 1970. In 1975, ECLAC also advanced an "integrated or human development" proposal for the Latin American region in the Evaluation of Quito (Bielschowsky, 1998). International support came from the Central American Institution of Nutrition (Instituto de Nutrición de Centroamérica y Panamá), which funded several Chilean consultants to advise on the nutrition component of the new fund.[36]

Although state actors may have been the drivers of FODESAF, the policy architecture also played a subtle yet significant role. First, payroll taxes became a key source of funding; without them, it would have been hard to finance the new programs. A proposal to raise income through direct taxes on companies did not go anywhere and sale taxes

implementing the Program of Nutrition and Health in marginal areas." See http://pln.or.cr/daniel/ddani02.htm (accessed September 12, 2012).
[35] Interview #13.   [36] Interview #11.

alone would not have been enough. Relying on payroll taxes made funding progressive as contributions came from the non-poor population.

More importantly, FODESAF's design responded in part to the financial needs of the rural health program – which in turn was a result of the reorganization of social insurance and other health services. Health Minister Weinstock, for example, enthusiastically supported FODESAF because it granted resources to what then became his flagship program (Solano, 2009). Bureaucratic pressures extended to other public agencies, which were incorporated in the bill to channel FODESAF's resources to the poor.[37] Bureaucratic authorities drew on congressional hearings to promote their own participation in the project.[38]

Finally, the program became an opportunity to push for the creation of non-contributory pensions, which the CCSS saw as the last step into the consolidation of a pension system for all. The inclusion of non-contributory pensions under FODESAF was negotiated between Oduber and legislator Rafael Ángel Calderón Fournier – emerging leader of the opposition – previously member of the Caja's board and later President of Costa Rica in the 1990s (see Chapter 7). In 1972, Calderón Fournier had participated in discussions within the Caja on the need to expand pensions to the rural poor. His political initiative to draw on the family allowances' bill to fund non-contributory pensions was shaped by this urge.

State Actors and Veto Management

While the need to pay more attention to the poor was not controversial, the funding of the family allowances program was contested from the start. Jiménez Veiga's initial bill relied exclusively on payroll taxes – even if the transfer would only reach some of the insured. His reasoning was straightforward: the CCSS was capable of collecting payroll taxes effectively and expanding other taxes would have met a stronger opposition. In his own words, "we have considered several

---

[37] This was a double edged sword: it put more pressure on Congress to approve the bill, yet it also altered the initial allocation of resources. For instance, while Oduber and his team agreed that children age 0 to 3 should be the main beneficiaries of nutrition programs, the creation of school dinners advocated by the Ministry of Education reduced available resources for the main target group.

[38] See for example, Álvaro Vindas-CCSS, RNC (V/1137–1138); Padre Alfaro-IMAS, Plan de Lucha contra la Miseria (1129–1132, IV/795–803, 875–884); MEP, comedores escolares (IV/735–744); INA (III/691–697, 707–712) (Legislative Assembly, 1973b).

alternatives ... to fund the program of family allowances, but we have determined that in our country the only secured way is through payroll taxes and through the subsequent administration by the Caja due to the collecting systems already established ... and the experience administrating social insurance" (CCSS, 1972). The bill raised negative reactions, particularly from business, which may explain why it was not submitted to Congress until the beginning of 1973.

When months later the second project entered Congress, business organizations like the Chamber of Industries were pleased with the shift from cash transfers to in-kind services. They argued that this approach would reduce poverty while also expanding private business (*La Nación*, May 25, 1974). An editorial in *La Nación* also echoed the need to provide services rather than transfers (*La Nación*, June 30, 1974: 2).

Business opposition voiced by the Chamber of Commerce concentrated on the expansion of payroll taxes (*La Nación*, June 30, 1974). In Congress its conservative allies had proposed an increase of sales taxes as an alternative to payroll contributions (Legislative Assembly, 1969: 1118).[39] At the end, the government and a large part of the opposition agreed on combining sources: an increase in five percentage points in payroll contributions complemented by sale taxes. This funding mechanism constituted an effective response to those concerned with the costs of payroll hikes on competitiveness and thus helped secure enough legislative support.[40]

As late as November of 1974 business and unions – representing insured workers who would fund but not benefit directly from FODE-SAF – were pushing for a tripartite commission to rework the entire law (*La República*, December 8, 1974). The government responded by speeding up the Congressional process and by incorporating changes that did not significantly alter the law while rejecting all others (Solano, 2009). Meanwhile, and beyond the legislative arena, the PLN's response to unions was forceful: in a paid advertisement in the journal *La Hora*, President Oduber argued that protestors were already enjoying Costa Rica's "social conquests." In his view, trade unions were acting as a privileged interest group and failing to show solidarity with low-income

---

[39] Meanwhile, left parties pushed for the creation of a new corporate income tax as a more progressive alternative (Solano, 2009).

[40] Eventually this formula gave the government more resources than initially planned: over 1 percent of the gross domestic product (GDP) during its first year FODESAF (Trejos, cited in Rovira, 1987).

groups (*La Hora*, 1974a: 3). Soon after the publication of Oduber's letter, a trade union close to the PLN and led by Luis Armando Gutierrez (later PLN deputy) backtracked and published an advertisement supporting the project, thus breaking the alleged workers' unity.[41]

6.5 Conclusion

The reforms presented in this chapter had a positive impact on universal outputs. In terms of access, between 1973 and 1984 health coverage grew by 32 percentage points – twice as much as in the previous decade – and health insurance reached 82 percent of the population. In terms of equity, the elimination of the wage ceiling increased the contribution of high-income groups. In terms of generosity, integration of hospitals into a single institution secured similar services for the whole population. The rural health program also helped reach the scattered population living far away from dispensaries and more complex medical facilities. In terms of quality, additional resources contributed to more investment and thus better services for all. By 1978, the impact of the health care system on the distribution of income was impressive: the poorest 60 percent of the population increased its share of national income by 2.3 percentage points when health care was considered, while the share of the top 10 percent decreased by 1.3 percentage points (Briceño and Méndez, 1982: 66).

In showing how the reforms moved Costa Rica in the right direction, we have relied on a set of counterfactual arguments. For example, the *removal of wage ceilings* could have been accompanied by free medical choice and competition for the insured between private practitioners rather than by expanded public facilities. The former market option was still available and supported by a few legislators in the early 1970s.[42] Such a path would have undermined universal outputs for two reasons. First, it would have fueled a fragmentation of benefits

---

[41] An editorial of the PLN-friendly *La Hora* also criticized the press and "those well-known groups that run the press in this country," and characterized the proposal for a tripartite commission as a stalling mechanism (*La Hora*, December 2, 1974: 4).

[42] Indeed, when the wage ceiling was removed the minority report argued that "a possible alternative is to negotiate an agreement with the medical association so that the private practices of the doctors, with free medical choice by the insured population, cover the deficiencies that the *Caja* infrastructure currently has" (Legislative Assembly, 1969: 310).

among the insured based on their income. Second, free medical choice would have kept the poor and their services in facilities apart from those available to the insured population. Also, hospitals could have theoretically remained under the Ministry of Health or could have been transferred to a state entity other than the social insurance agency, strengthening a two-tier system with distinct hospitals for the poor and non-poor. The fact that these options did not materialize largely reflected the actions of state actors and the influential role of the previous policy architecture.

The Costa Rican experience in the 1970s also has important policy implications, some of which we revisit in Chapter 9. It highlights the importance of complementing social insurance and social assistance, making sure that both are as linked as possible. Costa Rica was able to combine both in a unified manner – something that other countries should try as well. To do so, however, it is important that social assistance adopts broad targeting – based, for example, on regional criteria – and that interventions give the poor access to the same system as everyone else.

Yet the construction of a unified health care service in Costa Rica was not concluded by 1980. The creation of health posts first in rural communities and then in various cities was fundamental to incorporate the poor to state services, including the complex curative services provided by the CCSS. Yet the quality of these health posts was uneven and not everyone had access to the same services. Costa Rica had to rethink the way it provided its health care system, but this became harder after the debt crisis of the early 1980s.

7 | Contradictory Moves under Market Pressures since the 1980s

7.1 Introduction

Maintaining a pro-universal architecture became harder after 1980. Economically, the debt crisis hit Costa Rica earlier than any other Latin American country and abruptly diminished resources for social policy. Politically, the dominance of social democracy weakened: during the late 1980s the Partido Liberación Nacional (National Liberation Party, PLN) moved towards the center as its conservative wing became more influential and the right-of-center Partido Unidad Social-Cristiana won three of the four presidential elections held between 1990 and 2006. Internationally, ideas advocating state downsizing – as reflected by the World Bank-led structural adjustment loans – gained momentum.

Despite these obstacles, Costa Rica's policy architecture has remained relatively stable in terms of eligibility, funding, entitlements, and service provision. In 2013 social insurance was still funded with payroll taxes and spending in health care and pensions represented more than 10 percent of GDP. Solidarity endured: by the mid-2000s, around half of all contributions made by formal workers went to fund health care services for pensioners, independent workers, and poor families (Gottret, Schieber, and Waters, 2008). The top 20 percent of contributors accounted for almost half of the Caja's income (Estado de la Nación, 2005, cited in Sáenz *et al.*, 2011). Most medical facilities have stayed public and Costa Rica still guarantees an open basket defined by the public sector. Moreover, additional reforms during this period further unified the policy architecture: primary care services expanded nationwide and health care and pension insurance for the self-employed became mandatory.

Nevertheless, policy outputs are less universal today than they were two or three decades ago, primarily due to lessening quality and growing inequality in service provision. The outside option – the fifth component of the policy architecture – is largely responsible. The growth of private services and the spread of conflicting dual practices among CCSS doctors have threatened the other four components.

How can we explain the formal stability of four components of the architecture along with the growth of the outside option? The usual suspects of democratic institutions, social mobilization, and partisan ideology lack explanatory power. Policy changes in primary health care actually began under President Calderón Fournier (who otherwise pursued a pro-market policy agenda) and went unchallenged by other conservative administrations. Electoral competition reduced the chances of unpopular reforms, but can hardly explain why some measures entered the policy agenda – i.e. the creation of primary health care – and others did not – i.e. the contracting out of public services.

An influential view in the study of health care argues that the epidemiological and demographic transitions as well as technological breakthroughs increase demand for health care. To meet this growing demand – the argument goes – budgets would need to grow faster than what is politically feasible (see Callahan, 2008; for Costa Rica see Muiser and Vargas, 2012). As a result, waiting lists increase and passive privatization unfolds as "private provision increases to fill the gaps or even displace government services" (Clark, 2011: 5).

Epidemiological and demographic developments have indeed con-tributed to the growth of health spending as a proportion of GDP. Costa Ricans now live longer than they did two decades ago and suffer more from chronic illnesses that are expensive to treat. Yet there is evidence that these changes have not driven the growth of the outside option. First, the share of Costa Ricans over 65 years of age in the total population has not increased particularly fast: it was 5.6 percent in 2010 compared to 3.8 percent three decades before. This is also a smaller proportion than the average of 6.6 percent in Latin America (2009) where the importance of private spending in total health care has actually decreased (CEPAL, 2009; PAHO, 2012). Second, the expansion of the private sector has concentrated in outpatient services (Herrero and Durán, 2001), many of which are not particu-larly costly (e.g. gynecologist tests) or out of the ordinary (e.g. child delivery). The Caja still remains the sole provider of most complex and rare procedures (Martínez Franzoni and Mesa-Lago, 2003).

Third, waiting lists and poor quality affect relatively basic procedures like pap smears and other lab-tests (Clark, 2011).

To account for continuities and changes in Costa Rica's policy architecture, we rely on our state-centered approach while also considering the role of the previous architecture and international ideas. We show that the existence of a state actor with techno-political capacity – including the ability to adapt international ideas to domestic debates – explains the successful adoption of primary health care. The parallel absence of the same state actor contributed to the failure of a market-friendly reform in the management of hospitals and other health care units. In turn, this policy failure was a major factor behind the weakening of state capacity to provide high quality services and to regulate dual practice effectively.

The policy architecture constrained the possibilities for radical change through three channels: cross-class support for social security limited pro-market changes in eligibility, funding, and entitlements; doctors in the public sector were entrenched defenders of public service provision – even if, at the same time, their dual practice was eroding its effectiveness; and a large segment of the Caja's top bureaucracy fought to maintain control of resources and services. The policy architecture also contributed towards the transfer of all primary care facilities from the Ministry of Health to the Caja – in a unification drive similar to the one we discussed in Chapter 6 regarding hospitals.

The chapter is divided into five sections. Section 2 shows the negative effects of the economic crisis of the early 1980s, contrasting it with the positive impact of the economic model on social policy in previous decades. The crisis of the 1980s created bottlenecks in public health provision (e.g. waiting lists, dual practice) that worsened in the 1990s. We also review some of the government's short-term responses, including contradictory measures towards doctors. Section 3 discusses the expansion of primary health care services, which increased coverage, generosity and equity in health provision. Section 4 analyzes the managerial reform and the reasons behind its failure to improve services. Section 5 explores the growth of the outside option, linking it to the weakening of state institutions. Section 6 discusses old-age pensions aside from health care because by the 2000s, this program followed an independent policy process. In pensions, civil society was more active in policy design, but path dependence and the leadership of state actors still explain continuities and changes.

7.2 The Crisis, Short-Term Responses, and Long-Term Economic Change

Between the 1950s and the late 1970s, Costa Rica's economic model supported the expansion of welfare programs.[1] Public employment and incentives for small and medium firms, especially cooperatives, jointly generated a growing number of well-paid jobs. During the 1970s, for example, unemployment was low (5 percent) and informal jobs accounted for only 14 percent of the non-agricultural economic active population (Villasuso, 2008). Real wages grew steadily – e.g. between 1950 and 1979 the minimum wage increased at an annual average rate of 1.9 percent (Sánchez-Ancochea, 2004) – without necessarily affecting profits.

The expansion of formal employment contributed to a steady expansion of payroll tax revenues. As discussed in the previous chapter, in Costa Rica, this income source funded an increasing number of programs, including entitlements not directly related to contributions. Figure 7.1 reports the evolution of payroll tax rates between 1941 and 1980, including their remarkable increase after 1965 when contributions began funding new training and anti-poverty programs.

The growth of payroll taxes supported the expansion of Costa Rica's welfare effort: between 1958 and 1980, social spending as percentage of GDP increased from 7.0 percent to 14.9 percent, driven by the expansion of health, education, and social assistance. Meanwhile, in neighboring countries such as the Dominican Republic and El Salvador, social spending remained below 5 percent of GDP during the whole period.

Unfortunately, Costa Rica's inability to diversify exports away from coffee and bananas along with the rapid increase of imports led to a growing current account deficit: from US$74 million in 1970 to US$664 in 1980.[2] This deficit became unsustainable when global conditions deteriorated: from August 1980 to May 1982, the colon suffered a sharp devaluation of more than 600 percent and short-term foreign

---

[1] The next few paragraphs rely heavily on Martínez Franzoni and Sánchez-Ancochea (2013b).

[2] Unlike countries such as Singapore or Taiwan, and previously, Finland or Sweden, the Central American countries failed to transform human capital into more dynamic comparative advantages. By 1982, Costa Rican coffee and bananas still accounted for 56 percent of all export revenues.

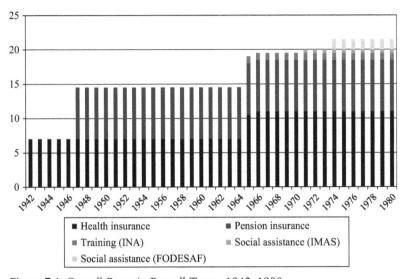

Figure 7.1 Overall Rates in Payroll Taxes, 1942–1980
Source: CCSS and Sistema Costarricense de Información Jurídica

debt grew rapidly (Villasuso, 2008). As a result the economy entered into a deep recession: between 1981 and 1982, real GDP decreased more than 10 percent.

The economic crisis of the 1980s disrupted the previous expansionary trend in social spending. Education outlays as percentage of GDP almost halved during the 1980s (from 6.2 percent to 3.7 percent) with a particular backlash in secondary education. For health care, the crisis could not have come at a worse time: after ten years of the most rapid expansion in coverage, facilities and services since the launching of social insurance in the 1940s (see Chapter 6), spending dramatically dropped – from 8.7 percent of GDP in 1980 to 5.0 percent in 1991 and 4.6 percent in 1995. A legal provision forbidding increases in investment by the CCSS had a negative effect on infrastructure and equipment throughout the 1980s and 1990s.[3] For example, the number of hospital beds per thousand Costa Ricans decreased from 3.3 in 1980 to just 1.8 in 1990. Waiting lists grew and contributed to

[3] Between 1989 and 1997, the Caja savings were above 50 percent of current income compared to the deficits run prior to 1980 (Contraloría General de la República, 1999).

mounting dissatisfaction (Abel-Smith, 1991) –although not to a reduction in overall public support for social insurance.

The Caja responded to the crisis with short-term adjustment measures and pilot experiments in funding and service provision. Under the leadership of the PLN techno-politician Guido Miranda – who was its executive president for eight years – the CCSS explored ways to reduce costs and increase efficiency through private involvement (Zamora and Sáenz, 1995). Firms were encouraged to have a general practitioner in their premises.[4] A mixed medicine program experimented with free medical choice funded with a combination of out-of-pocket spending and social insurance (Miranda, 1988). Also, between 1988 and 1991 outpatient services in three communities were allocated to the cooperatives COOPESALUD, COOPESAIN, and COOPESANA (see Abbreviations).

All these programs fragmented providers and benefits along occupational, income, and geographical lines. Yet they were small, pilot-like initiatives with limited impact on the overall architecture. For example by 1995 mixed medicine reached less than 7 percent of outpatient services (Herrero and Durán, 2001). The scaling up of these measures confronted opposition from the Caja's bureaucracy, which was then fully committed to maintaining the monopoly of the state as service provider.

Changes in doctors' working arrangements ultimately induced more fragmentation than the aforementioned market-friendly experiments. To cut back costs, the Caja eliminated most Saturday services, adding instead two extra hours to the regular working day from Monday to Friday. Institutional inertia reflected in individual and organizational routines prevented the effective use of these additional hours and, as a result, facilities lost an average of ten hours of service per physician per week.[5] Simultaneously, controls over working arrangements relaxed and "by the 1990s, it was possible to see chiefs of services operating mid-morning outside of the Caja."[6]

A doctor's strike in 1982 made matters worse. At the end of his term in office, President Rodrigo Carazo (1978–1982) had committed to a 2,000 colones pay raise – 35 percent higher than for any other public servant.

---

[4] This program had already begun in the 1970s, but during the 1980s there were deliberate efforts to involve more firms.
[5] Interview #9.   [6] Interview #9.

Yet in May 1982 deteriorating economic conditions forced the new government to backtrack from this promise.[7] Medical unions responded with a 42-day strike – the longest in the history of social insurance. The display of power was successful: in December, legal change to medical incentives established automatic increases in doctor's wages to preserve an agreed gap between their wages and those of all other public employees – a gap that still remains today. Unfortunately, medical performance, including the enforcement of working hours and the regulation of dual practices, was never on the table. Overall, the strike and its resolution displayed the doctors' strength and their capacity to protect their autonomy even under a narrower fiscal space.

Over the long run, the economic crisis and the policy reforms that followed also had dramatic consequences (Martínez Franzoni and Sánchez-Ancochea, 2013b). Although unemployment did not increase significantly during the 1990s and 2000s, unprotected, low quality jobs did. By the mid-2000s informal jobs accounted for 35 percent of the working population, compared to slightly over 20 percent in the early 1980s (Martínez Franzoni and Sánchez-Ancochea, 2013b). Because social programs continued to rely heavily on payroll taxes (see Figure 7.2), growing informality had a direct impact on shrinking financial resources for social programs. By 2010, the share of social security contributions in the total wage bill had still not regained its 1985 value, despite increased payroll tax rates (Table 7.1).

It is in this context of limited resources and orthodox stabilization, with a policy architecture expected to do as much as before but with considerably fewer resources that we must place the various reform efforts discussed in the rest of the chapter.[8]

7.3 Deepening Unification at an Odd Time: the Expansion of Primary Health in the 1990s

Despite difficult economic conditions, during the 1990s the establishment of the Basic Comprehensive Health Care Teams (Equipos Básicos

---

[7] Interview #9.
[8] The politics of austerity exacerbated these problems even more. For example, in August 1990, soon after starting his presidential mandate, President Rafael Angel Calderón Fournier (1990–1994) asked the Caja to implement cutbacks for 650 million colones as part of a 2 billion austerity plan.

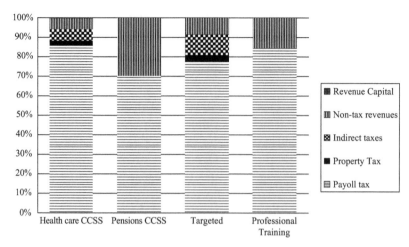

Figure 7.2 Social Policy Regime: Funding Source by Policy as Percentages, 2004
Source: Castro Méndez and Martínez Franzoni (2010)

de Atención Integral en Salud, EBAIS) improved coverage, generosity, and equity in health care. All across the country, each EBAIS brought together a team of doctors, nurses, and health technicians to serve 4,000 people (de Bertodano, 2003).[9] Their impact was significant, particularly in poor areas where the program first started. A study by Rosero-Bixby (2004: 1279) showed that, "the proportion with inadequate access [to outpatient services] dropped from 22% in 1994 to 13% in the year 2000."

The implementation of such an ambitious program is puzzling in the context of international pressures towards market-friendly reforms. In social policy, the international financial institutions (IFIs) sought to control costs, reduce what they saw as excessive benefits for the middle class, and expand private competition. Following the Chilean model and health economics, the World Bank promoted the creation of private health insurance as well as new management practices in public facilities – such as the separation between financing, purchasing, and provision of services (Clark, 2002; Rodríguez, 2005). In primary care, the World Bank supported the implementation of "essential services"

---

[9] Nationwide, the EBAIS were organized in ninety health areas, each of which had ten of these teams.

Table 7.1 *Costa Rica: Wages and Contributions to Social Policy Among Formal Workers, 1985–2008, Monthly Colones*

Year	Average wages	Payroll contributions	Contribution a (% average wages)
1985	197,117.9	19,854.5	10.07
1986	207,715.4	21,295.9	10.25
1987	195,203.0	16,247.4	8.32
1988	194,998.6	15,956.4	8.18
1989	202,381.2	16,951.7	8.38
1990	209,004.9	17,467.4	8.36
1991	202,603.8	17,315.3	8.55
1992	212,299.9	18,018.9	8.49
1993	227,983.4	19,732.2	8.66
1994	239,235.4	21,238.0	8.88
1995	234,502.0	21,113.0	9.00
1996	239,247.7	21,484.2	8.98
1997	235,824.0	21,002.3	8.91
1998	241,574.6	21,778.7	9.02
1999	261,101.4	23,850.5	9.13
2000	263,955.8	24,031.4	9.10
2001	234,237.4	21,568.8	9.21
2002	237,805.6	22,520.7	9.47
2003	239,210.6	22,963.6	9.60
2004	241,507.5	23,359.6	9.67
2005	234,234.1	22,714.0	9.70
2006	244,290.5	23,833.1	9.76
2007	252,238.8	24,729.9	9.80
2008	259,528.5	26,417.3	10.18

Source: own calculations with Central Bank Data

restricted to pregnancy-related care, family planning, control of tuberculosis, sexually transmitted diseases, and care of common serious illnesses among children (World Bank, 1993).

The key explanation of this puzzle lies in the existence of a small group of state actors who were committed to improving the model of primary care first implemented during the 1970s. Working within a World Bank-funded unit at the CCSS, they designed an ambitious proposal to be funded with international lending (Clark, 2002). The team was led by Álvaro Salas, then director of technical services of the

Caja, but the upgrading of primary health was the brainchild of Fernando Marín (Clark, 2002). Formerly a public servant at the Department of Technical Health Care Services (Dirección de Servicios Técnicos de Salud), he acted as a national consultant. He was supported by a group of techno-bureaucrats with ties to the main political parties including Xinia Carvajal from the Ministry of Health, Ana Guzmán and Norma Ayala from the Caja, and Jorge Fonseca from the Ministry of Planning.[10]

Policy design built on previous domestic experiences, including the Rural and Community Health Program (see Chapter 6) and the primary care units run by COOPESAIN, one of the medical cooperatives sub-contracted by the CCSS and which Marín had led. The group also selectively adopted international ideas. During 1992 they examined the Chilean, Cuban, British, and Swedish experiences, drawing on lessons from their primary health care models. Much like in the 1940s but based on a broader set of international examples, the Costa Rican team picked and chose specific dimensions from each case. This included the per capita allocation of resources from the British National Health Service (NHS) and the organization of primary care from the Cuban and Swedish experiences (Martínez Franzoni, 1999). These examples helped build an argument against the World Bank's minimalist version of primary care services and demonstrate the financial feasibility of a more generous approach.[11] The team also engaged critically with the Chilean model to argue against a market-driven health care system.

The World Bank rejected some of the measures the Costa Rican team put on the table. In particular, the Bank argued that the EBAIS should only include nurses and primary care assistants. The Costa Rican team responded that the country was in the midst of an epidemiological transition that made access to general practitioners (GPs) and specialists particularly important. Their claim was as much about public legitimacy as about service delivery: Costa Ricans would only deem services adequate if doctors were involved. The group of state actors also sought to persuade the World Bank that the EBAIS would improve efficiency by reducing the demand for more expensive curative services. Ultimately World Bank officials gave in: they saw Costa Rica as a low-cost laboratory for policy reform (Martínez Franzoni, 1999)

---

[10] Interview #14.   [11] Interview #14.

and were, in any case, more interested in reforming hospitals than in primary health care (Clark, 2002).

The pre-existing architecture contributed to several of the unifying features of the reform. In the process of creating the EBAIS, all existing primary health care facilities with its 1,600 workers were transferred from the Ministry of Health to the CCSS. Although other alternatives would have been theoretically possible (e.g. a regional division of labor between agencies or a functional split with primary units under the Ministry of Health and clinics and hospitals under the CCSS), they were more problematic for equity among regions and coordination between levels. These options were also constrained by the architecture. The Caja was now even more dominant than it was in the 1970s: it had more political influence and was in a much better position to absorb services than was the Ministry of Health.[12] According to Clark (2002: 8), "the transfer [to the CCSS] was critical for supplying sufficient resources for the EBAIS to work." Doctors from the Ministry of Health received higher benefits upon moving to the Caja and thus had no incentives to veto the transfer (Rodríguez, 2005).

The policy architecture also influenced decisions regarding funding: after the startup support from the World Bank loan (Legislative Assembly, 1994), new facilities were to be supported by payroll taxes and transfers from FODESAF. Not only did the reliance on payroll contributions contradict prevailing pro-market ideas but other options – including co-payments – were theoretically available. However, implementing co-payments or expanding indirect taxes was significantly harder than relying on well-managed payroll taxes – Costa Rica's traditional funding option.

In contrast, social actors played a small role in the creation of primary health care. This reform was not at the top of the socio-political agenda in the early 1990s and there were not major demands for an overhaul of the system. Trade unions and medical personnel were only informed after the overall design had been settled (Clark, 2002). At that point, trade unions challenged some of the

---

[12] In addition, international ideas in the context of market-friendly reforms emphasized the role of the ministries of health as regulators and supervisors while deterring their direct involvement in services (World Bank, 1993). These ideas had a direct influence in Costa Rica's transformation (Gobierno de Costa Rica, 1992).

components – e.g. the Colegio de Médicos regarded EBAIS as basic public health units – but failed to slow down the adoption and implementation of the measures.

Political ideology was not influential in the design phase and only played a marginal role during implementation. The reform was drafted under the Calderón Fournier administration, which was more interested in reducing government spending than in adopting progressive changes. Implementation started in 1994 just when a new administration took office. Led by José María Figueres Olsen (1994–1998), son of the founder of the PLN, Pepe Figueres, the new government made the expansion of EBAIS part and parcel of its political platform (Partido Liberación Nacional, 1993: 19–20). Figueres Olsen's most important role was to create space for technical actors: he promoted key members of the initial health care team into leadership positions. Fernando Marín was appointed vice-minister of Health and Alvaro Salas executive president of the Caja Figueres. Olsen also named Herman Weinstock – a doctor committed to a unified health care system as we showed in Chapter 6 – as Minister of Health.

These techno-politicians set the expansion of primary health care as their main task, starting with scattered rural communities, where access was most lacking. Coverage increased rapidly, from 36 percent of the population in 1995 to 69 percent in 2000. By 2005 basically every resident in Costa Rica had access to new primary health care services (Cercone and Pacheco Jiménez, 2008).

An intelligent and quick expansion of services, which carefully balanced technical needs and political expediency, contributed to the consolidation of the program even after the election of a less sympathetic president in 1998. The conservative Miguel Angel Rodríguez replaced the team in charge of the modernization process soon after being elected and slowed down the expansion of primary care units (Contraloría General de la República, 1999). Yet his administration could not reverse a program that was well underway.

7.4 Managerial Transformations: a Failed Attempt to Implement New Public Management

The same World Bank loan that funded the creation of the EBAIS supported the managerial transformation of public facilities, including hospitals where about 60 percent of the budget was allocated

(Rodríguez, 2005). This second reform was from the onset the priority for the IFIs. In particular, the World Bank proposed measures to improve planning capacity (i.e. generation of standardized information regarding health care demands) and manage services more effectively (i.e. resources associated to performance and needs rather than historical budgeting). Informed by health economics, the objective was to reduce transaction costs between principals (the central administration) and agents (hospitals and other health care facilities) (Andersen Consulting, 1996; Sojo, 1998) and to expand the autonomy of the latter. The plan also included pilot experiments with alternative managerial models such as contracting out, mixed medicine, free medical choice, and cooperatives (Legislative Assembly, 1994; World Bank, 1993).

On paper, the impact of these proposals on universalism was uncertain.[13] By redistributing resources to those units most in need, moving away from historical budgets, and reducing waiting lists, the reform could improve generosity (particularly quality) and equity.[14] By delivering managerial efficiency, the changes could indirectly contribute to reducing dual practices too. Yet if private delivery and fragmented health care provision increased, as implied in the initial piloting of alternative managerial models, the impact could be heterogeneous upon generosity and negative upon equity.

In practice, the reform had disappointing results. A process of deconcentration of hospitals and other facilities did take place.[15] Initially, a series of performance agreements (compromisos de gestión) were signed with seven hospitals. A Hospital Deconcentration Bill (Ley de Desconcentración Hospitalaria) approved in 1998 with bipartisan support gave legal status to this process, formally transferring prerogatives over budgets, personnel, and purchases to the hospitals.[16] The

---

[13] See financial component of the Loan Document, Law 7441, Part C, pp. 35–38 (Legislative Assembly, 1994).

[14] In Costa Rica, funding per capita was sixty times higher in some regions than others without any objective reason. The use of historical criteria to allocate resources perpetuated unfair inequalities and resulted in large inefficiencies (Cercone and Pacheco Jiménez, 2008).

[15] For deconcentration, we mean "the redistribution of management power and responsibilities from the central administration toward the units directly providing medical services within the same national institution" (Clark, 2002: 13).

[16] The law also created community councils (Juntas de Salud) to oversee the work of large hospitals and increase community involvement in decision making (Clark, 2002). The community councils were never particularly successful and

agreements between providers and headquarters were supposed to improve coordination and help allocate resources based on evidence-based criteria (de Bertodano, 2003).

Unfortunately administrative and financial autonomy was granted without an effective central coordination. Therefore, the primary goal of aligning health care demands with the allocation of resources was not accomplished. Instead, discretionary decision making and the duplication of support units (e.g. statistics, legal advice) spread across all levels of the social insurance agency. With the deconcentration of purchases, the Caja also lost economies of scale: as documented by public auditing agencies, health care facilities began making their own purchases, often over the counter and at much higher prices than before (see Martínez Franzoni and Mesa-Lago, 2003). The growing dispersion of power within the CCSS also created more opportunities for corruption and conflicting public–private relations.

How can we explain the failure of the managerial reform? Political preferences do not seem particularly helpful: between 1990 and 2002 governments of different persuasions supported the changes.[17] Instead, we need to consider the role played by state actors and learn from comparisons with their role in primary health care.

Rather than led by techno-political cadres, the design and initial implementation of the managerial reform was in the hands of an outsider expert, James Cercone. He was a well-prepared and technically savvy health economist at a time when health economics was used to legitimize reforms (Markoff and Montecinos, 1993). Yet he was hardly involved in partisan politics and apparently lacked the political leverage held by Fernando Marín – who had access to top leaders in the PLN and close ties to techno-political actors in the Ministries of Finance and Planning.

Also, unlike the case of primary care, recommendations drawn heavily on foreign expertise were not grounded on bureaucratic agreements. The initial ideas Costa Rica put on the table during negotiations were in fact rather raw. As an active participant of the reform process

by 2009 only 15,000 people participated in the election of its members out of a total eligible population of 1.7 million (Clark, 2010).

[17] President Figueres Olsen – who was more interested in primary health care (Interview #15) – was less supportive than the previous and subsequent conservative administrations. Nevertheless, a key component of the reform was approved during his administration.

told us: "the only component that was ready for implementation when the World Bank lent the money was a reformed primary health care model, precisely because the country had already advanced in proposals and reflections. All the other reforms [like the management reform] had to be designed when the execution of the loan begun."[18] Not surprisingly, half of the loan was devoted to hire international experts (Contraloría General de la República, 1999). The foreign consultancy Andersen Consulting – selected in a bidding process – played an active role in designing the reform based on Spain.[19]

While in primary health all techno-political efforts were geared towards a single goal (Rodríguez, 2005), the managerial reform suffered from conflicting views. For some people within the implementation team, the changes were first steps towards the promotion of public–private competition. In fact, performance agreements were supposed to open some twenty procedures to the private sector.[20] Others saw the reform as a way to discipline doctors and increase public efficiency without private involvement. Doctor Julieta Rodríguez, the Medical manager of the Caja during the PLN administration (1994–1998), for example, maintained that "if you go to any private clinic at 10 in the morning, there are colleagues that should be in the hospitals. For this reason, contract agreements turn hospitals into firms which, as such, cannot afford to do without half their assembly line" (*La Nación*, March 29, 1998). Rodríguez was skeptical of private provision: the purchasing of services "is a valid option, but one must be careful not to feed into vicious practices and corruption. The problem is that most of those who would sell services to the Caja, [actually] work at the Caja … It is necessary to produce as much as possible with the available resources and only purchase services to meet the unsatisfied demand" (*La Nación*, April 27, 1998).[21]

The lack of coherent leadership carried over to a second implementation phase. After the 1998 elections, Rodolfo Piza, a lawyer with ambassadorial experience but no knowledge or prior contact with social security, became Executive Director of the CCSS.[22] Within the

---

[18] Interview #14.   [19] Interview #15.   [20] Interview #15.
[21] Ana Sojo, an ECLAC officer close to the techno-political group in the Olsen administration, presents a similar pro-state view in a 1998 document (Sojo, 1998).
[22] See www.rodolfopizapresidente.com/index.php/rodolfo-piza/biografia (last accessed 12 August 2014).

new team – which did not include any of the previous reform leaders – there were no techno-politicians capable of driving the process, coordinate transformations that cut across different managerial departments, and build the bureaucratic support needed to implement change.

This lack of coherence was also evident among top bureaucrats. In public appearances in 2001, the director of the recently created Modernization Department was optimistic about the reform progress and stressed that the CCSS was moving towards a mixed – public and private – provision of services (see also Rodríguez, 2005). Almost at the same time, René Escalante, director of the Administrative Department, was concerned with the large number of performance agreements the CCSS was signing without the implementation of complementary strategic plans (Escalante 2001b in Martínez Franzoni and Mesa-Lago, 2003). Changes underway involved a myriad of contradictory measures. For example, performance agreements were defined between the Administrative Department and each health unit yet excluded the Medical Department – then in charge of the strategic organization of the health care network (Rodríguez, 2005).

A sudden flush of resources – not just from the World Bank but also from Spanish and Finish loans – contributed to bureaucratic expansion and dispersion. In 1994 an autonomous unit within the Caja began managing foreign loans. This unit later became the Modernization Department, an almost parallel institution (*La Nación*, July 8, 2004) responsible for managing foreign loans for US$170 million.[23] Right after a major corruption scandal broke within the Caja, the Modernization Department was split into Logistics – with an investment budget of US$87 million – and Infrastructure and Technology.

The pre-existing policy architecture also shaped the reform and helps explain its ultimate failure. The existence of a strong body of doctors almost all of whom worked for the Caja was particularly important. They resented that the "modernization" process lacked consultation – they were never informed about the negotiations with the World Bank (Clark, 2005) – and prioritized economic and administrative criteria over medical concerns. During the whole process, one of

---

[23] In addition there was US$40 million for building the new hospital in Alajuela; a World Bank loan for US$22 million, and the first part of a loan by the Central American Bank for Economic Integration for US$27.5 million.

their main concerns was the potential privatization of health care provision through contracting out. Public opinion was also against privatization: during the 1990s and early 2000s, an average of 70 percent of the population opposed the privatization of social insurance (Poltronieri, 2011). As late as 2011, 85 percent of the population preferred the CCSS to out-of-pocket services (*La Nación*, October 10, 2011).

At the same time as they protected the Caja as service provider, doctors revolted against any attempt to reduce their autonomy, constrain dual practice or regulate labor conditions. According to Clark (2002: 15), "the unions have steadfastly resisted any attempt to tie the salaries of medical personnel to performance indicators ... Hospital and clinic directors are also not able to force changes in working conditions previously negotiated (i.e. schedules) and so rely on new hires to work unpopular shifts."

The Caja's attempt to put an end to dual practice during working hours in Punta Arenas in the late 1990s had resulted in a massive medical strike. Years later, in 2003, the National Medical Union protested vociferously against a Caja campaign – involving private investigators – to reduce illegal and irregular practices like the *biombos* and mismanagement of waiting lists (*La Nación*, July 25, 2003).[24] The board of directors reversed course immediately (Clark, 2005).

This contradictory role of doctors – a central actor within the pre-existing policy architecture – deserves attention for several reasons. First, the Costa Rican experience highlights that interest groups can have opposite roles in policy reforms. By protecting on-going programs, doctors, trade unions, and public servants can prevent market-friendly, unequal measures. Yet by the same token, they may also become rent-seekers and contribute to the fragmentation of health delivery.[25]

In summary, the managerial reform contributed to fragmentation and weakened the delivery of universal outputs. Yet this was not caused by an ideological-driven process of privatization or by the expansion of competition among public units, but by the incoherence and disorganization of decision making in headquarters and health

---

[24] "*Biombos*" is a colloquial way of referring to a private, out-of-pocket use of public facilities.

[25] Given the need to confront doctors' rent-seeking behavior and secure a more effective reform, techno-political leadership was particularly damaging.

care facilities alike. Following managerial changes, doctors expanded their capacity to handle their own waiting lists and resources granted to hospitals were never linked to needs or results. Higher fragmentation in headquarters ended up with growing dual practice, lower quality of services, and increasing participation of private interests in purchase – a combined growth of outside options that we now discuss.

7.5 The Growth of Outside Options and their Implications for Universal Outputs

The contracting out of specific services initiated in the 1980s and the failure of the management reform of the 1990s weakened state capacities. In our view, this – more than any other factor such as technological innovations or political preferences – drove the growth of the outside option. Both private provision of services and the use of the public sector for private gain increased significantly. They reinforced each other: the growth of private providers increased the opportunities for doctors to develop dual practices, which further weakened state capacity and expanded demand for private services. The result was a vicious cycle that has undermined universal outputs. In elaborating this argument we had limited data regarding the behavior of doctors, a problem that transcends Costa Rica (Hanson and Berman, 1998).

7.5.1 The Expansion of Private Provision

In 1980, there were only three private clinics, which just focused on outpatient services and birth delivery: the Bíblica (founded in 1929), the Católica (1963), and the Santa Rita (1965). Since then, three large hospitals have been created (Santa María in 1989, Centro Internacional de Medicina [CIMA] in 2000, and Metropolitano in 2008) and the pre-existing ones have expanded their activities to new inpatient services. Some of the private hospitals created branches outside San Jose and the Central Valley and three hospitals and three clinics were accredited by the United States for medical tourism (Muiser and Vargas, 2012).

Spending figures reflect the expanded influence of private provision. Between 1991 and 2001, private spending grew rapidly (see Chapter 4). In the last decade, the expansion of private options continued with the share of out-of-pocket disbursements going from 21.4 percent in

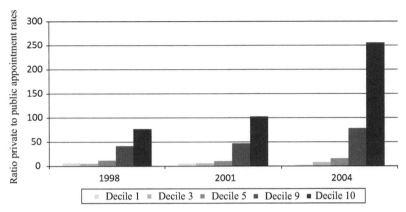

Figure 7.3 Appointments in Private and Public Sector by Income Decile, 1998–2004

Source: Based on household survey data in Rodriguez y Castillo, 2009

2000 to 31.1 percent in 2010 (WHO, 2012). Although still small, the supply of private insurance has expanded rapidly as well (Muiser and Vargas, 2012).

The upper middle class and the wealthy have been the primary drivers of the growing demand for private services. Almost 60 percent of all private health care spending in the early 2000s came from the wealthiest 25 percent of the population (Picado, Acuña, and Santacruz, 2003). Regarding appointments, Figure 7.3 offers data on their distribution between the private and public sectors. By 2004, the top decile stood out as the only one using outpatient private services more than public ones.[26]

The expansion of private providers has been a response to the economic crisis (see Section 2) and to the state's growing inability to provide quality services (Section 4).[27] According to PAHO, in 2001 three-quarters of public hospitals had at least one specialty with more than three months of waiting list (Connolly, 2002) and the situation has not improved

---

[26] Other social groups are starting to use private services as well. In fact, according to a survey from the University of Costa Rica, more than 65 percent of Costa Ricans were forced to pay for private services at some point. See www.ucr.ac.cr/noticias/2011/11/11/encuesta-de-opinion-publica-2011.html (last accessed 3 June 2015).

[27] Growing income inequality has likely contributed to the growth of private health care as well.

significantly in recent years (Carrillo *et al.*, 2011; Clark, 2010). Not surprisingly, Costa Ricans are increasingly dissatisfied with the state of hospitals: in 2007, 74 percent believed that hospitals were not being modernized, compared to only 36 percent in 2003 (Poltronieri, 2011). Public spending has been too focused on personnel and, as a result, infrastructure and equipment is lacking: for example, between 2000 and 2006 payroll-related spending increased from 54 percent to 62 percent of total spending (Carrillo *et al.*, 2011), while most renovations in infrastructure lagged behind four decades (Rodríguez, 2005). There are also many cases of poor management decisions in the context of weakening state capacity. For example, during the 1990s oncologists and the PAHO advised the CCSS to purchase magnetic resonance equipment (Jaramillo, 2013). Instead, in 2001 two private clinics purchased their own equipment and started selling services to the Caja. Within a few years the outsourcing bill was several times higher than the price of the equipment.

Private providers have also benefited from the growth of private medical education. While the training of specialists still takes place at the public University of Costa Rica, the number of higher education institutions teaching health-related disciplines (from general medicine to physiotherapy) has increased rapidly. Between 1990 and 1995 the number of new doctors more than doubled but the Caja lacked enough positions to hire them all (Cercone and Pacheco Jiménez, 2008). Paradoxically, professional bodies have at the same time acted as gatekeepers, preventing the entry of new doctors to selected specialties like anesthesiology.

7.5.2 *The Growth of Dual Practices*

Since the inception of the CCSS, some doctors worked simultaneously in the public and private sectors. Until the economic crisis of the 1980s, however, this dual practice was highly restricted (Martínez Franzoni and Mesa-Lago, 2003), but by 1997 a third of all doctors working for the Caja also practiced outside (Ickis, Sevilla, and Iñiguez, 1997, cited in Clark, 2005: 108).

Conflicting dual practice takes place when public professionals work less than required or act strategically to maximize private gains. In recent years, there have been two drivers behind the expansion of this behavior: decisions from the social insurance agency and broader changes in the demands and opportunities doctors face. The lack of any kind of regulation of dual practices has made things even more problematic.

The contracting out of state personnel is a case of conflicting dual practice directly encouraged by the CCSS. For example, when in 1998 the Caja had to deal with a four-month waiting list in pathological exams for cancer diagnosis, it began sub-contracting its own laboratory personnel after hours, at a higher rate than during regular hours. The idea was to complete 4,000 biopsies (Cambronero, Larios, and Muñoz, 2001), but, in practice, the decision generated perverse incentives. By 1999 the need for contracting out had actually increased and amounted to US$100,000, split among a few individuals. Overtime spending has increased across the board in recent years: by 2011, 16 percent of all spending in personnel went to overtime and a special commission for the reform of social security recommended to eliminate it as "a regular payment mechanism" (Carillo *et al.*, 2011: 20).

There are few publicly available examples of dual practices generated by doctors, partly because they result from illegal behavior. Yet the literature discusses different types and offers some remarkable illustrations (Clark, 2010; Martínez Franzoni and Mesa-Lago, 2003). In some instances, doctors may charge patients to jump positions in the waiting list. For example, there are examples of cancer patients being forced to choose between waiting five months for their surgery or paying US$3,000 to receive immediate treatment by the same specialist in charge of waiting lists. In other cases, physicians refer patients from social insurance to their private practice or to private companies in which they have vested interests. In 1997, for example, a legislative commission denounced that a US firm had invested in high-tech medical equipment for cancer treatment and strategically located its facilities at equal distance between three major Costa Rican hospitals. Caja physicians were invited to invest in the business and receive payments per referral. The initiative involved a former Minister of Health – at the time member of the health insurance board – as well as 350 doctors (Cambronero *et al.*, 2001).

Finally, there are cases of doctors using public facilities to treat private patients. Physicians have been known to deliver the babies of their fee-paying private patients in public hospitals. In 2014, the *New York Times* reported that two specialists used public equipment to transplant organs of private patients (*New York Times*, August 17,

2014). Across the board, specialists benefit from working in both settings: they receive a secure wage and benefit from access to expensive equipment in public facilities, while making profits in their private practice. All this behavior has been facilitated by the disorganization of the Caja – resulting from the way management reforms were implemented (see Section 4) – and doctors' growing autonomy.

7.5.3 The Outside Option and its Growing Role in Shaping Political Trajectories

An expanded dual practice has blurred the boundaries between the public and private sectors, and contributed to unmet timetables and weakened public performance (Socha, 2010). Overpriced medical inputs, purchases of non-essential services and waiting lists that go well beyond supply shortages are some examples of the conflicts of interest that currently undermine universalism. The expansion of the outside option will likely have negative consequences for universalism in the long run as well. The growing number of doctors with vested interests in private practice and of private hospitals is creating a powerful coalition against the current policy architecture. For the first time since the late 1940s, a political actor capable of advancing an alternative agenda based on active private involvement has emerged. This was evident in 2013 when representatives of this group met publicly to discuss the future of health care in a forum hosted by the private University of Medical Science (Universidad de Ciencias Médicas, UCIMED). Table 7.2 compares the current architecture to the proposals at that meeting.

Their recommendations would primarily affect benefits and providers with an implication on out-of-pocket funding as well. In the case of benefits, the UCIMED-sponsored group proposed to create a closed basket of services. Setting a dividing line between included and excluded services would lead to charges for the latter. In the case of providers, the emergent political actor proposed to move to a mixed system.

This announcement is a clear demonstration of our main argument: changes in the policy architecture do not only affect universal outputs directly, but also through changes in the landscape of influential actors. At present, in Costa Rica the process is conspiring against universalism: the initial growth of the outside option has strengthened

Table 7.2 *Policy Architecture: Existing and Proposed by Private Actors*

Dimensions	Current	Proposed
(1) What criteria makes people eligible?	Insured (mandatory workers, family or poor)	Unchanged
(2) Who pays and how?	Tripartite contributions and social assistance	Unchanged (plus co-payments of excluded services; see 3)
(3) Who defines the benefits and how?	State; all services	Negotiated; defined services as it is not possible to give everything to everybody
(4) Who/where is care provided?	Public facilities for all	Mixed, with public and private
(5) Management of an outside (market) option?	Outside option is growing and unregulated	Unchanged

Source: based on UCIMED (2013).

private actors (and doctors with vested interests in both the public and private sectors) who now pressure for further fragmentation, particularly regarding service provision. Further steps against the unification of the architecture are likely to follow, including out-of-pocket co-payments to complement social insurance fees, free choice of service providers, and the replacement of centralized allocation of social insurance for fees that go directly to providers.

7.6 Pensions as a Shadow Case

In pensions, the international consensus in favor of privatization was stronger than in health care.[28] The World Bank, in particular, made a global push for the reduction of state direct provision, the growth in contributions, and the gradual replacement of collective savings for individual ones (Demirguc-Kunt and Scharwz, 1995). By expanding

---

[28] By 2005, ten out of eighteen Latin American governments have implemented some form of pension privatization (Brooks, 2011). The pro-market blueprint was condensed in a World Bank Report, *Averting the Old Age Crisis: Policies to Protect the Old and Promote Growth*, published in 1994.

private options and leaving the state responsible for the poor alone, these recommendations affected generosity and equity in provision.

Costa Rica was not immune to these pressures. A second pillar based on individual savings for salaried workers was created in 2000. The measure increased fragmentation in benefits between salaried workers and the self-employed (who cannot participate in this pillar) and opened the door for the private sector to compete in the administration of individual funds.

Despite this market-friendly innovation, most other components of the policy architecture have remained relatively stable, and several reforms have actually contributed to deepen unification.[29] For example, the mandatory incorporation of the self-employed based on a combination of payroll taxes and public subsidies expanded eligibility. These subsidies are progressive: the higher the skill level of the worker, the higher their contribution and the smaller the state subsidy as a percentage of their salary. The reforms have also expanded eligibility by creating opportunities to access a pension even without making contributions for the required thirty years – a change that has been particularly beneficial for women. Last but not least, the size of non-contributory pensions has also increased significantly.

Explaining the lack of radical reforms and the contradictory effects of different changes through party politics is not easy. As discussed in previous sections, in the last two decades electoral alternation between center-left and right-wing (market-friendly) parties has been the norm. Some reforms to pensions were initially designed under one government and negotiated and implemented under a different one. Moreover, given the new international policy environment and the rightward move of Costa Rica's political system, more radical changes should have taken place.

To account for continuities and changes we instead show that state actors searched for feasible adaptations to changing economic and international conditions. Their options were always constrained by the previous policy architecture: for example, the privatization of the first pillar or the exclusive involvement of the private sector in the second pillar was simply out of the question.

---

[29] The first step towards unification after the crisis of the 1980s took place in 1992 when a myriad of tax-funded pension regimes for a select group of public servants – all of which were subsidized by the national budget – were shut down.

In this way, our shadow case generally confirms our previous findings with just one difference. Pension reform during this period is the only case in the seven decades we have considered in which organized civil society actors, primarily trade unions and businesses, but also cooperatives and women's organizations, played an active role in policy design. Their participation took place under a National Pact (Concertación Nacional, CN) called by the government in 1998; in the discussion of the subsequent law in Congress, and again in 2004–2005. These groups pushed for the maintenance of collective arrangements and the promotion of state participation in the policy architecture. They also advocated measures that strengthened the unification of the collective pillar.

7.6.1 *The Blueprint for Reform, 1996–1998*

Since the early 1990s issue framing focused on the contradictory needs to confront fiscal shortcomings and expand access, particularly among self-employed workers. The World Bank provided a loan that assisted in redesigning the system and played a key role in bridging domestic and international debates.

Like in the rest of the world, in its discussions with Costa Rican authorities during the Figueres Olsen administration, the World Bank advocated the creation of a multi-pillar system with a first pillar for the poor and mandatory individual savings for the non-poor. The World Bank's recommendations clashed with the views of a group of experts around Vice-President Rebeca Grynspan – a leading techno-political actor in this matter. Costa Ricans pushed for a first pillar, conceived as a contributory component of the system and not as a targeted one. During 1994 relations with the World Bank were strained but eventually the Bank agreed to explore different policy alternatives.[30]

The design of the reforms involved a small group of experts from the Vice-President's inner circle and from key public institutions such as the Pensions Supervision Agency (Superintendencia de Pensiones, SUPEN) and the Ministry of Labor. The CCSS was involved but with a much smaller role than in health care. The group was led in their day-to-day work by techno-politician Adolfo Rodríguez – a heterodox

---

[30] Interviews #16 and #10.

economist with a PhD from Belgium and a long-term association with the Minister of Finance (Fernando Herrero), the Minister of Planning (Leonardo Garnier), and Vice-President Grynspan.[31] Supported by funding from the World Bank, Rodriguez's team worked behind closed doors, pulling resources – information, knowledge, and contacts – from the various agencies to which they belonged. They also benefited from international expert advice from Rodolfo Saldain, former director of the Uruguayan social insurance agency.[32]

This techno-political group prepared several documents and policy recommendations and eventually delineated the basic blueprint of a multi-pillar system. It included an expanded first pillar with mandatory insurance for the self-employed, a second pillar based on individual contributions, and a more generous non-contributory pillar for the non-insured and elderly poor.[33] This proposal was in line with the approach of the ILO, which by the mid-1990s advocated a strong contributive collective saving pillar within a multi-pillar system.

In making their proposal, the team around Vice-President Grynspan was well aware of the constraints and limitations imposed by the previous architecture. The group went out of its way to protect the first pillar and prevent an increase in contributions or a reduction in entitlements – all measures that would have been unpopular for the cross-class alliance of insured workers. They also focused on expanding coverage among the self-employed as a means to increase the contributory base of the system. The amount of available options was also limited by the influence of the Caja, which opposed market-based options.

The proposal elaborated by the group under Grynspan's political leadership did not make it immediately to Congress. Yet its effects were long lasting: with few changes – mostly related to non-judicial mechanisms to enforce compliance with mandatory insurance – it became the blueprint for the 2000 Workers' Protection Law (Ley de Protección

---

[31] In addition to Adolfo Rodríguez, this group included Olivier Castro (head of the SUPEN), Irma García (expert, Ministry of Finance), Eugenio Solano (Ministry of Labor), and Fabio Durán (actuary CCSS).
[32] See www.saldain.com/equipo/rodolfo-saldain (last accessed March 19, 2015).
[33] To this initial blueprint unions would later add a set of measures that helped reduce evasion and underreported wages.

al Trabajor, LPT) and also informed the parametric changes in the collective pillar approved in 2005.

7.6.2 The Implementation of the Blueprint, 1998–1999

Having won the national elections by a very small margin, the Rodríguez administration was initially concerned with securing social support for its ambitious pro-market reform agenda. To this purpose, the new government invited civil society actors to the National Pact, particularly to discuss the liberalization of electricity and telecommunications.[34] Because pensions faced funding shortages and a proposal for reform had already been fleshed out, the administration included pensions as well.

Ronulfo Jiménez, a well-known liberal economist from the Academia Centroamericana (the most prominent neoliberal think tank in the country), was appointed to lead the negotiations on pensions. Jiménez placed the proposal elaborated by the Grynspan team between two alternative scenarios that were clearly less desirable. The first was a radical parametric change to the collective pension fund, which would entail a sharp increase in payroll contributions or a significant reduction in replacement rates.[35] The second Chilean-like model would turn pensions from collective to individual savings, involving high transition costs and negative effects on solidarity (Foro de la Concertación Nacional, 1998).

Given the options on the table, it is not surprising that all the participants agreed on the creation of a multi-pillar system. Regarding the first pillar, the final document included measures to strengthen the managerial capacities of the Caja promoted by trade unions. The document also proposed the incorporation of the self-employed and housewives to social insurance. Altogether, this package further unified coverage and funding.

Regarding the second pillar, the National Pact agreed from the start to rely on existing payroll taxes. In particular, it proposed that

---

[34] According to many specialists, this strategy backfired: calling for a National Pact actually strengthened rather than weakened vetoes to pro-market reforms (Interview #17).

[35] In 1996, Vice-President Grynspan and her team had stated this option as an alternative that was economically unfeasible due to the negative impact that the hike in payroll taxes would have on competitiveness (*La Nación*, July 5, 1996).

the 1.25 percentage points of mandatory individual savings already transfered to the Banco Popular, the 1 percentage point for the occupational hazards insurance, the half percentage point for the INA, and the 1.5 percentage points for severance payment, be reallocated to the second pillar. Workers were allowed to choose pension fund managers within a list that included private insurers, cooperatives, labor organizations (i.e. unions, self-help organizations), and the Caja.[36] After the conclusion of the National Pact, a small group of business and trade union leaders remained involved in negotiating the draft of the bill that President Rodríguez submitted to Congress. The pension reform thus involved social actors to a far greater extent than any of the other policy measures discussed in this book. That said, their contribution should not be exaggerated: as demonstrated in Table 7.3, the law sent to Congress on July 30, 1999 drew heavily on the blueprint initially proposed by Gryspan's expert team.

The law introduced measures to improve the finances of the first pillar through two channels. First, it included non-judicial mechanisms to enforce the payment of social security contributions by businesses.[37] Second, it created additional revenues for the first pillar – particularly to support the self-employed – by having public enterprises transfer up to 15 percent of their net profits to the collective fund. The role of public agencies as administrators of individual savings (as a default option when workers do not choose otherwise) was also reinforced.

7.6.3 Addressing the Pending Parametric Changes, 2004–2005

In March 2004, actuaries from the Caja made a dramatic public announcement: by 2005 the interests from the social security reserves would be used in full to meet pension obligations. By 2015, the statement went, these interests would not be enough and pensions would have to be paid directly out of the reserves. Finally, by 2022 reserves would run out and the collective savings funds would become a pay-as-you-go system (Martínez Franzoni, 2005). In a

---

[36] The age of eligibility for the non-contributory pillar was also lowered from 70 years of age in the initial proposal to 65 in the final one approved after the debates.

[37] If firms were in debt with the CCSS, they could not supply goods and services to the state or access the public records needed for private transactions (Legislative Assembly, 2000).

Table 7.3 *Pensions: Policy Instruments by Stages of the Policy Process*

Components of the policy architecture	Executive proposal to launch the National Pact (based on Grynspan's team earlier proposal)	Additions suggested by civil society organizations
(1) What criteria make people eligible?	Salaried workers	Adds timetable to complete the mandatory insurance of the self-employed
(2) Who pays and how?	Reallocation of savings already in place	Does not leave room to fund individual savings by shrinking collective savings
(3) Who defines the benefits and how?	Defined contribution	Proposes that non-contributory pensions cannot be lower than half of the minimum contributory pension
(4) Who provides?	Workers choose among private agencies overseen by SUPEN or the CCSS invest in private firms and workers get average gains	In addition to private financial companies, public banks, cooperatives, and other non-profit entities are included in the list of potential pension managers
(5) Management of an outside (market) option?	Corresponds to the voluntary third-pillar available to all workers (salaried and self-employed)	–

subsequent study, the ILO confirmed this trend but revised the cut-off years to 2011, 2022, and 2028.

In response to the crisis, the Caja's actuaries proposed to increase contributions and reduce benefits. Workers and business representatives in the Caja's board of directors opposed these measures. Business resented the proposed hike in contributions and workers were not fond of lowering replacement rates. Both groups – most notably and noisily

unions – demanded full implementation of the non-parametric measures included in the LPT.

Between April and December of 2004, a commission comprised of
state actors and civil society representatives met to explore different
options. It first discussed the diagnosis of the actuarial imbalance and
then made a set of proposals. In line with the actuaries' demands, the
starting point for the negotiations was the need to introduce parametric changes that increased contributions and reduced replacement
rates. Negotiators then drew on measures designed but never made
public by Grynspan's techno-political team and put now on the table
by the ILO, including the use of staggered replacement rates with
higher rates for those with lower income.

Between January and February of 2005, a technical group fine-
tuned the proposals that were then approved by the Caja's board of
directors in April.[38] The final reform was the result of a compromise
between all actors. Unions accepted increases in payroll taxes in
exchange for progressive replacement rates (i.e. the lower wages
were, the higher the proportion of the salary that would be replaced
upon retirement). The business sector backed off its initial attempt to
administer public pension funds. Overall, the policy reform primarily
reflected the role of techno-political rather than of societal actors:
most of its components came from state-driven suggestions already
discussed in the 1990s.

In 2011, the sustainability of the pension system was again in the
spotlight. State actors were now split between those who blamed poor
macro-economic conditions and a few who denounced an inactive
investment policy as well as the (illegal) transfer of resources from
pensions to health care. The lack of any public actor with the strength
and capacity to impose its views and advance workable solutions
painfully highlighted the growing weakness of the Costa Rican state.

7.7 Conclusion

Between 1950 and 1980, Costa Rica unequivocally moved towards a
unified policy architecture in health care (and, to a lesser extent,

---

[38] Advisers were Sergio Velasco (ILO), Fabio Durán followed by Adolfo Rodríguez
(from the Executive Presidency of the Caja), Carlos León (Defensoría de los
Habitantes), Juliana Martínez (Women's National Institute and unions), Marta
Rodríguez (unions), and Johnny Mora (cooperatives).

pensions) capable of delivering outputs more universal than in almost any other country across the South. More recently, the country's policy trajectory has been more contradictory. On the one hand, there has been continuity in four of the five components of the policy architectures – eligibility, funding, and the definition and delivery of services. Even more positively, some measures, like the creation of the EBAIS, the mandatory, subsidized insurance for the self-employed, the creation of more options to access contributory pensions, and the improvement in the generosity of non-contributory pensions, have promoted universalism. This progress is all the more surprising in the context of fiscal shortcomings, changes in international ideas, and a gradual rightward move in the country's party system. On the other hand, the weakening of state institutions, due to the combination of the economic crisis and failed management reforms, has driven a significant expansion of the outside option.

Although changes have been more complex and contradictory than in previous periods, similar actors and processes have influenced them. A small number of state actors – both techno-politicians with political skills and technical knowledge and techno-bureaucrats who occupy influential positions in various institutions – have shaped the characteristics and the degree of success of different measures.

Meanwhile, the pre-existing policy architecture created different actors with limited interests in market-friendly changes (beneficiaries, the Caja bureaucrats, doctors). Doctors have played a particularly prominent role in influencing both the continuities of most components of the policy architecture and the growth of the outside option. They successfully confronted any attempt at privatizing or contracting out services, while simultaneously protecting and expanding opportunities for dual practice. This double function – also identified by Mary Clark in several papers (see, for example, Clark, 2005) – makes their contribution to universalism particularly contradictory. In defending the Caja, they encouraged unification, but in protecting their own rents (i.e. higher wage increases than other public servants, conflicting dual practice), they have deepened fragmentation.

More generally, our study of reforms in the last three decades reinforces two of this book's main arguments. First, in assessing implications for universalism, we ought to consider the interplay between different components of the policy architecture. In particular, unification in eligibility, funding, definition of benefits, and/or provision can do little if it is not accompanied by the effective regulation of the outside option. Second, gradual changes in the architecture also modify the set of actors with policy influence. In Costa Rica, the emergence of new private actors in health care and pensions are likely to further undermine the unified policy architecture in the long run. It is not the Caja that is under threat but its universal trajectory.

PART IV

Conclusions

8 | *Actors and Ideas in Comparative Perspective*

8.1 Introduction

In the previous three chapters, we explained how Costa Rica built a unified, pro-universal policy architecture and why it has recently confronted growing tensions. Our analysis confirmed that democracy and progressive political leadership were important factors behind this result. Electoral competition kept social policy at the forefront of the policy agenda and progressive changes accelerated – particularly after 1970 – during periods of left-of-center governments. Yet the existence of a dominant progressive party and political leaders like José Figueres – often taken as ultimate drivers of Costa Rica's exceptionalism (Huber and Stephens, 2012; Sandbrook *et al.*, 2007) – can hardly account for the unification of the policy architecture. As we showed in Chapters 5 and 6, pressures from social movements also have limited explanatory power: in the 1940s collective actors were primarily demanding labor rights rather than social services, and in the 1970s they focused almost exclusively on access to land and better wages.

Instead, our analysis highlighted the combined role of state actors and international ideas in (re)shaping this architecture. At times bureaucrats and at other times political appointees, they all had in common direct access to political power, links to international policy ideas, and capacity to make bureaucratic change happen. In the 1940s, a small group close to President Rafael Ángel Calderón Guardia created social insurance for salaried workers by adapting ideas promoted by the ILO. In the 1970s, the social assistance funds, FODESAF became an innovative instrument of "targeting through universalism" thanks to the intervention of an expert team. Supported by President Daniel Oduber, these experts were in tune with international ideas that advocated the allocation of social services to the poor rather than transfers alone. During the 1990s, the existence of a state actor with political backing and a coherent agenda grounded on expert knowledge explains the expansion of primary health care nationwide, while its absence partly determined the failure of a managerial reform largely concentrated on hospitals.

Does this explanatory model stand when looking at cases other than Costa Rica? In this chapter, we explore this question by revisiting policy formation in Mauritius, South Korea, and Uruguay. Rather than seeking to account for all relevant changes in the three countries over many decades, ours is a robustness check. We explore whether state actors with connections to progressive political leaders and access to international ideas contributed to changes in the policy architecture. We pay primary attention to the case of health care, but make references to pensions when useful to add empirical variation and analytical leverage to the argument.

8.2 Explaining the Foundational Architectures

As we argued in Chapters 1 and 4, the foundational architectures – the blueprint of policy instruments set up by states in an initial effort to organize social benefits – partly shapes subsequent trajectories. We thus start our analysis by considering how they came about in Mauritius, South Korea, and Uruguay. We focus on how useful the drivers we identified in Costa Rica are for explaining the other three cases (Table 8.1).

The experience of South Korea illustrates how difficult it is to create pro-universal policy architectures under authoritarianism. The Park Chung-hee administration focused almost exclusively on promoting economic growth and had limited incentives to implement generous social policies (Kwon, 1995; Ringen *et al.*, 2011). The authoritarian character of the regime and its high concentration of power also explain why state actors involved in social policy formation failed to advance their agenda. In 1962, for example, the Committee for Social Security within the Ministry of Social Affairs proposed the creation of social insurance for workers in large companies. Their proposal was informed by the Japanese experience (Jeong and Niki, 2012) and gave prevalence to financial feasibility over equity (Kwon, 2007). Yet the military junta – hardly open to persuasion and policy debates – rejected it as "too idealistic" and costly, particularly for the middle class (Kwon, 2007: 151).

Table 8.1 *Factors Behind Foundational Architectures in Health Care*

Explanatory factors	Mauritius	South Korea	Uruguay
Characteristics of the architecture	Public health with dual practice and a prominent outside option	Mandatory firm-level social insurance in companies without state funding support and a social assistance health care program for the poor	Tax-based public health for the poor and unregulated, private mutual funds for the middle-class
Date	Early 1950s	1977	1910
Political regime	Newly created democratic institutions still under colonial rule	Authoritarian regime	Semi-democratic institutions
Parties/political leaders in power	Left-of-center political party sharing power with Colonial authorities	Military government led by General Park Chung-hee	Catch-all party under progressive leader José Batlle y Ordoñez
Driving actors in the policy process	Few state actors with technical expertise around progressive leaders. Significant influence of British experts with no bureaucratic connections. Not trace of social movement influence in policy design	Social policy proposals within the Ministry of Health and Social Affairs. Veto from the President and the Minister of Finance who were focused on economic growth	Team of doctors around the Minister of Health. No active participation of social actors
Influential international ideas	British ideas regarding social assistance. A few years later key role of ideas adapted from the NHS under the Titmuss report	A fragmented Japanese model of social insurance	French ideas of public assistance and public health

In the late 1970s, a few state actors proposed measures that would provide services for all. In particular, leading members at the Ministry of Health pushed for the creation of a single, unified social insurance fund, but their influence on the President was limited and their plans failed (Kwon, 2007). Political authorities were only willing to adopt the plan that had been designed fifteen years before, which benefited only a small number of workers. This way, the regime could secure much needed social legitimacy (Wong, 2004) with minimal fiscal implications.

The Mauritian case also reveals the importance of democracy and progressive leadership as preconditions for generous social policies (Seekings, 2011). Technocratic proposals for pensions and health insurance put forward in the early 1940s did not get anywhere due to absence of electoral competition. These proposals were fleshed out with much detail by foreign consultants, but met with limited state support. According to a high-ranking official in 1943, "from time to time, experts have made Reports which have never been fully implemented, and devised schemes which have never been completed" (Council of Government of Mauritius, 1943).[1]

Advances only took place when colonial authorities allowed (partial) electoral competition. In 1948, (literate) Mauritians elected the majority of members to the newly created Legislative Council. The electoral contest contributed to the reemergence of the Labour Party, which "campaigned on a platform inspired in large part by its British counterpart: social security and old-age pensions, compulsory education, housing and limited nationalisation" (Seekings, 2011: 172).

The new political environment facilitated the expansion of health services already available. Yet it did not contribute to regulation of the outside option – primarily private GP services for the upper middle class and the rich. Stronger regulations would have required supporting ideas and more effective state actors, neither of which were available. In terms of ideas, proposals coming from Britain distinguished between the poor and high-income groups: public provision should concentrate on the former, leaving private services for the latter. Even after the publication of the Beveridge report – which promoted universal health

---

[1] In 1942, for example, London and Port Louis exchanged correspondence on how to build social insurance: the Colonial office offered to send an expert and the governor asked for actuary calculations for the creation of a pension system (Colony of Mauritius, 1948).

care for the UK – recommendations for the colonies concentrated on social policy interventions that contributed to increased productivity of the working class (Seekings, 2011).

In terms of actors, during the late 1950s and early 1960s, only a few Mauritians combined political influence and technical expertise in social policy. There were some "great men" like Seewoosagur Ramgoolam – a doctor trained in the United Kingdom (Joynathsing, 1987; Sandbrook *et al.*, 2007) – but few experts with public sector experience around them. This was partly an inheritance of the earlier colonial period, when British expatriates handled almost all management posts in the public administration (Minogue, 1976).

In fact, most of the ideas that entered into the public agenda came instead from British experts without close ties to political elites. The most important were Richard Titmuss and Brian Abel-Smith, world-class academics who had been actively involved in the creation of the British NHS (Sheard, 2012). Their report – the widely cited Titmuss report (Titmuss and Abel-Smith, 1968) – recommended the creation of the National Health Service of Mauritius, which would have resulted in a unified policy architecture. Unfortunately Titmuss and Abel-Smith were outsiders based in London and without enough institutional embeddedness and political support to advance their long-term agenda.[2]

The case of pensions is similar to health care: the emergence of democracy resulted in the creation of generous programs, but the lack of expertise limited its overall impact on universalism. The discussion on both non-contributory and contributory pensions began in the early 1940s in light of Fabian ideas and the experience of Great Britain and its colonies (Seekings, 2011).[3] Yet their adoption was repeatedly postponed due to opposition from London and concerns about pensions' fiscal costs.

---

[2] Also, the Labour Party elite, which was influenced by Fabian ideas of redistribution, was primarily concerned with expanding opportunities for the poor and did not want to threaten the private sector (Bowman, 1991).

[3] In October 1943, a report by the Government Actuary of Great Britain mentioned "that the colonies of Barbados and Trinidad and Tobago instituted non-contributory schemes of old age pensions in 1937 and 1939 respectively. Both schemes were framed closely on the model of the non-contributory old age pensions law of Great Britain with appropriate modifications as to pensionable age, rates of pensions, etc." (Colony of Mauritius, 1948).

The situation changed dramatically after the 1948 elections when the new members of the Legislative Council pressured for a rapid adoption of old-age transfers. Non-contributory pensions – with low generosity – were then created under the administration of the Public Assistance Department "as a stopgap measure to be used until a 'proper' system of social insurance could be set up" (Willmore, 2006: 70). Yet contributory pensions were not adopted until twenty-six years later, in part because they involved a more technically demanding design and were heavily dependent on qualified experts.[4] In fact, in 1976 Mauritius did not even have a formal Government Actuary Service (Abel-Smith, 1976). At no time did politicians question the existence of private arrangements for high-income groups (Mootoosamy, 1981).

In Uruguay, back when the foundational policy architecture was established, three of the factors in our model (democratic institutions, progressive political leadership, and capable state actors) were present, but enabling ideas were not. As a result, the foundational architecture was created with significant fragmentation between services for the poor and the non-poor.

The election of José Batlle y Ordóñez in 1903 opened the door for a progressive state agenda that simultaneously launched industrial, rural, fiscal, and social reforms. Tuition for secondary and university education – for the benefit of the middle class and also the poor – was eliminated, and labor rights were introduced (Vanger, 1980). In the absence of strong organized civil society pressures, Batlle y Ordóñez put the building blocks of "a particular type of welfare state, one that was statist ... anticipatory and paternalistic" (Filgueira, 1995: 11).

In health care, the Batlle y Ordóñez administration created the National Public Assistance to manage public hospitals previously in the hands of the Catholic Church. The aim was to guarantee services to the poor as a matter of right and not charity (Morás, 2000). Decisions

---

[4] Contributory pensions were designed by external experts. Abel-Smith and Tony Lynes were invited to Mauritius in February 1976 and published their results just two months later (Abel-Smith and Lynes, 1976; Government of Mauritius, 1976). Two Mauritian actuaries hired by the government prepared financial estimates, but Abel-Smith "was not happy with their conclusions" (Abel-Smith, 1976). At the end, contributions were too low and benefits promised were too generous – features that no state actor has been able to change since then (Chapter 4).

were made by a group of doctors around the Minister of Health, José Scosería, a physician with close ties to the President who had led the Council of National Charity and Public Beneficence since 1903. Some of these doctors were part of the government while others like Luis Morquio advised from the outside. According to Birn (2008: 321), they "studied in Europe, took part in burgeoning international networks, and hosted prominent European scientists." Scosería himself would in years later work in the Geneva-based Committee of Hygiene of the League of Nations. The new institutional setting was "consciously modeled after France's Assistance Publique" (Birn, 2012: 423) and was focused almost exclusively on the poor. Meanwhile, the non-poor started accessing private mutual societies with minimal state regulation.

The lack of international ideas promoting universalism was also evident in the case of pensions, a sector in which Uruguay was one of the pioneers in Latin America (Mesa-Lago, 1978). Following the Bismarckian principles and ILO recommendations dominant in the 1920s, Uruguay created old-age insurance funds for specific occupations – e.g. teachers, armed forces, public servants. This may have been a good way to secure rights for different groups, but consolidated the fragmentation of the policy architecture. In contrast, in Costa Rica social insurance was founded decades later at a time when the ILO was promoting an idea whereby the entire working population – both blue and white collar - be reached by a single national insurance.

8.3 Explaining the Transformation of the Policy Architecture

In this section, we focus on recent reforms, particularly in health care, considering the relative contribution made by each of the four factors in our model (Table 8.2). We first discuss the two countries that have moved towards less fragmentation in their policy architecture, followed by Mauritius where – as in Costa Rica – the opposite has been the case. As discussed in Chapter 4, the fact that South Korea and Uruguay made the most progress towards unification in recent years demonstrates that globalization is by no means an insurmountable barrier to achieve universal policy outputs.

Much of the literature on South Korean social policy focuses on the role of democratization to justify the recent expansionary phase (see also Chapter 4). Wong (2004: 15), for example, argues that the

Table 8.2 *Factors Behind the Transformation of Architectures in Health Care*

Explanatory factors	Mauritius	South Korea	Uruguay
Changes in architecture	State provides incentives for further expansion of private providers and the outside option	Unification into a single insurer. Low state funding and private provision of services remain	Significant pro-unification reform with the creation of the National Health System
Period	1990s–2000s	1998 onwards	Late 2000s
Political regime	Democracy	Democracy	Democracy
Parties/political leaders in power	Different coalitions with steady presence of left-of-center parties	Key role of the progressive President Kim Dae-jung, elected in 1998	Left-of-center Frente Amplio had majority in Congress and occupied the presidency since 2005
Driving actors in the policy process	Many proposals elaborated by international actors with limited influence from domestic ones. State actors unable to cope with outside option or build a coherent position regarding management reforms	Experts from civil society pressured for unification and built close links to Kim's party. Pro-unification experts also occupied key posts in the Kim administration	Techno-political actors from Frente Amplio in close interaction with providers and medical organizations
Influential international ideas	Several models discussed but Singaporean experience particularly attractive	Move away from Japanese ideas towards consideration of a larger number of experiences	Local adaptation of ideas regarding institutional autonomy of hospitals and influence of health economics

"democratic breakthrough mattered most in Taiwan and South Korea by redirecting the trajectory of social policy reform towards universalism." Yet this is not totally accurate: in fact, advances towards unification of the policy architecture only took place when democratic institutions were combined with progressive political leaders and with influential experts within and outside the state.

The fact that democracy was not enough becomes evident when comparing the attempts to unify national health insurance in 1989 and 1998. In 1989, after the first democratic elections, opposition political parties – allied to progressive social policy experts from the newly created Association of Social Security Studies – approved a law for the unification of all health funds and the expansion of health care to the self-employed. Yet a high-ranking bureaucrat, Kim Jong-Dae, and other members of the Ministry of Health and Social Affairs in favor of a decentralized system, talked the President into rejecting the project (Wong, 2004). He vetoed the law and only extended social security to the self-employed through new funds.

In contrast, all the required factors for unification were present in 1998, when a single health care fund was created (Hwang, 2006; Kwon, 2007; Kwon and Reich, 2005; Wong, 2004). First, the progressive leader, Kim Dae-jung, had just been elected. He had close ties to the National Solidarity Alliance for the Integration of Health Insurance – which later became the Health Solidarity Coalition (Wong, 2004) – that was pushing for unification since 1994. This social organization was not a social movement as much as a group of "expert-activists. [It] comprised a sophisticated corps of policy experts, who were capable of providing tenable policy alternatives" (Wong, 2004: 101). They included university professors like Yang Bong-Min and former bureaucrats like Che Heung-Bong. Experts borrowed ideas from a diversity of countries rather than from Japan alone as in previous decades. According to Jeong and Niki (2012: 67), policy experts "found themselves with ready access to overseas institutions other than those in Japan ... [They] played a substantial role in studying foreign medical institutions and introducing these ideas into South Korea" (Jeong and Niki, 2012: 67).

Second, the Minister of Health and Social Affairs in the Kim administration – Chun Myung-Kee – was a strong advocate of integration (Jeong and Niki, 2012). Another progressive techno-pol, Lee Sang-Young, became director of the Ministry's health insurance division, where all ranking bureaucrats supported unification (Kwon, 2007; Wong, 2004). Third, external conditions were also more favorable as we discussed in Chapter 4: the 1997 financial crisis questioned the sustainability of several health care funds and opened the door for new policy options in the context of tripartite negotiations between business, trade unions, and the state.

Policy formation behind South Korea's health care reforms thus confirms the importance of democracy and progressive leadership as macro-factors and actors and ideas as drivers in the context of incentives created by the policy architecture.[5] Yet, contrary to Costa Rica, in South Korea technical proposals often came from civil society rather than from within the state. This apparent contradiction between our Costa Rican-based state-centered explanation and South Korea's policy process reflects diverging historical trajectories. By the 1990s, the latter was still a young democracy with a strong bureaucracy, which had striven for economic growth as its single objective over the course of several decades. Given the strength of business groups and other vested interests (e.g. insurance funds, hospitals) in the context of a fragmented architecture, social organizations were bound to play a more active role in proposing and securing policy change.[6]

In Uruguay the policy architecture for health care has changed significantly in recent years. In 2008, following the ascent of a left-wing coalition to power, a reform that unified benefits between public and private providers and expanded access, particularly for children, was introduced. In order to assess the role of different drivers in explaining the success of this reform, it is useful to compare it with a failed attempt a few years earlier, during the right-of-center administration of Julio María Sanguinetti (1995–2000).

The 1995 reform aimed to eliminate public subsidies for private services, invest in more and better public hospitals, and encourage medical choice (i.e. beneficiaries would choose whether to channel

---

[5] The combination of democratization, progressive leadership, and ideas from social policy experts was also behind reforms in pensions (Lee, 2008). Even in this case, state actors from the bureaucracy remained key shapers of social policy, particularly in a second phase of legislation. At the same time, international ideas no longer came exclusively from Japan and social and state actors had opportunities to study other experiences.

[6] In fact, as we discussed in Chapter 4, key features of the policy architecture including powerful private providers and doctors have constrained further change after the reform of the late 1990s and explains remaining fragmentation.

their contributions through mutual associations or public hospitals). It also involved a total separation between public facilities and private mutual associations so that members of the latter could not access the former. In order to increase public sector productivity, the reform proposed to make labor conditions for health workers more flexible (Filgueira and Moraes, 2001).

The reform failed for two reasons. On the one hand, the proposal was introduced at a time when pressures from the architecture regarding costs and quality were relatively small: "health care was not considered a problem and the crisis of the mutual associations was regarded as solvable" (Fuentes, 2010: 131).

On the other hand, a techno-political actor with political skills and the capacity to adapt international ideas was absent. A single appointed official, Alfredo Solari, led the reformist attempt in his capacity as Minister of Health. He lacked a strong advising team and never developed a clear strategy to gain political and social support. Proposals relied excessively on market-friendly ideas of public-private competition and choice, largely alien to the Uruguayan public. Measures were unlikely to reduce costs, shorten waiting lists or improve services, and threatened almost all interest groups involved without creating hardly any winners. The mutual associations opposed the elimination of public subsidies, the left-wing Frente Amplio was against the decision to restrict access to public services, and trade unions challenged measures that would reduce labor rights (Fuentes, 2010; Filgueira and Moraes, 2001).

Solari's proposal drew on World Bank recommendations and did not have much bureaucratic assistance or support. According to Fuentes (2010: 130), "there was never a diagnostic of the system or a proper marketing of the proposal: there was only support from the International Financial Institutions."

Conditions were much more favorable in 2008. First, the problems created by the pre-existing policy architecture were more dramatic and visible to many. The 2001 economic crisis had threatened the survival of a large number of mutual associations and weakened the state's fiscal position. Costs of services had increased and quality had dropped (Chapter 4).

Second, the Frente, now in government, proposed the reform. The Frente had close links to trade unions and professional associations in the health sector and had the capacity to aggregate the agendas of various stakeholders (Fuentes, 2010; Pribble, 2013). Yet strong ties between the government and interest groups could have led to stagnation instead of change, as happened in education (Pribble, 2013).

Third, and even more importantly, President Tabaré Vázquez granted power to a group of state actors with technical capacity, political connections, and bureaucratic expertise. The team included four doctors and one economist (Setaro, 2013). They were members of different political parties who had aided Vázquez when he was mayor of Montevideo. The Minister of Health, María Julia Muñoz, for example, was a doctor who specialized in infectious diseases, epidemiology, and public health. She had taught for twenty years at the University of the Republic, worked for the President in the municipality, and led one of the largest mutual associations in the country for a year.

Muñoz and her team organized a number of issue-focused working groups with representation from social actors and public institutions – an effective mechanism to cope with vetoes. Agreements reached by these working groups were consolidated into a single plan by the Minister's team, which was the only one with a comprehensive perspective of the reform. During the design process a group of young (health) economists supported the techno-political actor. Coming from the main university of Uruguay, they joined the bureaucracy and contributed to streamline the old structure of the Ministry of Health (Setaro, 2013).

The role of international ideas in Uruguay is surprisingly absent in the literature. However, the technical expertise in health economics of the whole group is beyond doubt. The reform embraced and adapted dominant paradigms, including the need to create a "national integrated system," "local health care systems," and "managerial and health delivery models" (Setaro, 2013). Uruguay's new funding is also based on a capitation system, an internationally renowned idea.

In Mauritius, there were many proposals to improve public provision and increase revenues in the last decades but they did not go anywhere until recently. In the 1970s, the accent was placed on the rationalization of the system and the expansion of the primary level. In 1977, for example, Abel-Smith was hired to explore the creation of a "Free General Practitioners National Health Service." The proposal limited the number of public and private doctors that each patient attended, reduced dependence on the secondary level and included measures to increase equity (Abel-Smith, 1977). Abel-Smith's proposal aimed to take advantage of the growing number of doctors – a significant constraint on growth until then.

In the 1980s and early 1990s, attention was devoted to funding and management issues. In 1988 the government embarked on a comprehensive review of the health system (Valyadon, 2002). Professors Victor Rodwin from New York University and Dominique Jolly from Faculte Broussais-Hotel-Dieu were hired to provide their expert advice. They became members of a task force led by the Minister of Health with representatives from different ministries. In tune with dominant international ideas, this task force recommended service decentralization, management reform, and additional financial sources (Valyadon, 2002).[7]

Between 1993 and 1997 the government undertook another major review with technical assistance from international financial institutions and participation from international experts. Abel-Smith was again partly involved in preparing technical inputs that informed the debate (Coopers and Lybrand, 1995). Options for a national health insurance as well as managerial reforms (including decentralization in the public sector) were revisited (Abel-Smith, 1994; Valaydon, 2002).

Yet none of these proposals were pursued and, for a long time, changes were minimal: while public spending gradually increased, the outside option remained strong and health insurance was not enacted. Significant changes had to wait until the 2000s and entailed expanded access to private provision rather than the strengthening of public delivery. They included, for example, permission to draw on individual saving accounts (the National Savings Fund) to purchase private health insurance. Support to the outside option was seen as a way to reduce pressures on the public sector, gain support from the middle class, and fuel private investment (*African Business Monitor*, 2012).

How can we explain the failure of the various proposals? And the recent promotion of the outside option? As we showed in Chapter 4, the policy architecture is particularly important to answer these questions. The existence of dual private-public arrangements limited the opportunities for integration: low-income groups were unwilling to be

---

[7] Measures on the table included the creation of a national health insurance inspired by the Singapore's Central Provident Fund, which would provide access to public and private providers (Deerpalsing, 1988).

charged by social insurance for services they already had, while high income groups were satisfied with private provision. The co-existence of strong public and private sectors also created powerful vetoes against management reforms and the regulation of the outside option – just like in Costa Rica. In 2002, for example, a manager of the Ministry of Health argued that "the biggest Mafia preventing the health sector to function properly is [the] medical Mafia – whether it be within MOH [Ministry of Health] at headquarters, in hospitals or outside. It has been in [the] interest of certain groups of people, mostly medical groups and also other groups to prevent the public health service to function properly ... Because if it did, then there would be no work outside for the same Mafia who belonged to the health/ medical *public service and to the private service* outside" (cited in Valaydon, 2002: 197, italics in the original).

Yet the failure to introduce unifying reforms – actually any kind of significant reform – can also be explained by the lack of coherent state leadership. Valaydon (2002) shows that power struggles within the Ministry of Health were frequent and that top bureaucrats like the permanent medical administrators opposed changes. His interviews to high-ranking members of the Ministry of Health in the late 1990s highlighted "conflict of leadership, unclear assignment of responsibilities, lack of coordination and collaboration, including turf issues and conflict of interest" (p. 183). Moreover, in recent decades, the center of power within the government shifted to state actors in the economic area, including the Board of Investment of Mauritius. This board has actively pursued medical tourism and has supported the growing role of medical private insurance. In early 2015, its managing director praised the fact that "an increasing number of the local population has medical insurance cover and hence have recourse to private clinics for medical treatment" (*Financial Express*, 2015). Social movements, on the other hand, have not been particularly active in health care and have not been a source of reform ideas like in South Korea.

Since the early 1990s, the menu of international ideas has not been particularly supportive for unification either. At the macro-level, Singapore has become a source of inspiration for Mauritian policy-makers, who aim to recreate its economic model and institutions (Frankel, 2010; World Bank, 1992). In health care, the Singaporean experience with a capitalization fund and a public-private mix was often mentioned as a possible option during the 1990s (Coopers and

Lybrand, 1995; Deerpalsing, 1988) and has informed recent measures. Meanwhile, World Bank's ideas supported managed competition and the expansion of private provision (Valaydon, 2002).

8.4 Conclusion

In Chapters 3 and 4 we discussed the role of the policy architecture in promoting universal outputs. Depending on how a country secures access and funding, defines benefits, provides services, and regulates the outside option, outputs will be more or less universal. In particular, the more unified all these components are, the better. By strengthening specific actors and creating different opportunities and constraints, policy architectures also shape subsequent trajectories.

But how are policy architectures initially shaped? Under what circumstances are opportunities for the unification of the policy architectures maximized? In Chapters 5, 6, and 7 we explored these two questions by reconstructing Costa Rica's long-term trajectory. We relied on inductive research based on primary data and elaborated a mid-range theory based on four factors: electoral competition and progressive leadership as macro-political conditions and state actors and international ideas as drivers of policy change. At least in the Costa Rican case, politicians were responding to social and electoral pressures in promoting new programs, but the specific measures adopted were the design of state actors embedded in international debates.

In this chapter, we have evaluated how well our explanation travels to Mauritius, South Korea, and Uruguay – all countries that have been praised in the literature for their generous social policies but have performed differently in terms of universalism (see Chapters 3 and 4). Our analysis – which focused on health care – confirmed the importance of our variables – both the two macro-factors and the two that are missing links in the literature. In the foundational stage, the combination of democracy and progressive leadership explains why social policy was more expansionary in Mauritius and Uruguay than in South Korea. Yet even in the presence of these enabling factors, the foundational architecture was not unified in any of the cases because either effective state actors or supporting ideas or both were lacking (see Table 8.3).

In the last two decades, Mauritius' policy architecture went from being less to more fragmented, while the opposite happened in South

Table 8.3 *Foundational Architecture: Stylized Depiction of Explanatory Model*

Country	Democracy	Progressive leadership	State actor with political support, bureaucratic links, and international embeddedness	International ideas encourage a unified architecture	Unified architecture?
Mauritius	Yes	Yes	No	Contradictory	No
South Korea	No	No	No	No	No
Uruguay	Yes	Yes	Yes	No	No

Korea and Uruguay.[8] As discussed in Chapter 4, incentives and constraints generated by the previous policy architecture created at times new demands from users, but we found no evidence that collective actors drove the pro-universal agenda. Instead, we stress the role of state actors that responded to pressures for the architecture with a policy menu that favored universal outputs in South Korea and Uruguay but not in Mauritius.

At the same time, the analysis in this chapter adds some caveats to our Costa Rican-based model. First, non-state experts may at times have the capacity to advance a unification agenda. In particular, in South Korea, state actors worked together with policy experts from social movements to unify all insurance funds into a National Health System. Second, some foundational architectures create more interest groups than others. Uruguay, where there were many social actors with veto power is a case in point: these actors had to be involved in the policy debate if a reform was going to pass. Third, the international policy menu often offers contradictory options. In fact, in the last three decades, many of the prevailing ideas (e.g. competition in delivery, expansion of private options, medical choice) have discouraged rather than encouraged unification. The interaction between actors and ideas

---

[8] It is important to stress that when discussing the most recent period we do not explore policy outputs but trajectories alone. For example, despite improvements, the South Korean policy architecture is still far from unified due to limits in benefits and dominance of private providers. In Uruguay, the unification of benefits across an array of providers is still in the making.

Table 8.4 *Transformations in the Architecture: Stylized Depiction of Explanatory Model*

Country	Democracy	Progressive leadership	State actor with political support, bureaucratic links, and international embeddedness	International ideas encourage a unified architecture	Moves towards unification of the architecture
Mauritius	Yes	Yes	No	No	No
South Korea	Yes	Yes	Yes, but social policy actors were more important	Yes, although contested	Yes
Uruguay	Yes	Yes	Yes, but also active participation of interest groups	Yes, thanks to local adaptation	Yes

is then all the more important: successful state actors must be able to use ideas from abroad selectively and adapt them successfully to the domestic context.

Before concluding, let us remind the reader of our objectives and recognise a limitation of the analysis. In this book, we have intentionally left aside structural factors (e.g. class composition, economic structure, characteristics of the elite, income inequality) that may condition the opportunities for expansionary social policies (Sandbrook *et al.*, 2007). Instead, our aim all along has been to explain social policies that deliver specific (universal) outputs thanks to a concrete architecture. To this purpose we chose countries which have, at one point or another, implemented expansionary social policies, and which are thus likely to have benefited from positive structural preconditions.

Last but not least, this chapter had to confront the dearth of research on the role of state actors (whether technopols or high ranking bureaucrats) and international ideas in social policy in Mauritius, South Korea, and Uruguay. Much research seems to assume that provided there is political will, change will take place in a relatively unproblematic fashion. This assumption downplays how and by whom policies are designed and implemented. Our book is partly an invitation to pay more attention to this missing link.

9 | The Quest for Universalism: Implications for Contemporary Policymaking

9.1 Introduction

During the 1980s and 1990s the aspiration of delivering social services and transfers for all was abandoned in most of the South. New programs were primarily targeted to low-income groups, while the rest of the population was encouraged to rely on the market. Fortunately things have gradually changed since the early 2000s. A growing concern with equity – in the context of international attention to inequality and its costs (Piketty, 2013; Wilkinson and Pickett, 2009; World Bank, 2006) – together with new social demands have led to a renewed attention to universalism. In Latin America, the change of mood was triggered by the ascent of left-wing parties to power.

In most cases, these policy efforts have focused exclusively on increasing coverage. At the national level, new programs have extended to the poor only *some* of the rights that other groups already had. At the international level, debates around the post-MDGs agenda have paid more attention to access than to closing the gaps between countries in the level and quality of benefits. Defining universalism without strong concern for generosity and equity reinforces hierarchical differences, with some people receiving more generous benefits than others.

Albeit positive to bring new options to the center stage, this approach to universalism is a far cry from the comprehensive normative use, which calls for similar benefits for all based on general taxation and the principle of citizenship and residency. Influenced by the Nordic successful record, this broad definition has been linked to many positive results, including a higher redistribution of income, increases in social cohesion and more competitive economies (Chapter 2).

Unfortunately, policymakers across the South face mounting obstacles to develop this social-democratic ideal: fiscal resources are limited, electoral cycles are short, the need to show immediate results is high, unmet social demands are pressing, and initial levels of social inequality significant. In creating and reforming policies, governments must thus deal with tough trade-offs. Should they place resources in non-contributory basic services just for those in need? Or should they undertake costly reforms that reach everyone, seeking to mix the poor and the middle class? For example, should they introduce nurseries for poor children alone or develop broad childcare programs that aspire to incorporate the middle class? Do governments have sufficient fiscal space for the latter and, if not, how can they create it? If programs start off by reaching the poor, will the non-poor be willing to join them later?

To address these dilemmas, in this book we started from a different approach to universalism, one that is ambitious but also based on a practical understanding of the challenges state and social actors face in the South. In our view, a social policy is universal when it incorporates everyone to similar, generous services and transfers, *independently of the instruments used*. If universalism is defined as a desirable policy output and not as a specific kind of (often costly) program, different interventions (i.e. social insurance, social assistance, targeted programs) may contribute to build it. Our conceptualization also views universalism as a long-term process; what matters most is the direction of change and, as a result, reconciling different objectives becomes feasible.

How can social policies generate these desirable outputs in the South? To answer this question, the second part of this book (Chapters 3 and 4) turned to the experience of Costa Rica, Mauritius, South Korea, and Uruguay, where social policy has been robust but the degree of universalism has varied. In comparing these four countries, we aimed to identify factors beyond electoral competition and ideology that shape the characteristics of social policy. We highlighted the synchronic and dynamic role of policy architectures, exploring the constraints and opportunities foundational architectures offer for subsequent change. Building on the case of Costa Rica, in the third part of the book (Chapters 5 to 7), we focused on the drivers of policy architectures at key moments in time. We highlighted the central role of state actors and their capacity to adopt and adapt international ideas to meet domestic demands. Comparing these lessons with policy trajectories over the long run in Mauritius, South Korea, and Uruguay confirmed the general validity of our model for other contexts (Chapter 8).

In this concluding chapter, we begin with an overview of our contribution to the determinants of universalism in the South, addressing macro-political preconditions, defining the concept of policy architectures and identifying the actors that shape them. We then explore the implications our findings have for the design (or reform) of policy architectures. We conclude with the implications of our findings for future research agendas.

9.2 From Democracy to Universal Outputs: Missing Links

Historically grounded analysis shows that the creation of social programs often takes place during periods of authoritarianism (Mares and Carnes, 2012). However, programs that aim to secure entitlements for the whole population are specific types that tend to appear under semi-democratic or democratic regimes (Huber, Mustillo, and Stephens, 2008; Huber and Stephens, 2012).

Our evidence confirms that electoral competition facilitates the adoption of social policies with universal outputs; left-wing political parties and progressive political leadership also make an important contribution. For example, South Korea moved decisively towards the reduction of fragmentation in its policy architecture – and thus towards universalism – only when the first progressive leader, Kim Dae-jung, from the Democratic Party, was elected president. In Uruguay, Tabaré Vázquez of the leftist Frente Amplio succeeded in implementing a pro-universalistic reform in health care, which conservative parties had previously avoided or failed to accomplish. During much of the period considered, Costa Rica and Mauritius have been unique among their respective Central American and African neighbors partly because of their democratic institutions and social-democratic leadership.

Nevertheless, the existence of electoral competition and progressive parties and leaders does not guarantee universalism in social policy. As the Chilean and Uruguayan record before the 1970s demonstrates, electoral competition can go along with policies that provide unequal benefits and exclude large segments of the population. During the past decade many countries with progressive parties in office did not move social policy in a universalistic direction.

This is why this book has focused on missing links between macro-political factors and universal policy outputs in countries with a record of robust social policy. Instead of placing social actors at the centre of our analysis – as does much of the literature on the North – our empirical analysis has called attention to the role of policy architectures as well as the state actors and ideational inputs behind them. We define policy architectures as the combination of instruments addressing eligibility, funding, delivery, provision, and the outside option of specific social policies. The effects of these architectures upon universalism do not result from each single component, but from their interaction (Chapter 3).

Policy architectures play a double role in transforming (or failing to transform) electoral pressures into universal outputs. At a specific moment in time, the more unified the architecture, the more universal the policy outputs are likely to be (Chapter 3). In the long run, as explained in Chapter 4, policy architectures create distinct opportunities and constraints for the building of universalism. On the one hand, they empower some actors over others and create a set of political, fiscal, and economic incentives that influence the direction of reform. On the other hand, policy architectures define the alternatives that social and state actors can credibly pursue.

Our analysis of this missing link borrows from and contributes to two distinct literatures in the social sciences. Latin American sociologists introduced the concept of architecture to loosely refer to the combination of policies and programs in a specific country (Filgueira, 2007b; Filgueira *et al.*, 2006). Our conceptualization focuses on single policies and offers a more systematic exploration of its different components. It also describes with more detail the way different instruments interact to generate certain policy outputs.

We also rely on historical institutionalism and the literature on path dependence in policy formation. Starting from the work of Pierson (1994) and others, a large body of scholarly work has emphasized the role of institutions and actors in limiting dramatic change in social policy (see Amenta, 2003 for a review). A wide array of variables may favor stability, including the type of actors that have been empowered, the influence of social policies on economic interests, and the institutional veto points in the political system (Estévez-Abe, Iversen, and Soskice, 2001; Huber and Stephens, 2001).

Our argument regarding the long-term implications of architectures is closest to Jennifer Pribble's analysis of policy legacies. In her work, legacies play two roles (Pribble, 2013). The first is to explain the type of problems that exist at a moment in time: for example, if social spending in education is low in time 0, there will be overcrowding in time 1. Policy legacies also shape the power structure, strengthening some actors and weakening others. Our approach emphasizes a third role of architectures in narrowing down the set of alternatives available. In Costa Rica, for example, dependence on payroll taxes made other funding alternatives less appealing – a matter that relates to the cognitive processes involved in policy formation as studied by Weyland (2007). More importantly, by specifying the different components of the architecture (what is being offered, by whom, and for whom), we can identify actors and alternatives in different contexts – something that is harder to do within the framework of policy legacies.

The two bodies of research from the fields of social policy and historical institutionalism should speak to each other more systematically than they currently do. One of our main theoretical contributions is making this link clear. Each decision policymakers take when designing a program affects one or more components of the architecture – eligibility, funding, entitlements, providers, and the outside option – at a given moment in time. Every one of these decisions also shapes subsequent trajectories and makes further advances more or less likely.

Considering the outside option as a fundamental component of the policy architecture is an additional contribution of our study. The outside option does not simply create segmentation between those who can resort to the market and those who cannot. It also affects the way the public sector operates, gradually eroding access, funding, and benefits. By linking public policies and private alternatives and by highlighting the regulatory role of the state, we provide a more accurate picture of how health care, education, and other social services actually work. We also call for a broad understanding of the outside option: it should not only include private providers but also the use of the public sector for private gains.

How are policy architectures designed? How do they evolve over time? We drew from the case of Costa Rica as the one country in our sample that built the most unified policy architecture to explore these questions. In Costa Rica, a single social security fund created in the early 1940s incorporated the working class and put in place incentives for the subsequent expansion of coverage to higher income groups. The creation of a dominant institution in charge of providing services and transfers, the Caja Costar-CCSS also shaped how social assistance was organized in the 1970s. Payroll taxes helped overcome historical difficulties to raise taxes and became the most prominent funding source for social insurance and social assistance.

Democratic institutions created the preconditions to design and reform Costa Rica's policy architecture. Yet the specific measures introduced were not shaped by collective actors or by the preferences of political leaders. In the 1940s, for example, President Rafael Ángel Calderón Guardia's initial reaction after his election was to create an array of social assistance measures targeted to the poor such as the distribution of free shoes. Calderón Guardia had less influence in turning the country's attention to social security or in shaping its foundational architecture.

We argue that the characteristics of pro-universal policies can be better explained by focusing on relatively small teams of state experts. Some of them are high-ranking members of the bureaucracy while others are political appointees with technical expertise, that is, techno-politicians. Contrary to contemporary views (e.g. Joignant, 2011), our analysis shows that the latter need not be ministers or vice-ministers; what is important is that they enter the policy process with close access to and full support from political leaders. State actors must also be politically savvy, capable of identifying potential vetoes and engaging with them.

In discussing the role of these state actors we highlight the relevance of expertise, which comes from training but also from access to foreign experiences, ideas, and models (Weyland, 2004). The state actors examined in this book acquired ideas from abroad, translating them into domestic conditions. Their participation in networks and organizations, in conferences and in publications played an important role in spreading shared norms (Sugiyama 2011). The international availability of pro-universal ideas at some points in time was particularly important.

The analyses we presented in Chapter 7 underlines how Costa Rican state actors and their relative power and coherence has also shaped policy formation in recent periods of economic crisis. In the presence of a coherent team of top bureaucrats with political support, a primary health care system that expanded coverage and generosity was enacted. In contrast, a managerial reform based on health economics and new public management failed partly due to a weaker and more uncoordinated state actor, unable to deal with powerful vetoes. This failed reform – together with underspending in social programs in the

1980s – more than the direct action of neoliberal politicians, weakened services and opened the door to a systematic growth of the outside option. In Chapter 8 we proved that the analytical model based on democracy and progressive leadership as preconditions, and state actors with political support and favorable international ideas as drivers, travels – with some modifications – to the cases of Mauritius, South Korea, and Uruguay.

Even if we emphasize the role of policy architectures and state actors at specific moments in time, we are aware that these actors emerge under context-dependent circumstances. History, levels of development, state-society relations, and many other factors determine the presence or absence of state actors and shape the institutions where they operate. For example, in Costa Rica, an emerging elite of middle class professionals and small and medium landowners launched a process of state-building in the late 1940s, which facilitated the growth of autonomous state actors with expertise and professionalism – a point we have developed elsewhere (Martínez Franzoni and Sánchez-Ancochea, 2013a). In many other countries in the South, on the other hand, state institutions have been weak and the existence of progressive expert knowledge limited – partly due to the deployment of repressive strategies.

9.3 Using Architectures Effectively to Build Universalism

It is useful to explore now the practical implications of our analysis. In the following pages, we develop a set of key ideas that can assist those policymakers interested in promoting universalism in social policy. We build on the principle that universal outputs cannot be achieved instantly through quick fixes, but depend on setting appropriate long-term trajectories. The analysis draws on examples from services, including health care but also early child education and care as an emerging policy that most governments are addressing for the first time. We also consider CCTs and pensions.

9.3.1 Policy Architectures Should Promote Unified Services

The optimum way to secure universal outputs is through tax-funded, generous services and transfers for all together with a small and regulated outside option – that is, the "Scandinavian way." Yet building these kinds of policies requires high fiscal and institutional capacity to start with. Not surprisingly, just a few countries in the North and very few countries in the South have achieved it.

The Costa Rican case shows that creating payroll contributions may face fewer obstacles than increasing general taxes. In fact, it is not the instrument that matters the most, but the degree of unification each instrument reaches. Under unified policy architectures, contributions are independent of benefits, which are the same for everyone and, if possible, supplied by a single provider. All of these conditions can potentially be met through different eligibility principles and funding mechanisms. For example, in the case of health care, a country can have contributory and non-contributory systems for workers and the poor, but it should make sure that the basket of services and the type of providers are the same (i.e. everyone enters the same hospitals through the same doors). In contrast, separating services for the poor from those for the middle-class completely, like in the case of Mexico with *Seguro Popular*, runs the risk of consolidating fragmentation.

Thus, in the absence of tax-based programs relying on citizenship principles, contributory-based social insurance, targeted measures, and co-payments can jointly contribute to build policy architectures that deliver universal outputs. In what follows, we detail the conditions under which these tools – often present in most countries across the South – can make this positive contribution.

(1) Contributory-based Social Insurance

When it comes to instruments that promote universalism, social insurance programs based on payroll taxes are normally rejected because of how closely they link benefits to contributions. This assessment draws from the historical experience of many Southern countries: in South America, for example, occupation-based social insurance programs with multiple funds provided different benefits to different groups. In Central America, health care insurance has been organized under a single fund since the beginning, but with sharp distinctions between the services available to insured workers and those received by their dependents.

Yet Costa Rica provides evidence that unified contributory systems are possible. In the case of Uruguay, the 2008 reform unified the contributory-based policy architecture by placing all contributions into a single health care fund. Concerning old-age transfers, Argentina provides an example of recent unification: since 2008 the Sistema Integrado Previsional Argentino absorbs all individual savings into a single fund. Even the self-employed who do not meet these contributions are entitled to a similar pension.[1]

To fuel universalism, contributory systems must delink contributions and benefits as much as possible and combine eligibility based on people's status as workers with other criteria to incorporate the rest of the population as beneficiaries. Delinking contributions and benefits, which is often criticized by those fixated with individual incentives, also helps the state pool resources, thus generating economies of scale. In the case of pensions, to ensure generosity and equity, the state should set maximum pensions and guarantee generous minimum ones.

(2) Targeting Within Universalism

Under the residual view of state policy that dominated during the 1980s and 1990s, using targeted instruments to promote universal outputs is neither possible nor desirable: the poor and non-poor are to remain apart under public and private services, respectively. Yet, under a different, non-neoliberal view, targeted measures may contribute to universalism. The key principle is that they are used to incorporate beneficiaries *to the same entitlements available to everyone else.* To this purpose, targeting based on geographical areas or other ecological criteria – exactly what has happened in Costa Rica since the 1970s – may be more effective than means testing.

Let's draw from the case of CCTs to illustrate the differences between current approaches and our own recommendation based on the previous analysis. Many CCTs have provided the poor with benefits for the first time and have reinforced the state's commitment to the expansion of public health care and education. Yet because these services continue to embody the notion of "poor services for poor people", CCTs have done very little to expand equity. To enhance the contribution of CCTs to universal outputs, the prevailing notion of conditionality should be revisited, from conditioning beneficiaries to conditioning the state's service supply. Transfers should be expanded at the same time as services are improved through performance

---

[1] Those granted pensions in this way are expected to complete contributions by continuing to pay their fees upon retirement.

standards. The spatial expansion of CCTs could also be linked to the creation of better facilities in the most needed areas.

(3) User Fees

As we have argued in this book, particularly when referring to South Korea, co-payments reduce equity between beneficiaries and affect generosity. Therefore, the notion that user fees can contribute to universal trajectories may sound counter intuitive. Yet, under certain conditions, user fees can effectively expand funding and contribute to the quality of services in a non-segmented fashion.

The case of childcare can illustrate our point. Public "overspending" in attractive facilities – which may not be indispensable for good services – may often be needed to attract various segments of the middle class and to strengthen cross-class coalitions. Yet constructing attractive infrastructure is costly and demands a considerable expansion of the available resources. User fees can become a desirable option to raise those funds and secure involvement of the middle class provided three conditions are met. First, they must be progressive and charged to families who can afford them. Second, resources coming from user fees should be pooled together with all other income sources and help fund *all* facilities and not just those directly used by payers. Last but not least, only state authorities should know who is being charged with user fees and who is not.

9.3.2 Every Country May Start from a Different Place

In thinking about how to unify policy architectures, policymakers must chose measures that can affect the largest number of components, are politically feasible, and can trigger positive trajectories. In some cases, countries should start by unifying funding, in others by allowing the poor access to services already available for the non-poor, and in others by regulating the outside option. There is no single recipe.

Chile's health care reform constitutes a case in point. The country emerged from the Pinochet's dictatorship with a dual system. The main public provider had fewer resources, but serviced more people (who also suffered more medical troubles) than the private sector. Ideally, to promote universalism, Chile should have moved towards the unification of providers. Yet given the strength of private interest groups, this was rather difficult. Instead, in 2004, the Lagos administration defined a standard basket of benefits for everyone with the approval of the Universal Access Plan with Explicit Guarantees (Plan de Acceso Universal de Garantías Explícitas, AUGE). The reform entailed expanding funding for the public sector, overseeing the implementation of the guarantees among private providers, and reducing discrimination based on health risks. Obstacles to reach universal outputs in Chile are still plenty (Castiglioni, 2012), but AUGE moved the country towards unification.

This does not mean that "anything goes" and that all expansionary reforms will always contribute to unification. In particular, we remain skeptical of reforms that expand services for the poor through new programs, while simultaneously maintaining separate services for the non-poor. Contrary to what Cotlear *et al.* (2014) maintain, we fear that this approach will not create incentives for future unification, instead consolidating segmentation both in the short and long terms.

9.3.3 State Intervention Must Effectively Deal with the Private Threat

Neoliberal globalization posed numerous threats to universalism. Fiscal bottlenecks reduced social spending and lowered the quality of public services. Public sector reform reduced the management capacity of the central government. Deregulation and privatization expanded private providers with little interest in the equitable provision of services and transfers. Some segments of the middle class – larger in some countries than others – abandoned the state, preferring to use private providers.

As a result, promoting similar services for all no longer depends exclusively on reforming the state. Regulating the private sector effectively may be just as important. Regulation should in many instances include taxation that increases price and expands the amount of resources available to improve public services. Private providers should also be more transparent so that it is easier to distinguish between real differences in quality (say, more prompt medical attention or more qualified personnel) and differences that are accessories to the core services involved (e.g. more comfortable and diverse accommodation options in hospitals). Regulation should also reduce conflicting dual practice by limiting the amount of time doctors and other public servants are allowed to work in the private sector as well as the fees they can charge.

Regulating the outside option will discourage its use, thus reducing segmentation between high-income groups and the poor. It is also an important strategy to prevent the weakening of public provision. A powerful private sector creates more opportunities for dual practice and strengthens interest groups that support segmentation in funding, benefits, and provision.

Governmental regulation of different outside options can often generate as much if not more positive effects on people's wellbeing than the expansion of public services per se. This is clearly shown by El Salvador's recent record. The administration of Mauricio Funes (2009–2014) implemented measures to improve primary health for the rural poor – mostly by expanding facilities managed by the Ministry of Health – and increased investment in infrastructure and medical equipment in the hospitals managed by social security. These decisions had a positive effect on specific groups, but were never integrated into a single, unified strategy.

In contrast, the regulation of pharmacies had a more direct effect on improving access, quality and equity. In El Salvador, pharmacies act as a powerful outside option as many people resort to them to solve their health problems. Unfortunately, this drains public resources: as a result of inappropriate prescriptions and unfinished treatments – partly due to the high cost of drugs – many people end up in public hospitals with bigger issues to solve. By reducing the price of selected medicines, the General Law of Medicine weakened pharmacies while promoting a cross-class alliance among beneficiaries. By making prescriptions for key medicines mandatory, the Law also created incentives for more people to get their prescriptions from trained professionals. In addition, regulating access to over-the-counter medicine helps the public sector avoid many health problems that follow from the use of non-prescribed drugs.

9.3.4 The Pursuit of Universal Outputs Involves Thinking about the Future

Electoral cycles put pressure on policymakers to deliver results, including honoring commitments regarding the expansion of social spending. Unfortunately, electoral politics also involves risks, including perverse incentives to avoid reforms that only have long-term benefits. In social policy, electoral calculations usually push governments to increase coverage rather than equity and generosity. The main risk is that, from the onset, the expansion of coverage with uneven benefits can result in further fragmentation of provision, particularly in services.

Governments should instead recognize that pro-universal programs will not be built overnight. Their gradual expansion requires effective political trajectories, keeping in mind that "the order of factors does change the product." Progressive governments should put in place policy architectures capable of strengthening actors that demand a further equitable expansion of the programs.

In this process, difficult trade-offs between the short and long terms must be confronted. This is clear, for example, when thinking about early child education and care for children from 0 to 3 years of age. One way to expand these services rapidly is to fund a combination of public and private providers. Yet this strategy may be counterproductive to promote equity. Once the state funds different service providers, how can service fragmentation be avoided? Will all providers offer exactly the same services? Won't they charge for additional services or discriminate in favor of children from favorable backgrounds? The expansion of coverage at a slower pace but based on a single provider and/or on a diverse set of providers with strong regulation of private ones may do more to guarantee progress in all dimensions of universalism.

Of course this is easier said than done: children of low-income families and full-time working parents need to have services sooner rather than later. The challenge is then to identify temporary measures that expand access while also encouraging steps towards further unification – exactly what social security in Costa Rica did in the 1940s. What is at stake – and what politicians may easily forget in the absence of state actors capable of reminding them – is the building of policy trajectories, not just benefits per se.

9.4 Conclusion: Towards Future Research Agendas on Universalism

In the process of suggesting new ways to think about universalism, our research has probably raised more questions than provided answers. We hope that our book can open future lines of research among sociologists, political scientists, political economists, and other public policy experts. Our ideas could also help policymakers approach social policy in more creative ways in the future.

Given the high concentration of income across the South, the top 5 percent is likely to use private services and to stay away from public ones. Yet what happens with the following 5 percent or with the second income decile? Can people in these income brackets be enticed to the public sector? The answers to these questions will be country specific and partly driven by income distribution. A better understanding of the social structure in each country, including divisions within the middle classes, will be particularly important. Studies based on household surveys could determine current patterns of consumption of services and levels of public transfers and consider implications for the unification of the policy architecture.

Hopefully, this book will also encourage studies of the policy architecture for health care, pensions, education, and other services and transfers in different countries. To design better and more sustainable social policies, we ought to consider how different interventions affect eligibility, funding, the definition of benefits, and the characteristics of providers. By studying these components together, researchers can compare degrees of fragmentation across countries. Policymakers will also be able to design credible political strategies towards unification: some countries may need to pool different funding mechanisms while others should first create a more common basket of benefits.

Analysis of the policy architectures should always incorporate a careful consideration of the outside option, including private provision but also particular vested interests within the public sector. The outside option undermines universal outputs by weakening the commitment to the public sector, reducing pressures to improve the quality of services, and worsening public provision from the inside (e.g. conflicting dual practices in health care, conflicting practices in the management of individual saving funds in pensions). The existence of the outside option is by no means unique to Costa Rica, Mauritius, and South Korea: for example, a study of health care spending in six Latin American countries reveals that out-of-pocket spending represents between 32 percent and 60 percent of all health care spending (Debrott, 2014). Private education and private pension funds are also on the rise in many middle income countries in the South. We need to better understand how and why the outside option is increasing in different sectors and countries, how public and private provision interact with each other, and how the latter can be more effectively regulated.

Since building unified architectures takes time, we also need more research on long-term trajectories. When considering countries in the South, it is hard to find historical evidence of programs that, departing from the extreme poor, were able to scale up to the rest of the population. The problems derived from building social security by reaching the professional middle class first are also well known. Based primarily on the case of Costa Rica, we have argued that architectures should initially incorporate people that are neither poor nor part of the upper middle class. We would like to encourage more studies that test and refine this claim and explore trajectories in different countries.

Further research concerning the type of incentives likely to align short-term electoral cycles with effective long-term trajectories is also needed. Tensions between expanding coverage and improving generosity and equity deserve special attention. Politicians are under great pressure to deliver results quickly for as many people as possible. Yet, if our argument is correct, segregated incorporation of the poor may lead to segmented outputs over the medium and long run.

Who shapes the policy architectures? Are state actors always the driving force as in the Costa Rican case? Or are political parties and their characteristics more important as Pribble (2013) argues? Do social movements have the technical expertise and policy influence to shape architectures in some cases? Studies that place the policy process in historical perspective can answer these questions, illuminating how techno-political actors emerge and how the composition of state actors evolves over time. Elsewhere we have highlighted the role of state building in expanding the number of progressive techno-politicians as well as gradually empowering high ranking bureaucrats in the Costa Rican case (Martínez Franzoni and Sánchez-Ancochea, 2013a). But is this the norm elsewhere in the South? In the recent wave of Latin American leftist governments, has the presence and the role of techno-politicians been as important as we claim? Research on state actors should also be placed within the study of state institutions more generally; as we showed in Chapter 7, the weakening of these institutions harms the public sector's capacity to promote universal outputs.

Creating more equitable societies is one of the most urgent challenges of our time and social policy has a key role to play in meeting it. Providing everyone with high quality, comprehensive health care, education, pensions, and other social rights is not only an ethical responsibility, but also an intelligent way to facilitate economic growth and social cohesion. Success in this task will necessarily take time, but it can certainly be achieved with patience and the right strategy.

References

Abel-Smith archive (1960). "Interview with Dr Dufourgmentel," March 30. London School of Economics.

Abel-Smith, Brian (1976). "Letter to Mr Osgleby," July 29. Abel-Smith archives: London School of Economics.

(1977). "A Free General Practitioners National Health Service," Confidential mimeo for the Ministry of Health. Abel-Smith archives: London School of Economics.

(1991). "Report 3 Visit to Costa Rica," Mimeo, Abel-Smith archive: London School of Economics.

(1994). "Confidential Brief on Health Insurance. Review of Social Services. Brief on Health Insurance Scheme." *Report to the Technical Committee of High Officials*. Abel-Smith archives: London School of Economics.

Abel-Smith, Brian and Lynes, Tony (1976). "Report on a National Pension Scheme for Mauritius," Port Louis: Government Printer, Abel-Smith archives: London School of Economics.

Abel-Smith, Brian and Titmuss, Kay (1987). *The Philosophy of Welfare*. London: Allen & Unwin.

African Business Monitor (2012). "Mauritius: Unions Oppose a Slew of Privatizations." Available at http://africanbusinessmagazine.com/africa-within/countryfiles/mauritius-unions-oppose-slew-of-privatisations (accessed January 19, 2015).

Agartan, Tuba (2012). "Marketization and Universalism: Crafting the Right Balance in the Turkish Healthcare System." *Current Sociology*, 60(4): 456–471.

Amenta, Edwin (2003). "What we Know about the Development of Social Policy: Comparative and Historical Research in Comparative and Historical Perspective." In James Mahoney and Dietrich Rueschemeyer (eds.), *Comparative Historical Analysis in the Social Sciences* (91–131). Cambridge University Press.

Andersen Consulting (1996). "Marco Conceptual del Sistema de Asignación de Recursos." Doc. A1. Caja Costarricense de Seguro: San José, Costa Rica.

Andrenacci, Luciano and Repetto, Fabián (2006). "Un camino para reducir la desigualdad y construir ciudadanía." In Carlos Gerardo Molina (ed.), *Universalismo básico. Una nueva política social para América Latina* (93–114). Washington, DC: Banco Interamericano de Desarrollo/ Planeta.

Antía, Florencia; Castillo, Marcelo; Fuentes, Guillermo; and Midaglia, Carmen (2013). "La renovación del sistema de protección uruguayo: el desafío de superar la dualización." Paper presented at the Political Science Congress. Montevideo, Uruguay, October 7–11.

Anttonen, Anneli; Häikiö, Liisa; and Stefánsson, Kolbeinn (eds.) (2012). *Welfare State, Universalism and Diversity.* Cheltenham: Edward Elgar.

Arbulo, Victoria; Pagano, Juan Pablo; Rak, Gustavo; and Arias, Laura (2012). *El camino hacia la Cobertura Universal en Uruguay: Evaluación y revisión del financiamiento del Sistema de Salud uruguayo.* Pan American Health Organization (PAHO).

Arza, Camila (2012). "Towards a Rights-based Policy? The Expansion of Old-Age Pension Coverage in Latin America". Draft. CONICET/ FLACSO-Argentina.

Avelino George; Brown, David; and Hunter, Wendy (2005). "The Effects of Capital Mobility, Trade Openness, and Democracy on Social Spending in Latin America, 1980–1999." *American Journal of Political Science,* 49: 625–641.

Bachelet, Michelle (2011). *Social Protection Floor: For a Fair and Inclusive Globalization.* Geneva: International Labour Organization.

Barrán, José Pedro (1992). *Medicina y sociedad en el Uruguay del Novecientos. Volumen 1. El poder de curar.* Montevideo: Ediciones de la Banda Oriental.

Barrientos, Armando and Lloyd-Sherlock, Peter (2002). "Non-Contributory Pensions and Social Protection." *Issues in Social Protection. Discussion Paper 12.* Geneva: International Labour Organization (ILO).

Béland, Daniel and Lecours, André (2008). *Nationalism and Social Policy: The Politics of Territorial Solidarity.* Oxford University Press.

Béland, Daniel and Waddan, Alex (2013). "Social Policy Universality in Canada and the United States." Paper Presented at the Conference on the Political Economy of Social Policy in North America: Convergence Towards Universalism? St Antony's College, Oxford, March 1.

Béland, Daniel; Blomqvist, Paula; Andersen, Jørgen Goul; Palme, Joakim; and Waddan, Alex (2014). "The Universal Decline of Universality? Social Policy Change in Canada, Denmark, Sweden, and the United Kingdom." *Social Policy and Administration,* 48(7): 739–756.

Bergh, Andreas (2004). "The Universal Welfare State: Theory and the Case of Sweden." *Political Studies,* 52: 745–766.

Bertodano de, Isabel (2003). "The Costa Rican Health System: Lost Cost, High Value." *Bulletin of the World Health Organization*, 81(8): 626–627.

Bielschowsky, Ricardo (1998). "Evolución de las ideas de la Cepal." *Revista de la CEPAL*, No. extraordinario: 21–47.

Birdsall, Nancy (2010). "The (Indispensable) Middle Class in Developing Countries; or, The Rich and the Rest, Not the Poor and the Rest." Working Paper 207. Center for Global Development.

Birn, Anne-Emmanuelle (2008) "Doctors on Record: Uruguay's Infant Mortality Stagnation and Its Remedies, 1895–1945." *Bulletin of the History of Medicine*, 82(2): 311–354.

(2012). "Uruguay's Child Rights Approach to Health: What Role of Civil Registration." *Proceedings of the British Academy*, 182: 412–447.

Borzutsky, Silvia (2002). *Vital Connections: Politics, Social Security and Inequality in Chile*. South Bend: University of Notre Dame Press.

Bowman, Larry (1991). *Mauritius: Democracy and Development in the Indian Ocean*. Boulder and San Francisco: Westview Press.

Brady, Henry and Collier, David (eds.) (2014). *Rethinking Social Inquiry: Diverse Tools, Shared Standards*. Lanham: Rowman and Littlefield.

Briceño, Edgar and Méndez, Eduardo (1982). "Salud pública y distribución de ingreso en Costa Rica," *Revista de Ciencias Económicas*, 2(1 and 2): 49–70.

Brooks, Sarah (2009). *Social Protection and the Market in Latin America: The Transformation of Social Security Institutions*. Cambridge University Press.

(2011). "Globalization and Pension Reform in Latin America." *Latin American Politics and Society*, 49(4): 31–62.

Brown, David and Hunter, Wendy (1999). "Democracy and Social Spending in Latin America, 1980–1992." *The American Political Science Review*, 93(4): 779–790.

Buchelli, Marisa; Ferreira-Coimbra, Natalia; Fortesa, Álvaro; and Rossi, Ianina (2006). *El acceso a la jubilación o pensión en Uruguay: ¿cuántos y quiénes lo lograrán?* Montevideo: CEPAL.

Bunwaree, Sheila (2005). "State–Social Relations: Re-engineering the Mauritian Social Contract." Draft Paper. University of Mauritius.

Burn-Murdoch, John and Bernard, Steve (2014). "The Fragile Middle: Millions Face Poverty as Emerging Economies Slow." *Financial Times*, April 13. Available at www.ft.com/cms/s/2/95fb1cca-c181-11e3-83af-00144feabdc0.html#axzz3DCjQtfmf, accessed April 13, 2014.

Caja Costarricense de Seguro Social (1942a). Act 1, January 23. San José: CCSS.

(1942b). Act 109, December 11. San José: CCSS.

(1943). Untitled article. *Su Seguridad: Revista oficial de la* Caja Costarricense de Seguro Social, 7:5 (October–December). San José: CCSS.

(1962). Acta 2836, Junta Directiva, August 2. San José: CCSS.

(1969a). Acta 4545, Junta Directiva, November 6. San José: CCSS.

(1969b). Acta 4055, Junta Directiva, December 12. San José: CCSS.

(1969c). Acta 3984, Junta Directiva, July 8. San José: CCSS.

(1970a). Acta 4092, Junta Directiva, March 10. San José: CCSS.

(1970b). Acta 4116, Junta Directiva, May 7. San José: CCSS.

(1970c). Acta 4115, Junta Directiva, May 5. San José: CCSS.

(1970d). Acta 4127, Junta Directiva, May 29. San José: CCSS.

(1970e). "Universalización del seguro social" (Vindas Report), submitted to Legislative Assembly, July. San José: CCSS.

(1972). Acta 4468, Junta Directiva, May 30. San José: CCSS.

(2014). Data provided by the Dirección Actuarial y Económica, September. San José: CCSS.

Callahan, Daniel (2008). "Health Care Costs and Medical Technology." In Mary Crowley (ed.), *From Birth to Death and Bench to Clinic: the Hastings Center Bioethics Briefing Book for Journalists, Policymakers, and Campaigns* (79–82). Garrison: The Hastings Center.

Cambronero, Juven; Larios, Manuel; and Muñoz, Walter (2001). "Comisión especial que proceda a: analizar la calidad de servicios, compra de servicios privados, utilización de recursos de la CCSS, para la enseñanza universitaria privada, medicamentos y pensiones." Expediente N°13.980: Asamblea Legislativa, San José, Abril 26.

Carrillo, Rafael; Martínez Franzoni, Juliana; Naranjo, Fernando; and Sauma, Pablo (2011). "Informe del equipo de especialistas nacionales nombrado para el análisis de la situación del seguro de la salud de la CCSS." *Recomendaciones para restablecer la sostenibilidad financiera del seguro social*. San José, September.

Carroll, Barbara and Carroll, Terrance (2000). "Trouble in Paradise: Ethnic Conflict in Mauritius." *Commonwealth and Comparative Politics*, 38(2): 25–50.

Casas, Antonio and Vargas, Herman (1980). "The Health System in Costa Rica: Toward a National Health Service." *Journal of Public Health Policy*, 1(3): 258–279.

Castiglioni, Rossana (2000). "Welfare State Reform in Chile and Uruguay: Cross-class Coalitions, Elite Ideology, and Veto Players." Prepared for delivery at the 2000 Meeting of the Latin American Studies Association, Miami, March 16–18.

(2005). *The Politics of Social Policy Change in Chile and Uruguay: Retrenchment versus Maintenance, 1973–1998*. New York: Routledge.

(2012). "Social Policy Reform and Continuity under the Bachelet Administration." In Jordi Diez and Susan Franceschet (eds.), *Comparative Public Policy in Latin America* (247–271). University of Toronto Press.

Castro Méndez, Mauricio and Martínez Franzoni, Juliana (2010). "Un modelo exitoso en la encrucijada: límites del desencuentro entre régimen laboral y de bienestar en Costa Rica." *Revista Centroamericana de Ciencias Sociales*, 7(1): 70–122.

Centeno, Miguel (1994). *Democracy within Reason: Technocratic Revolution in Mexico*. University Park: Pennsylvania State University Press.

CEPAL (2007). *Panorama social de América Latina 2007*, Santiago: CEPAL.

(2009). *Proyecciones de población*. Latin American Demographic Observatory. Available at www.cepal.org/publicaciones/xml/7/38297/od7_proyeccion_poblacion.pdf.

Cercone, James and Pacheco Jiménez, José (2008). "Costa Rica: 'Good Practice' in Expanding Health Care Coverage – Lessons from Reforms in Low- and Middle Income Countries." In Pablo Gottret, George J. Schieber, and Hugh Waters (eds.), *Good Practices in Health Financing: Lessons from Reforms in Low- and Middle Income Countries*. Washington, D.C.: The World Bank.

Choi, Young Jun (2008). "Pension Policy and Politics in East Asia." *Policy and Politics*, 36(1): 127–144.

Clark, Mark (2002). "Health Sector Reform in Costa Rica: Reinforcing a Public System." Prepared for the Woodrow Wilson Center Workshops on the Politics of Education and Health Reforms. Washington D.C, April 18–19.

Clark, Mary (2005). "Health Reform, Doctors and the Physician Labor Market in Costa Rica." *The Latin Americanist*, Fall: 125–148.

(2010). "The Recentralization of Health Care Reform in Costa Rica." Occasional Paper Prepared for the Center for Inter-American Policy and Research (CIPR). Department of Political Science, Tulane University, July 21.

(2011). "The DR-CAFTA and the Costa Rican Health Sector: A Push Toward Privatization?" *The Latin Americanist*, September: 1–23.

Collier, David, Brady, Henry; and Seawright, Jason (2004). "Sources of Leverage in Causal Inference: Toward an Alternative View of Methodology." In David Collier and Henry Brady (eds.), *Rethinking Social Inquiry* (161–201). Maryland: Rowman and Littlefield.

Colony of Mauritius (1948). *Social Insurance Schemes in Mauritius. Correspondance Exchanged between the Government of Mauritius and the Colonial Office*. Port Louis: Government Printer. Abel-Smith archive: London School of Economics.

Congreso Constitucional de la República de Costa Rica (1941a). Comisiones del Congreso, Dictamen de Creación de la Caja de Seguro Social, October 16.

(1941b). Decreto de Creación de la Caja de Seguro Social, October 31.

Congreso de la República de Uruguay (1943). Decreto de Ley No 10.384, February 13.

Connolly, Greg (2002). "Costa Rican Health Care: A Maturing Comprehensive System." Global Health Council. Available at www.cehat.org/rthc/paper5.htm, accessed August 2013.

Contraloria General de la República de Costa Rica (CGR) (1999). *Panorama de la Reforma del Sector Salud*. San José: CGR.

Coopers and Lybrand (1995). *Study on the Development of a Health Insurance Scheme in Mauritius, Technical Proposal to the Government of Mauritius*. Abel-Smith archives: London School of Economics.

Cornia, Giovanni (2010). "Income Distribution under Latin America's New Left Regimes." *Journal of Human Development and Capabilities*, 11(1): 85–114.

Corporación Andina Fomento (CAF) (2012). "Finanzas públicas para el desarrollo: fortaleciendo la conexión entre ingresos y gastos." *Reporte de Economía y Desarrollo*. Bogotá: CAF-Banco de Desarrollo de América Latina.

Cortés, Alberto and León, Andrés (2008). "Costa Rica: conflictividad social y distribución, 1950–2005." *Research Report, Policy Regime and Poverty Reduction, Costa Rican Case*. Geneva: UNRISD.

Cotlear, Daniel *et al.* (2014). "Overcoming Social Segregation in Health Care in Latin America." *The Lancet*, Series Universal Health Care Coverage in Latin America, October 16, 1–9.

Council of Government of Mauritius (1943). *A Statement on Public Health in Mauritius*. Port Louis: Government Printer.

Creedman, Theodore (1994). *El gran cambio: de León Cortés a Calderón Guardia*. San Jose: Editorial Costa Rica.

Cueto, Marcos (2004). "The Origins of Primary Health Care and Selective Primary Health Care." *Public Health Then and Now*, 94(11): 1864–1874.

Danson, Mike; McAlpine, Robin; Spicker, Paul; and Willie Sullivan (2012). "The Case for Universalism: An Assessment of the Evidence on the Effectiveness and Efficiency of the Universal Welfare State." The Jimmy Reid Foundation.

David, Antonio and Petri, Martin (2013). "Inclusive Growth and the Incidence of Fiscal Policy in Mauritius – Much Progress, but More Could Be Done." IMF Working Paper.

Deacon, Bob (2010). "From the Global Politics of Poverty Alleviation to the Global Politics of Welfare State Rebuilding." *Crop Poverty Brief*, June.

Deacon, Bob; Cimadamore, Alberto; Grønmo, Sigmund; Koehler, Gabriele; Lie, Gro Therese; O'Brien, Karen; Ortiz, Isabel; Pogge, Thomas; and St. Clair, Asuncion (2013). "Mobilizing Critical Research for Preventing and Eradicating Poverty". *Crop Poverty Brief*, January.

Debrott, D. (2014) "Consumo efectivo de los hogares en salud. Resultado de estudios piloto en seis países deAmérica Latina." Serie Estudios Estadísticos no. 83, CEPAL.

Deerpalsing, Munkoomar (1988). "Proposals for the setting up of a National Health Insurance Scheme for Mauritius," mimeo. Abel-Smith archives: London School of Economics.

Demirguc-Kunt, Asli and Scharwz, Annta (1995). "Costa Rican Pension System: Options for Reform." Policy Research Working Paper 1483. Policy Research Department Finance and Private Sector Development Division. Washington: World Bank.

Devi, Sharmila (2008). "Mauritius Counts Health Successes." *The Lancet*, 371(9624): 1567–1568.

Deyo, Frederic (1989). *Beneath the Miracle. Labor Subordination in the New Asian Industrialization*. Los Angeles: University of California Press.

DFID (2011). *Cash Transfers: Evidence Paper*. Policy Division. London: DFID, UKAid.

Diario de Costa Rica (1941). "Previstos todos los aspectos de la implantación de los seguros sociales en Costa Rica." October 2: 1–6.

——— (1942). "La United Fruit Company pagará el seguro social en sus actividades bananeras en Costa Rica." March 11: 1, 5.

——— (1942). "La Caja Costarricense de Seguro Social expone las razones que tiene para oponerse al Proyecto de los Empleados Municipales, tendiente a que se les exima del Seguro Social." July 21: 3.

——— (1942). "La Municipalidad de Heredia, en sensacional acuerdo, se pronuncia en contra de la Ley de Pensiones Municipales y a favor del Seguro Social." July 30: 1, 6.

——— (1942). "La Municipalidad de Cartago pide al Congreso no aprobar la reforma al Artículo 43 de la Ley de Seguro Social." August 5: 1, 8.

——— (1942). "Anuncio CCSS." September 18: 5.

——— (1943). "Los empleados de aduanas piden ley especial de pensiones." August 2: 9.

——— (1943). "Puntarenas también rendirá homenaje al autor de las Garantías Sociales." September 2: 2.

——— (1943). "Las organizaciones obreras y campesinas del país apoyan el Proyecto de Reforma a la Ley del Seguro Social." September 5: 13.

——— (1943). "Puntarenas: base inconmovible del Código de Trabajo." September 9: 2.

Diaz-Arias (2009). "Social Crises and Struggling Memories: Populism, Popular Mobilization, Violence, and Memories of Civil War in Costa Rica, 1940-1948." PhD Dissertation, Department of History, Indiana University.

Diccionario Biográfico de Chile (1942). Santiago de Chile: La Nación, SA.

Dion, Michelle (2010). *Workers and Welfare: Comparative Institutional Change in Twentieth-Century Mexico*. University of Pittsburgh Press.

Dommen, Edward and Dommen, Bridgit (1999). *Mauritius: an Island of Success: a Retrospective Study 1960–1993*. Wellington: Pacific Press.

ECLAC (2007). *Social Cohesion: Inclusion and a Sense of Belonging in Latin America and the Caribbean*. Santiago: ECLAC.

Eisenstadt, Shmuel N. (1966). *Modernization: Protest and Change*. Englewood Cliffs: Prentice-Hall.

Erikson, Erik (2015). *Welfare in Paradise? The Effects of the Private Health Sector on Universality in Health-Care in Mauritius*. Thesis for the MPhil in Development Studies, University of Oxford.

Esping-Andersen, Gosta (1990). *The Three Worlds of Welfare Capitalism*. Princeton University Press.

Esping-Andersen, Gosta and Korpi, Walter (1987). "From Poor Relief to Institutional Welfare State: The Development of Scandinavian Social Policy." In Robert Erikson; Erik Jorgen Hanson; Ringen Stein; and Hannu Uusitalo (eds.), *The Scandinavian Model. Welfare States and Welfare Research* (39–74). London: M. E. Sharpe.

Estévez-Abe, Margarita, Iversen, Torben, and Soskice, David (2001). "Social Protection and the Formation of Skills: A Reinterpretation of the Welfare State." In Peter Hall and David Soskice (eds.), *Varieties of Capitalism: The Institutional Foundations of Comparative Advantage* (145–183). Oxford University Press.

Ewig, Christina (2010). *Second-Wave Neoliberalism: Gender, Race and Health Sector Reform in Peru*. University Park: Penn State University Press.

Ewig, Christina and Kay, Stephen (2011). "Postretrenchment Politics: Policy Feedback in Chile's Health and Pension Reforms". *Latin American Politics and Society* 53(4): 67–99.

Ferreira Francisco *et al.* (2012). *Economic Mobility and the Rise of the Latin American Middle Class*. Washington, D.C.: World Bank (Latin America and Caribbean Studies).

Figueres Ferrer, José (1970). *Presidential Speech*. May 8. San José, Costa Rica.

Filgueira, Fernando (1995). "A Century of Social Welfare in Uruguay: Growth to the Limit of the Batllista Social State." *Democracy and Social Policy Series*. Working Paper 5, Kellogg Institute of International Studies, University of Notre Dame.

(1998). "El nuevo modelo de prestaciones sociales en América Latina: Residualismo y ciudadanía estratificada." In Brian Roberts (ed.), *Ciudadanía y Política Social* (71–116). San José: FLACSO.

(2005). "Welfare and Democracy in Latin America: the Development, Crises and Aftermath of Universal, Dual and Exclusionary Welfare States." UNRISD Working Paper, 21.

(2007a). "The Latin American Social States: Critical Juncture and Critical Choices." In Yusuf Bangura (ed.), *Democracy and Social Policy* (136–163). New York: Palgrave/UNRISD.

(2007b). "Cohesión, riesgo y arquitectura de protección social en América Latina." *CEPAL Series de Política Social*, 135.

Filgueira, Fernando and Moraes, Andrés (2001). "Contextos y estrategias de las reformas institucionales en la Seguridad Social, la Educación y la Salud en Uruguay." *Revista Uruguaya de Ciencias Políticas*, 12: 97–122.

Filgueira, Fernando; Molina, Carlos; Papadópulos, Jorge; and Tobar, Federico (2006). "Universalismo básico: una alternativa posible y necesaria para mejorar las condiciones de vida." In Carlos Gerardo Molina (ed.), *Universalismo básico. Una nueva política social para América Latina* (19–58). Washington, D.C.: Inter-American Development Bank.

Financial Express (2015). "Mauritius has the Potential to Transform Itself into a Medical Hub for the Region," January 10. Available at www.financialexpress.com/article/healthcare/market/mauritius-has-the-potential-to-transform-itself-into-a-medical-hub-for-the-region/28485.

Fischer, Andrew (2012). "Inequality and the Universalistic Principle in the Post-2015 Development Agenda." Institute of Social Studies (The Hague), Erasmus University Rotterdam, November.

Frankel, Jeffrey (2010). "Mauritius: African Success Story." NBER Working Paper 16569.

Fraser, Nancy (1994). "After the Family Wage: Gender Equity and the Welfare State." *Political Theory*, 22: 591–618.

Frenk, Julio (2006). "Bridging the Divide: Global Lessons from Evidence-based Health Policy in Mexico." *Lancet*, 368: 954–961.

Foro de la Concertación Nacional (1998). "La reforma del Sistema Nacional de Pensiones: una propuesta." San José, July 14.

Forteza, Alvaro; Apella, Ignacion; Fajnzylber, Eduardo; Grushka, Carlos; Rossi, Ianina; and Sanroman, Graciela (2009). "Work Histories and Pension Entitlements in Argentina, Chile and Uruguay." Social Protection Discussion Paper 926. Washington, D.C.: Banco Mundial.

Fuentes, Guillermo (2010). "El sistema de salud uruguayo en la post dictadura: análisis de la reforma del Frente Amplio y las condiciones que la hicieron possible." *Revista Uruguaya de Ciencia Política*, 19(1): 119–143.

(2013). "La creación del Sistema Nacional Integrado de Salud en Uruguay (2005–2012): impulso reformista y freno de puntos y actores de veto." Tesis de Doctorado en Gobierno y Administración Pública, Instituto Universitario de Investigación Ortega y Gasset, Madrid. Mimeo.

García Repetto, Ulises (2011). "La descapitalización de las Cajas de jubilaciones en el Uruguay: el empapelamiento de las Cajas: 1943–1967." Instituto de Economía- Facultad de Ciencias Sociales y Administración-Área de Historia Económica, Montevideo.

Giedion, Ursula, Alfonso, Eduardo Andres, and Díaz, Yadira. (2013). *The Impact of Universal Coverage Schemes in the Developing World: a Review of the Existing Evidence.* Universal Health Coverage (UNICO) Studies Series, no. 25. Washington, D.C.: The World Bank.

Gobierno de Costa Rica (1992). "Proyecto Rectoría y Fortalecimiento del Ministerio de Salud." San José, Costa Rica: Unidad preparatoria del proyecto Reforma del Sector Salud. Programa de Mejoramiento de los Servicios de Salud. CR-0120/BID. August.

Goñi, Edwin; López, Humberto; and Servén, Luis (2011). "Fiscal Redistribution and Income Inequality in Latin America." World Bank Policy Research Paper, 4487.

Goodman, Roger and Peng, Ito (1996). "The East Asian Welfare State: Peripatetic Learning, Adaptive Change and Nation-Building." In Gosta Esping-Andersen (ed.), *Welfare States in Transition. National Adaptations in Global Economies* (192–225). London: Sage.

Gottret, Pablo; Schieber, George; and Waters, Hugh (eds.) (2008). *Good Practices in Health Financing: Lessons from Reforms in Low- and Middle Income Countries.* Washington D.C.: The World Bank.

Gough, Ian (2013). "Social Policy Regimes in the Developing World." In Patricia Kennett (ed.), *A Handbook of Comparative Social Policy* (205–224). Cheltenham: Edward Elgar Publishing Ltd.

Government Medical and Dental Officers Association (Undated). *The Health and Social Services in Mauritius.* Abel-Smith Archives: London School of Economics.

Government of Mauritius (1976). *White Paper: The National Pension Scheme, Port Louis: Government Printer.* Abel-Smith archives: London School of Economics.

Grunberg, Isabelle (1998). "Double Jeopardy: Globalization, Liberalization and the Fiscal Squeeze." *World Development*, 26: 591–605.

Haggard, Stephan and Kaufman, Robert (2008). *Development, Democracy, and Welfare States: Latin America, East Asia, and Eastern Europe.* Princeton University Press.

Hall, Peter (1993). "Policy Paradigms, Social Learning, and the State: The Case of Economic Policymaking in Britain". *Comparative Politics*, 25(3): 275–296.

Hanlon, Joseph; Barrientos, Armando; and Hulme, David (2010). *Just Give Money to the Poor: The Development Revolution from the Global South*. Sterling: Kumarian Press.

Hanson, Kara and Berman, Peter (1998). "Private Health Care Provision in Developing Countries: a Preliminary Analysis of Levels and Composition." *Health Policy and Planning*, 13: 195–211.

Henderson, Jeffret; Hume, David; Hossein, Jalilian; and Phillips, Richard (2003). "Bureaucratic Effects: 'Weberian' State Structures and Poverty Reduction." CPRC Working Paper, 31.

Hernández-Naranjo, Gerardo (2010). "Reseña de las elecciones presidenciales de 1970." *Proyecto Atlas Electoral de Costa Rica 1953–2006*. San José: Instituto de Investigaciones Sociales (IIS).

Herrero, Fernando and Durán, Fabio (2001). "El sector privado en el sistema de salud de Costa Rica." *Serie Financiamiento del Desarrollo 109*. Santiago: CEPAL.

Hoeven, Rolph von der (2012). "MDGs Post-2015: Beacons in Turbulent Times or False Lights?" Paper prepared for the UN System Task Team on the Post-2015 UN Development.

Holzmann, Robert and Hinz, Richard (2005). *Old Age Income Support in the 21st Century: International Perspective on Pension System and Reform*. Washington, D.C.: World Bank.

Hopenhayn, Martín (2007). "Cohesión social: una perspectiva en proceso de elaboración." In CEPAL (ed.), *Cohesión social en América Latina y el Caribe: una revisión perentoria de algunas de sus dimensiones* (37–47). Santiago de Chile: CEPAL, Colección documentos de proyecto.

Hospitales de Costa Rica (1977). "Traspasados a la Caja los Hospitales San Juan de Dios, Psiquiátrico Nacional y Sanatorio Chacon Paut." *Hospitales de Costa Rica*, 14: 3.

Huber, Evelyne (1996). "Options for Social Policy in Latin America: Neoliberal versus Social Democratic Models." In Gosta Esping-Andersen (ed.), *Welfare States in Transition* (141–192). London: Sage Publications.

——— (2002). *Models of Capitalism. Lessons for Latin America*. University Park: Penn State University Press.

Huber, Evelyne and Stephens, John D. (2001). *Development and Crisis of the Welfare State: Parties and Policies in Global Markets*. University of Chicago Press.

——— (2012). *Democracy and the Left: Social Policy and Inequality in Latin America*. University of Chicago Press.

Huber, Evelyne; Mustillo, Thomas; and Stephens, John D. (2008). "Politics and Social Spending in Latin America and the Caribbean." *The Journal of Politics*, 70(2), 420–436.

Hwang, Gyu-Jin (2006). *Pathways to State Welfare in Korea: Interests, Ideas and Institutions*. London: Routledge.

(2007). *The Rules of the Game: The Politics of National Pensions in Korea*. International Development Department School of Public Policy University of Birmingham.

(2012). "Explaining Welfare State Adaptation in East Asia: The Cases of Japan, Korea and Taiwan." *Asian Journal of Social Science*, 40: 174–202.

Institute of Development Studies (IDS) (2012). "Where will the World's Poor Live? Global Poverty Projections for 2020 and 2030." IDS Focus Policy Briefing 26, August.

International Labour Organization (ILO) (2007). "Visions for Asia's Decent Work Decade: Sustainable Growth and Jobs to 2015." Paper Presented at the Asian Employment Forum: Growth, Employment and Decent Employment. Beijing, August 13–15.

(2011). "International Labour Conference, Meeting Number 100ᵃ Reunion." *Report IV. Floor of Social Protection for Social Justice and Equitable Globalization*. Geneva: International Labour Organization.

(2012). *The Strategy of the International Labour Organization. Social Security for all. Building Social Protection Floors and Comprehensive Social Security Systems*. Geneva: International Labour Organization.

International Labour Review (1936). "The Labour Conference of the American States which are Members of the International Labour Organisation." *International Labour Review*, 33(2):446–684.

Itzigsohn, José (2000). *Developing Poverty. The State, Labor Market Deregulation, and the Informal Economy in Costa Rica and the Dominican Republic*. University Park: Pennsylvania State University.

Jara, Antonio (2002). "Médicos y Seguridad Social en Costa Rica durante las décadas de 1950 y 1960." *VI Congreso Centroamericano de Historia*, Universidad de Panamá, July 22–26.

Jaramillo, Juan (2003). *Historia y evolución del Seguro Social de Costa Rica. Su primer hospital Dr Rafael Ángel Calerón Guardia*. San José: Editorial Nacional de Salud y Seguridad Social.

(2013). *La crisis en el seguro social en Costa Rica*. San José: Universidad de Costa Rica.

Jeong, Hyoung-Sun and Niki, Ryu (2012). "Divergence in the Development of Public Health Insurance in Japan and the Republic of Korea: a Multiple-Payer versus a Single-Payer System." *International Social Security Review*, 65(2): 51–73.

Jeong, Hyoung-Sun and Shin Jeong-Woo (2012). "Trends in Scale and Structure of Korea's Health Expenditure over Last Three Decades (1980–2009): Financing, Functions and Providers." *Journal of Korean Medical Science*, 27: S13–20.

Joignant, Alfredo (2011). "The Politics of Technopols: Resources, Political Competence and Collective Leadership in Chile, 1990–2010." *Journal of Latin American Studies*, 43: 517–546.

Joynathsing, Mohipnarain (1987). "Mauritius". In John Dixon *Social Welfare in Africa*. New York: Routledge.

Kessean, Hemant and Juwaheer, Thenike (2010). "Comparing Healthcare in Private Clinics vs Public Hospital Services Sector." International Research Symposium in Service Management, Le Meridien Hotel, Mauritius, August 24–27.

Kaufman, Robert and Segura-Ubiergo, Alex (2001). "Globalization, Domestic Politics, and Social Spending in Latin America: a Time-Series Cross-Section Analysis, 1973–1997." *World Politics*, 53(4): 553–587.

Kharas, Horni (2010). "The Emerging Middle Class in Developing Countries." Working Paper 285. OCDE Development Centre.

Kim, Kyo-Seong and Lee, Young-Jae (2010). "Developments and General Features of National Health Insurance in Korea." *Social Work in Public Health*, 25(2): 142–157.

Kim, Seong Sook (2013). "Pension Reform Options in Korea." IMF International Conference, Tokyo, January.

Kim, Won Sub and Choi, Young Jun (2013). "Revisiting the Role of Bureaucrats in Pension Policy-making: the Case of South Korea." *Government and Opposition*, 1–27.

Kim, Yeon-Myung (2006). "Towards a Comprehensive Welfare State in South Korea: Institutional Features, New Socio-Economic and Political Pressures, and the Possibility of the Welfare State". Asia Research Centre, Working Paper 14.

—— (2010). "Developments and General Features of National Health Insurance in Korea." *Social Work in Public Health*, 25(2): 142–157.

Korpi, Walter and Palme, Joakim (1998). "The Paradox of Redistribution and Strategies of Equality: Welfare State Institutions, Inequality, and Poverty in the Western Countries." *American Sociological Review*, 63(5): 661–687.

Krishna, Anirudh (2010). *One Illness Away: Why People Become Poor and How They Escape Poverty*. Oxford University Press.

Kwon, Huck-Ju (1995). *The "Welfare State in Korea": the Politics of Legitimation*. Thesis submitted to the Faculty of Social Studies, University of Oxford.

—— (2007). "Advocacy Coalitions and Health Politics in Korea." *Social Policy and Administration*, 41(2): 148–161.

Kwon, Soonman (2000). "Health Care Financing and Delivery for the Poor in Korea." *International Review of Public Administration*, 5(2): 37–45.

—— (2002). "Achieving Health Insurance for all: Lessons from the Republic of Korea." ESS Paper No 1. Social Security Policy and Development Branch. Geneva: ILO.

(2007). "The Fiscal Crisis of National Health Insurance in the Republic of Korea: in Search of a New Paradigm." *Social Policy and Administration*, 41(2): 162–178.

Kwon, Soonman and Holliday, Ian (2007). "The Korean Welfare State: a Paradox of Expansion in an Era of Globalisation and Economic Crisis." *International Journal of Social Welfare*, 16: 242–248.

Kwon, Soonman and Reich, Michael (2005). "The Changing Process and Politics of Health Policy in Korea." *Journal of Health Politics, Policy and Law*, 30(6): 1003–1025.

La Hora (July 28, 1970). "Médicos satisfechos por solución a la crisis." San José.

(March 17, 1971). "Voracidad fiscal se agudiza con ruptura de topes." San José.

(March 26, 1971). "Única esperanza es el compromiso público de Jiménez." San José.

(December 2, 1974). "Cámaras, miseria y gobierno." San José.

La Nación (February 24 ,1971). "Ministro Orlich: Sistema unificado de salud." San José.

(March 9, 1971a). "Cautela ante la universalización." San José.

(March 9, 1971b). "Ruptura de topes es perjudicial." San José.

(March 10, 1971a). "Estamos de acuerdo con la ruptura de topes en el Seguro Social." San José.

(March 10, 1971b). "Incluir a estudiantes mayores de dieciocho años en el Seguro Social." San José.

(March 12, 1971). "La clase trabajadora debe respetar y apoyar la ruptura de topes." San José.

(March 13, 1971). "Quién paga los beneficios sociales." San José.

(March 14, 1971a). "Fuerte desembolso a trabajadores con supresión de topes al Seguro." San José.

(March 14, 1971b). "Se puede extender la seguridad social a nuevas zonas del país." San José.

(March 14, 1971c). "El Partido Demócrata Cristiano ante la universalización del Seguro Social." San José.

(March 16, 1971). "Rompimiento de topes en el Seguro Social." San José.

(May 25, 1974). "País no está preparado para soportar el régimen de asignación familiar." San José.

(June 30, 1974). "Pobreza extrema y seguridad social." San José.

(November 1, 1974). "Hay que llegar a un solo sistema de medicina: Oduber." San José.

(December 6, 1974). "Oduber: Miles de hogares costarricenses no conocen las conquistas sociales." San José.

(July 5, 1996). "Reforma global aguarda pensiones." Available at www.nacion.com/archivo/Reforma-global-aguarda-pensiones_0_1400 260090.html, accessed August 24, 2014.

(March 29, 1998). "Caja rezagada ante cáncer." San José.

(April 27, 1998). "Privatizar la CCSS no es prioridad." San José.

(July 25, 2003). "Entrevista con Eliseo Vargas, Presidente Ejecutivo de la CCSS." Available at www.nacion.com/ln_ee/2003/julio/25/entrevista.pdf, accessed August 2014.

(July 8, 2004). "CCSS cierra la gerencia de modernización." Available at www.nacion.com/ln_ee/2004/julio/08/pais1.html.

(October 10, 2011). "Usuarios ven a la Caja como la institución más benefactora." Available at Downloads/2011%2010%2003%20La%20Naci%C3%B3n.pdf.

La Prensa Libre (March 10, 1971). "Estamos de acuerdo con la ruptura de topes en el Seguro Social." San José.

(March 11, 1971). "Sindicalismo es medio de desarrollo social." San José.

(March 12, 1971a). "Niego mensaje de subversión." San José.

(March 12, 1971b). "Lesión seria al desarrollo es la ruptura de topes." San José.

(March 16, 1971). "No title." San José.

(March 17, 1971a). "No title." San José.

(March 17, 1971b). "CCSS." San José.

(March 18, 1971). "No title." San José.

(March 19, 1971a). "Eliminación de topes: serie de interrogantes sin respuesta." San José.

(March 19, 1971b). "No me defiendas compadre." San José.

(March 19, 1971c). "CCSS." San José.

(March 22, 1971a). "Exposición del señor Ministro de Trabajo y Bienestar Social sobre el proyecto de eliminación de topes del Seguro Social." San José.

(March 22, 1971b). "CCSS." San José.

(March 23, 1971a). "CCSS." San José.

(March 23, 1971b). "Comité de Lucha pro-Reforma al Código Penal y Legislación Social apoya ruptura de topes." San José.

(March 24, 1971a). "Ruptura de topes no es una amenaza." San José.

(March 24, 1971b). "Eliminar topes donde se sirve." San José.

(March 24, 1971c). "Eliminación de topes y algunas conclusiones." San José.

(March 25, 1971a). "Eliminación de topes y algunas conclusiones II." San José.

(March 25, 1971b). "No title." San José.

(March 26, 1971a). "Junta de Pensiones y Jubilaciones del Magisterio Nacional." San José.

(March 26, 1971b). "Ruptura: paso trascendental." San José.

(March 26, 1971c). "No title." San José.

(March 26, 1971d). "Eliminación de topes y una conclusión final." San José.

La República (December 5, 1974). "No puedo hablar con quienes ignoran la solidaridad humana." San José.

(December 8, 1974). "Respuesta grosera y con mucha demagogia de Oduber." San José.

La Tribuna (October 21, 1941). "Debemos adaptar en Costa Rica la ley de seguro social no en forma total sino parcialente." San José.

(October 22, 1941). "Invitada Costa Rica a un congreso interamericano de previsión social." San José.

(July 2, 1942). "Acuerda la Municipalidad de Heredia el ingreso al Seguro Social de todos sus empleados y obreros." San José.

(August 27, 1942). "Un millón de colones tiene el depósito la Caja del Seguro Social para atender los tres primeros seguros." San José.

(September 25, 1942). "El Banco Nacional pide al Ejecutivo excluir a sus empleados de los beneficios del seguro social." San José.

Lange, Matthew (2003). "Embedding the Colonial State: a Comparative-Historical Analysis of State Building and Broad-Based Development in Mauritius." *Social Science History*, 27(3): 397–423.

Lee Jooha (2008). *Welfare Reform in Korea after the Economic Crisis.* DPhil in Social Policy, University of Oxford.

Legislative Assembly (1969). *Expediente No. 3899: Proyecto para la eliminación de topes de la seguridad social.* San José.

(1972). *Comisión de Asuntos Sociales: Audiencia Junta de Proyección Social.* San José, July 11 and 13.

(1973a). *Ley No. 5349: Ley de Traspaso de Hospitales.* San José

(1973b). *Expediente 5246: Creación del régimen de asignaciones familiares en Costa Rica (FODESAF).* San José.

(1974a). *Ley No. 5541: Normas Traspaso Hospitales a la Caja Costarricense de Seguro Social por la Junta de Protección Social.* San José, July 17.

(1974b). *Ley No. 5349: Universalización del Seguro de Enfermedad y Maternidad.* San José, October 3.

(1994). *Ley 7441: Aprobación del contrato de préstamo 3654-CR y sus anexos suscripto entre el Gobierno de la República y el Banco Internacional de Reconstruccion y Fomento para financiar el proyecto de reforma del Sector Salud.* San José, August 3.

(2000). *Ley 7983: De Protección al Trabajador.* San José, February 3.

Lehoucq, Fabrice (2010). "Political Competition, Constitutional Arrangements and the Quality of Public Choices in Costa Rica." *Latin American Politics and Society*, 52(4): 54–77.

(2012). *The Politics of Modern Central America: Civil War, Democratization and Underdevelopment.* Cambridge University Press.

Lewis, Colin and Lloyd-Sherlock, Peter (2009). "Social Policy and Economic Development in South America: an Historical Approach to Social Insurance." *Economy and Society*, 38(1): 109–131.

Lingayah, Siramloo (1995). "The Origins and Development of Social Service Provisions in Mauritius." PhD Thesis, School of Social Work and Health Science Middlesex University.

Litsios, Socrates (2002). "The Long and Difficult Road to Alma-Ata: a Personal Reflection." *The Politics of the World Health Organization*, 32(4): 709–732.

Lo Vuolo, Ruben (2005). "Social Protection in Latin America: Different Approaches to Managing Social Exclusion and their Outcomes". Paper presented at the ESRC Seminar Series Social Policy, Stability and Exclusion in Latin America, London, June 2–3.

Madrid, Raul (2003). *Retiring the State*. Stanford University Press.

Mahoney, James (2010). "After KKV: the New Methodology of Qualitative Research." *World Politics*, 62(1): 120–147.

Mallet, Alfredo (1980). *Social Protection of the Rural Population*. Consultant, International Social Security Association.

Mares, Isabela and Carnes, Matthew (2012). "Social Policy in Developing Countries," *Annual Review of Political Science*, 12: 93–113.

Markoff, John and Montecinos, Verónica (1993). "The Ubiquitous Rise of Economists." *Journal of Public Policy*, 13(1): 37–68.

Martí Bufill, Carlos (1960). *Acta 2451 CCSS, 26 de agosto, art 3*. San Jose: CCSS.

Martínez Franzoni, Juliana (1999). "Poder y Alternativas: la disponibilidad de agendas internacionales en las reformas de salud en Costa Rica (1988–1998)." *Revista Uruguaya de Ciencia Política*, 12: 123–144.

(2005). "Reformas recientes de las pensiones en Costa Rica: Avances hacia una mayor sostenibilidad financiera, acceso y progresividad del primer pilar de pensiones." *XI Informe del Estado de la Nación*. San José: Programa Estado de la Nación.

(2008). "Welfare Regimes in Latin America: Capturing Constellations of Markets, Families and Policies." *Latin American Politics and Society* 50(2): 67–100.

Martínez Franzoni, Juliana and Mesa-Lago, Carmelo (2003). *Las reformas inconclusas: pensiones y salud en Costa Rica: avances, problemas y recomendaciones*. San José: Fundación Ebert.

Martínez Franzoni, Juliana and Sánchez-Ancochea, Diego (2013a). *Good Jobs and Social Services*. Hampshire: Palgrave Macmillan.

(2013b). "Can Latin American Production Regimes Complement Universalistic Welfare Regimes? Implications from the Costa Rican Case." *Latin American Research Review*, 48(2): 148–173.

(2014). "The Double Challenge of Market and Social Incorporation: Progress and Bottlenecks in Latin America." *Development Policy Review*, 32(3): 275–298.

(2015). "Public Social Services." In Janine Berg (ed.), *Labour Market Institutions and Inequality: Building Just Societies in the 21st Century*. Cheltenham: Edward Elgar.

Mata, Leonardo and Murillo, Sandra (1980). "Canasta básica del costarricense." *Revista médica del Hospital Nacional de Niños*, 15(1): 101–114.

Mata, Leonardo and Rosero, Luis (1988). "National Health and Social Development in Costa Rica: A Case Study of Intersectoral Health." PAHO Technical Paper no. 13.

McGuire, James (2010). *Wealth, Health and Democracy in East Asia and Latin America*. Cambridge University Press.

Meisenhelder, Thomas (1997). "The Developmental State in Mauritius." *The Journal of Modern African Studies*, 35(2): 279–297.

Meltzer, Allan and Richard, Scott (1981). "A Rational Theory of the Size of Government." *Journal of Political Economy*, 89(5): 914–927.

Mesa-Lago, Carmelo (1978). *Social Security in Latin America: Pressure Groups, Stratification and Inequality*. University of Pittsburgh Press.

(1985). "Health Care in Costa Rica: Boom and Crisis." *Social Science and Medicine*, 21(1): 13–21.

(2008). *Reassembling Social Security: A Survey of Pensions and Health Care Reforms in Latin America*. Oxford University Press.

Meseguer, Covadonga (2009). *Learning, Policy Making and Market Reforms*. Cambridge University Press.

Milberg, William (1998). "Globalization and its Limits." In Richard Kozul-Wright and Robert Rowthorn (eds.), *Transnational Corporations and the Global Economy* (431–437). New York: St. Martin's Press.

Ministry of Health (1971). *Plan Nacional de Salud, 1971–1980*, vol. 1, y. 2. San José: Ministerio de Salubridad Pública.

(1973). *Programa de salud en comunidades del área rural de Costa Rica*. San José: Dirección General de Salud.

(2002). "White Paper on Health Sector Development and Reform." Ministry of Health and Quality of Life: Republic of Mauritius.

Ministry of Health and PAHO (1977). *Coordinación e integración del Sector Salud*. San José: Ministry of Health/PAHO.

Minogue, Martín (1976). "Public Administration in Mauritius." *Journal of Administration Overseas*, 15(3): 160–166.

Miranda, Guido (1988). *La Seguridad Social y el Desarrollo en Costa Rica.* San José: Caja Costarricense de Seguro Social.

Miranda Gutiérrez, Guido and Asís Beirute, Luis (1989). *Extensión del Seguro Social a la zona rural en Costa Rica.* San José: CCSS - EDNASSS.

Mkandawire, Thandika (2006a). "Targeting and Universalism in Poverty Reduction." *Social Policy and Development Programme Paper 23.* Geneva: UNRISD.

(2006b). *Social Policy in a Development Context.* Geneva: UNRISD.

Moene, Karl-Ove and Wallerstein, Michael (2001). "Targeting and Political Support for Welfare Spending." *Economics of Governance*, 2: 3–24.

Mohs, Edgar (1983). *La salud en Costa Rica.* San José: Editorial Universidad Estatal a Distancia.

Molina, Carlos Gerardo (ed.) (2006). *Universalismo básico.* México, DC: Editorial Planeta Mexicana.

Molina, Iván (2007). *Anticomunismo reformista.* San José: Editorial Costa Rica.

(2008). *Los pasados de la memoria: el origen de la reforma social en Costa Rica (1938–1943).* Heredia: EUNA.

Moon, Hyungpyo (2008). *The Role of Social Pensions in Korea.* Seoul: Korea Development Institute.

Mootoosamy, Sandrasegaram (1981). "Developing the Social Security System: the Experience of Mauritius." *International Social Security Review*, 34(4): 446–461.

Morás, Luis Eduardo (2000). *De la tierra purpurea al laboratorio social: Reformas y Proceso Civilizatorio en el Uruguay (1870–1917).* Montevideo: Ediciones de la Banda Oriental.

Morgan, Lynn (1990). "International Politics and Primary Health Care in Costa Rica." *Social Science and Medicine*, 30(2): 211–219.

Muiser, Jorine and Juan José Vargas (2012). *Health Care Financing and Social Protection in Latin America: the Design of the Costa Rican Health Financing System in View of Financial Risk Protection.* San José: La Net/La Red.

Neubourg, Chris de (2009). "Social Protection and Nation-Building: an Essay on Why and How Universalist Social Policy Contributes to Stable Nation-States." In Peter Townsend (ed.), *Building Decent Societies: Rethinking the Role of Social Security in State Building* (63–120). Geneva: ILO/Palgrave Macmillan.

New York Times (August 17, 2014). "Transplant Brokers in Israel Lure Desperate Kidney Patients to Costa Rica." Available at www.nytimes.com/2014/08/17/world/middleeast/transplant-brokers-in-israel-lure-desperate-kidney-patients-to-costa-rica.html?smprod=nytcore-ipad&smid=nytcore-ipad-share, accessed August 17, 2014.

Ocampo, José Antonio and Malagón, Jonathan (2011). "Los efectos distributivos de la política fiscal en América Latina." *Pensamiento Iberoamericano* 10: 71–101.

Oduber, Daniel *et al.* (1968). "Patio de Agua. Manifiesto Democrático para una Revolución Social." Available at http://mapasdecostarica.info/edel/Patio_de_Agua.pdf, accessed March 17, 2015.

OECD (2009). "Korea Profile, International Organization of Pension Supervisors." Available at www.oecd.org/site/iops/research/39625977.pdf, accessed on December 4, 2013.

(2013). "Country Profile Mauritius." Available at www.oecd.org/site/iops/research/MauritiusPensionSystemProfile.pdf, accessed November, 2013.

(2014). "Social expenditure." Available at http://stats.oecd.org/Index.aspx?DataSetCode=SOCX_AGG, accessed March 21, 2014.

Oxfam (2015). "Having It All and Wanting More." *Oxfam Issue Briefing*, Oxford: Oxfam.

Padilla, Guillermo (1966). "El seguro social en Costa Rica: su origen y sus primeros cinco años." *La Nación*, December 10, 30, 31, 90.

PAHO (2012). *Health in the Americas, 2012.* Washington: Pan American Health Organization.

Palmer, Steven (2003). *Popular Medicine to Medical Populism: Doctors, Healers and Public Power*, Durham: Duke University Press.

Papadópulos, Jorge (1992). *Seguridad social y política en el Uruguay.* Montevideo: CIESU-Valgraf.

(2013) "Uruguay." In Rafael Rofman; Ignacio Apella; and Evelyn Vezza (eds.), *Más allá de las pensiones contributivas: catorce experiencias en América Latina* (227–258). Buenos Aires: World Bank.

Parahoo, A. K. (1986). "A Sociological Analysis of the Organisation, Distribution and Uses of Health Care in Mauritius." PhD Thesis, University of Keele.

Park, Yong Soo (2011). "The Social Welfare Reform During the Progressive Regimes of South Korea: Theoretical Implications." *The Social Science Journal*, 48: 13–28.

Partido Liberación Nacional (PLN) (1993). *Programa Liberacionista para el Bienestar de los Costarricenses. Gobierno de José María Figueres 1994–1998.* San José: PLN.

Peabody, John; Lee, Sung-Woo; and Bickel, Stephen (1995). "Health for All in the Republic of Korea: One Country's Experience with Implementing Universal Health Care." *Health Policy*, 31: 29–42.

Pérez, Marcelo (2009). "La reforma del sistema de salud en el primer gobierno de izquierda en la historia del Uruguay: los desafíos del cambio."

Licenciatura Thesis, Instituto de Ciencia Política, Facultad de Ciencias Sociales, Universidad de la República.

Pezzini, Mario (2012). "An Emerging Middle Class". Available at www.oecdobserver.org/news/fullstory.php/aid/3681/An_emerging_middle_class.html#sthash.UUUKSh3j.dpuf.

Picado, Gustavo; Acuña, Edwin; and Santacruz, Javier (2003). *Gasto y financiamiento de la salud en Costa Rica: situación actual, tendencias y retos*. San José: OPS.

Pierson, Paul (1994). *Dismantling the Welfare State?: Reagan, Thatcher and the Politics of Retrenchment*. Cambridge University Press

Piketty, Thomas (2013). *Capital in the Twenty-First Century*. Cambridge: The Belknap Press of Harvard University Press.

Piza, Rodolfo (2014). Presidential Candidate Personal Website. Available at www.rodolfopizapresidente.com/index.php/rodolfo-piza/biografia, accessed August 12, 2014.

Poblete Troncoso, Moisés (1940) *Rapport Mission en Amerique Central*. Santiago de Chile, January 20.

Poltronieri, Jorge (2011). *Proyecto de Investigación Estructuras de la Opinión Pública, Comunicado de prensa, Encuesta de opinión pública XXIII – Panorama global*. San José: CIRMA/UCR.

Pontusson, Jonas (2005) "Varieties and Commonalities of Capitalism". In David Coates (ed.), *Varieties of Capitalism, Varieties of Approaches* (163–188) New York: Palgrave Macmilian.

Poveda, Jorge (1973). *La Union Medica Nacional: Fundamento Histórico*. San José

Pribble, Jennifer (2011). "World Apart: Social Policy Regimes in Latin America." *Studies in Comparative International Development*, 46: 191–216.

——— (2013). *Welfare and Party Politics in Latin America*. Cambridge University Press.

Programa Estado de la Nación (2013). Compendio estadístico de estadísticas sociales. Available at www.estadonacion.or.cr/estadisticas/costa-rica/compendio-estadistico/estadisticas-sociales, accessed July 30, 2013.

Ramesh, M. (2003). "Health Policy in the Asian Nies." *Social Policy and Administration*, 37(4): 361–375.

——— (2008). "Reasserting the Role of the State in the Healthcare Sector: Lessons from Asia." *Policy and Society*, 27: 129–136.

Republic of Mauritius (1971). *Four Year Development Plan*. Vol 1. Republic of Mauritius: Port Louise.

Ringen, Stein; Kwon, Huck-ju; Yi, Ilcheong; Kim, Taekyoon; and Lee, Jooha (2011). *The Korean State and Social Policy: How South Korea Lifted*

Itself from Poverty and Dictatorship to Affluence and Democracy. New York: Oxford University Press.

Rodríguez, Adolfo (2005). *La reforma de salud en Costa Rica.* Documento de Trabajo. Santiago: CEPAL.

Rosenberg, Mark (1979). "Social Security Policy Making in Costa Rica." *Latin American Research Review*, 14(1):116–133.

(1981). "Social Reform in Costa Rica: Social Security and the Presidency of Rafael Calderón Guardia." *The Hispanic American Historical Review*, 61(2): 278–296.

(1983). *Las luchas por el seguro social en Costa Rica.* San José: Editorial Costa Rica.

Rosero-Bixby, Luis (1986). "Infant Mortality in Costa Rica: Explaining the Recent Decline." *Studies in Family Planning*, 17(2): 57–65.

(1991). "Studies of the Costa Rican Model I: Peace, Health, and Development in Costa Rica." Paper presented at the Seminar: Peace, Health, and Development. Goteborg, Sweden, December 5.

(2004). "Evaluación del impacto de la reforma del sector salud en Costa Rica mediante un estudio cuasiexperimental." *Rev Panam Salud Pública*, 15(2): 94–103.

Rothstein, Bo (2008). "Is the Universal Welfare State a Cause or an Effect of Social Capital?" QoG Working Paper Series, 16.

Rovira, Jorge (1987). *Costa Rica en los años 80.* San José: Porvenir.

Rowthorn, Robert and Kozul-Wright, Richard (1998). *Transnational Corporations and the Global Economy.* New York: St. Martin's Press.

Roychowdhury Viveka (2015). "Mauritius has the potential to transform itself into a medical hub for the region." *Express Healthcare*, January 10. Available at www.financialexpress.com/article/healthcare/market/mauritius-has-the-potential-to-transform-itself-into-a-medical-hub-for-the-region/28485.

Rudra, Nita (2007). "Welfare States in Developing Countries: Unique or Universal." IGIS Research Seminar Series. George Washington University, April.

(2008). *Globalization and the Race to the Bottom in Developing Countries: Who Really Gets Hurt?* New York: Cambridge University Press.

Rudra, Nita and Haggard, Stephan (2005). "Globalization, Democracy, and Effective Welfare Spending in the Developing World." *Comparative Political Studies*, 38(9): 1015–1049.

Sáenz, Lenin; Meneses, Rodrígo; Martínez, Hazel; Hilje, Carmen; and Murillo, Mainrad (1981). *Salud En Costa Rica (Evaluación De La Situación En La Década De Los 70).* San José: Departamento de Publicaciones del Ministerio de Salud.

Saénz, María del Rocío; Acosta, Mónica; Muiser, Jorine; and Bermúdez, Juan Luis (2011). "Sistema De Salud De Costa Rica." *Salud Pública de México*, 53(2): 156–167.

Saldain and Asociados (2015). "Rodolfo Saldain." Available at www.saldain .com/equipo/rodolfo-saldain, accessed March 19.

Sánchez-Ancochea, Diego (2004). "'Leading Coalitions' and Patterns of Accumulation and Distribution in Small Countries." A Comparative Study of Costa Rica and the Dominican Republic under Globalization. PhD Dissertation. New York: New School for Social Research.

Sandbrook Richard; Edelman, Marc; Heller, Patrick; and Teichman, Judith (2007). *Social Democracy in the Global Periphery: Origins and Prospects*. New York: Cambridge University Press.

Secretaría de Gobernación, Policía, Trabajo y Previsión Social (1941). Letter to Congress, July 15.

(1943). Letter to Congress, no date.

Seekings, Jeremy (2007). *Welfare State-Building in Mauritius: Action and Inaction in a Sugar Dependent Economy, 1936–1978*. University of Cape Town/Yale University, February.

(2010). "The ILO and Welfare Reform in South Africa, Latin America, and the Caribbean, 1919–1950." In Magaly Rodríguez; Jasmien Van Daele; Geert Van Goethem; and Marcel van der Linden (eds.), *ILO Histories: Essays on the International Labour Organization and its Impact on the World During the Twentieth Century* (145–173). Schweiz: Peter Land Publishers.

(2011). "British Colonial Policy, Local Politics and the Origins of the Mauritian Welfare State 1936–1950." *Journal of African History*, 52: 157–177.

Segura-Ubiergo, Alex (2007). *The Political Economy of the Welfare State in Latin America*. New York: Cambridge University Press.

Sennett, Richard (2003). *Respect: the Formation of Character in an Age of Inequality*. Westminster: Penguin books.

Setaro, Marcelo (2004). "Vigilar y cuidar el bien común. El rol de rectoría del Sistema de Salud desde una perspectiva comparada." Masters Thesis, Instituto de Ciencia Política, Montevideo.

(2013). "La economía política de la reforma del sector salud en Uruguay (2005–2012). Innovación y continuidad en la construcción de un Estado Social con inspiración desarrollista." PhD Thesis in Social Science, Universidad de la República, Montevideo.

Shapiro, Ian; Swenson, Peter; and Donno, Daniela (eds.) (2008). *Divide and Deal: The Politics of Distribution in Democracies*. New York University Press.

Shaver, Sheila (1998). "Universality or Selectivity in Income Support to Older People? A Comparative Assessment of the Issues." *Journal of Social Policy*, 27(2): 231–254.

Sheard, Sally (2012). *The Passionate Economist: How Brian Abel-Smith Shaped Global Health and Social Welfare*. London: Policy Press.

Shifter, Jacobo (1979). *La fase oculta de guerra civil*. San José: EDUCA.

Silva, Patricio (2010). *In the Name of Reason: Technocrats and Politics in Chile*. University Park: Penn University Press.

Skocpol, Theda (1991). "Targeting Within Universalism: Politically Viable Policies to Combat Poverty in the United States." In Christopher Jencks and Peterson, Paul (eds.), *The Urban Underclass* (411–436). Washington, D.C.: The Brookings Institution.

  (1992). *Protecting Soldiers and Mothers: the Political Origins of Social Policy in the United States*. Cambridge: Harvard University Press.

Socha, Karolina (2010). "Physician Dual Practice and the Public Health Care Provision." *Health Economics Papers*.

Sojo, Ana (1998). "Los compromisos de gestión en salud de Costa Rica con una perspectiva comparative." *Revista de la CEPAL*, 66: 73–103.

Solano, Héctor (2009). "La política de creación del Fondo de Asignaciones Familiares en Costa Rica (1973–74)." In Andrés Martínez; Guillermo Meneses; José Miguel Salas; and Héctor Solano (eds.), *Memoria del Seminario de Graduación Formación del régimen de política social costarricense durante la época dorada (1970–1975)* (Chapter IV). Dissertation to obtain the degree of Licenciatura in Political Sciences, University of Costa Rica.

Sonoo, Janaki (2012). "Impact of Medical Tourism on Health Sector in Mauritius." *Consultant and Head National Blood Transfusion Service*, Mauritius.

Stiglitz, Joseph (2013). *The Price of Inequality*. London: Penguin.

Stuckler, David; Feigl, Andrea B; Basu, Sanjay; and McKee, Martin (2010). "The Political Economy of Universal Health Coverage." Background Paper for the Global Symposium on Health System Research. Switzerland.

Sugiyama, Natasha (2011). "The Diffusion of Conditional Cash Transfer Programs in the Americas." *Global Social Policy*, 11(2/3): 250–278.

Tanzi, Vito (2004). "La globalización y la necesidad de una reforma fiscal en los países en desarrollo." Documento de divulgación IECI, 06, Instituto para la Integración de América Latina y el Caribe. Inter-American Development Bank.

Titmuss, Richard (1958). *Essays on the Welfare State*. London: Allen and Unwin.

Titmuss, Richard and Abel-Smith, Brian (1968). *Social Policies and Population Growth in Mauritius*. London: Frank Cass.

Townsend, Peter (2011). *Building Decent Societies: Rethinking the Role of Social Security in State Building.* Geneva: ILO/Palgrave Macmillan.

Trabajo (October 18, 1941). "De pie la clase trabajadora a luchar por la Ley de Seguro Social." San José.

(May 9, 1942). "Brillante la Jornada del 1° de Mayo en Puntarenas." San José.

(September 12, 1942). "Los Seguros de Enfermedad, Maternidad y Cuota Mortuaria han comenzado a hacerse efectivos." San José.

(February 6, 1943). "El Seguro Social no es puro cuento." San José.

(April 3, 1943). "Imponente Manifestación Popular en Turrialba." San José.

Trejos, Juan Diego (1991). "La Política Social y la Valorización de Los Recursos Humanos." In Roberto Hidalgo; Leonardo Garnier; Guillermo Monge; and Juan Diego Trejos (eds.), *Costa Rica: Entre la Ilusión y La Desesperanza* (163–215). San José: Ediciones Guayacán.

UCIMED (2013). "Conclusiones." *I Foro Nacional Hacia el Fortalecimiento de los Servicios de Salud Públicos y Privados.* San José, November 4, 3 pages.

UNRISD (2010). *Combating Poverty and Inequality: Structural Change, Social Policy and Politics.* Geneva: United Nations Research Institute for Social Development.

Uy.press (October 9, 2013). "Almorzando con María Susana. Ministra Muñiz: No caer en la experiencia de Costa Rica, cuyo sistema de salud hoy es inviable." Available at www.uypress.net/uc_45108_1.html, accessed on March 21, 2014.

Vadakin, James (1958). *Family Allowances: an Analysis of Their Development and Implications.* Coral Cables: University of Miami Press

Valaydon, Biua (2002). "Health Sector Reform and the Civil Service System in Mauritius: Analysis of Barriers to Management Reform in the Ministry of Health from 1988 to 1999." PhD Dissertation, Graduate School of Public Service, New York University.

Vanger, Milton (1980). *The Model Country. José Batlle y Ordoñez of Uruguay, 1907–1915.* Boulder: Lynne Rienner.

Valenzuela, Samuel (2006a). "Demografía familiar y desarrollo. Chile y Suecia desde 1914." In Samuel Valenzuela; Eugenio Tironi; and Timothy Scully (eds.), *El eslabón perdido. Familia, modernización y bienestar en Chile* (97–136). Madrid: Taurus.

(2006b). "Diseños dispares, resultados diferentes y convergencias tardías. Las instituciones de bienestar social en Chile y Suecia." In Samuel Valenzuela; Eugenio Tironi; and Timothy Scully (eds.), *El eslabón perdido. Familia, modernización y bienestar en Chile* (359–430). Madrid: Taurus.

Vargas, Herman; Turcios, María Isabel; and Salgado, Patricia (1979). "Análisis del gasto en Salud en el Sector Público de Costa Rica (1957–1977)."

Paper Presented at the Primer Seminario Latinoamericano de Medicina Social. Universidad de Costa Rica.

Villegas, Hugo (1977). "Extensión de la Cobertura de Salud en Costa Rica." *Bol of Sanu Panam*, 83(6): 537–544.

(2004). "Atención integral de la salud en Costa Rica. La década de los setenta: desafíos y estrategias en el siglo XXI." In Guido Miranda and Carlos Zamora (eds.), *La construcción de la seguridad social*. San José: EUMED.

Villasuso, Juan Manuel (2008). "Medio siglo de economía política y política económica en Costa Rica." Background Paper for the UNRISD Program Public Policy Regime and Poverty Reduction.

Vittas, Dimitri (2003). "The Role of Occupational Pension Funds in Mauritius." Policy Research Working Paper 3033. The World Bank Financial Sector Operations and Policy Department, April.

Walker, Carol (2011). "For Universalism and Against the Mean Test." In Alan Walker; Adrian Sinfield; and Carol Walker (eds.), *Fighting Poverty, Inequality and Injustice: a Manifesto Inspired by Peter Townsend* (133–152). Bristol: The Policy Press.

Weyland, Kurt (2004). "Conclusion." In Kurt Weyland (ed.), *Learning from Foreign Models in Latin America Policy Reform* (241–283). Washington D.C: Woodrow Wilson Center Press.

(2005). "Theories of Policy Diffusion: Lessons from Latin American Pension Reform." *World Politics*, 57(2): 262–295.

(2007). *Bounded Rationality and Policy Diffusion*. Princeton University Press.

Wilkinson, Richard and Pickett, Kate (2009). *The Spirit Level: Why More Equal Societies Almost Always Do Better*. London: Bloomsbury Publishing.

Willmore, Larry (2003). "Universal Pensions in Mauritius: Lessons for the Rest of Us". *DESA Discussion Paper No. 32*.

(2006). "Universal Age Pensions in Developing Countries: The Example of Mauritius." *International Social Security Review*, 59(4): 67–89.

(2007). "Universal Pensions for Developing Countries." *World Development*, 35(1): 24–51.

Wong, Joseph (2004). *Healthy Democracies. Welfare Politics in Taiwan and South Korea*. Ithaca: Cornell University Press.

World Bank (1992). *Mauritius: Expanding Horizons*. Washington D.C.: A World Bank Country Study.

(1993). *Health Sector Reform: Social Security System Project*. Washington D.C: World Bank.

(2003). *Inequality and Poverty in Latin America: Breaking with History?* Washington D.C.: World Bank.

(2004). *Mauritius Modernizing an Advanced Pension System*. Washington D.C.: World Bank.
(2006). *World Development Report: Equity and Development*. Washington D.C.: World Bank.
(2013). *World Development Indicators*. Available at http://databank .worldbank.org/data/views/variableSelection/selectvariables.aspx?source= world-development-indicators, accessed March 21, 2014.
(2014). "Speech by World Bank Group President Jim Yong Kim on Universal Health Coverage in Emerging Economies." Available at www.worldbank.org/en/news/speech/2014/01/14/speech-world-bank-group-president-jim-yong-kim-health-emerging-economies, accessed March 21, 2014.
World Health Organisation (WHO) (2006). *World Health Survey 2003: India*. New Delhi: WHO.
(2010). *Health Systems Financing and the Path to Universal Coverage*. Geneva: WHO.
(2012). *World Health Statistics 2012*. Geneva: WHO.
(2013) *World Health Statistics*. Geneva: WHO.
Yashar, Deborah (1997). *Demanding Democracy: Reform and Reaction in Costa Rica and Guatemala, 1870s–1950s*. Princeton University Press.
Zamora, Carlos and Saénz, Luis Bernardo (1995). *Variaciones en los servicios de salud bajo diferentes modalidades de atención*. San José: CCSS.

Interviews

Interview #1: Former high ranking state official. August 11, 2011. San José, Costa Rica.
Interview #2: Personal communication: Former high ranking state official. October 15, 2012. San José, Costa Rica.
Interview #3: Former high ranking state official. November 20, 2012. San José, Costa Rica.
Interview #4: Former high ranking official in the CCSS. November 2012. San José, Costa Rica.
Interview #5: Former high ranking state official. November 19, 2012. San José, Costa Rica.
Interview #6: Public health expert and former state official. November 16, 2012. San José, Costa Rica.
Interview #7: Former state official. November 5, 2012. San José, Costa Rica.
Interview #8: Former high ranking state official. November 23, 2012. San José, Costa Rica.
Interview #9: Former high ranking state official. October 12, 2010. San José, Costa Rica.

Interview #10: Former high ranking state official. August 3, 2011. San José, Costa Rica.

Interview #11: Former high ranking state official. September 11, 2011. San José, Costa Rica.

Interview #12: Former high ranking state official. August 4, 2011. San José, Costa Rica.

Interview #13: Former high ranking state official. September 17, 2011. San José, Costa Rica.

Interview #14: Senior researcher. July 21, 2010. San José, Costa Rica.

Interview #15: Former high ranking state official. October 1, 2010. San José, Costa Rica.

Interview #16: Former member of the PLN. September 22, 2010. San José, Costa Rica.

Interview #17: Senior researcher. July 22, 2010. San José, Costa Rica.

Index